Infinite Value

Infinite Value

Accelerating Profitable Growth Through Value-Based Selling

Mark Davies

Bloomsbury Business
An imprint of Bloomsbury Publishing Plc

B L O O M S B U R Y

LONDON · OXFORD · NEW YORK · NEW DELHI · SYDNEY

Bloomsbury Business
An imprint of Bloomsbury Publishing Plc

50 Bedford Square	1385 Broadway
London	New York
WC1B 3DP	NY 10018
UK	USA

www.bloomsbury.com

Bloomsbury and the Diana logo are trademarks of Bloomsbury Publishing Plc

First published 2017

British Library Cataloguing-in-Publication Data
A catalogue record for this book is available from the British Library.

ISBN: PB: 978-1-4729-3529-8
ePDF: 978-1-4729-3530-4
ePub: 978-1-4729-3532-8

Library of Congress Cataloging-in-Publication Data
A catalog record for this book is available from the Library of Congress.

Cover design by Steve Stacey
Cover image © Bigstock

Typeset by Fakenham Prepress Solutions, Fakenham, Norfolk NR21 8NN
Printed and bound in India

Professor Lynette Ryals
Vice Chair To Assembly at Cranfield University

I left corporate life to develop my advisory and consulting practice in January 2008. In September 2008, Lehman Brothers filed for Chapter 11 (bankruptcy), and sparked the worst economic crisis since the Great Depression. My target client organisations switched to "survive-mode" and stopped spending on training, consulting, coaching and speaking assignments. My audacious business model was squashed in one cruel blow.

Lynnette offered me collaborative opportunities with the incredible Cranfield School Of Management and its world-class network of scholars, clients and other associates. It is hard to place a value on this act of kindness and my on-going work with the Cranfield sales & marketing community. Infinite Value may just about do it justice.

Thank you, Lynette.

Mark Davies
5th October 2016

Contents

Foreword

When I joined IBM as my first job in 1979, no one could say we weren't close to our customers. We listened to their needs carefully, asking searching questions throughout the customer firm. We made sure they were buying the right hardware and software for them, and helped them with their internal business case. We held their hands in implementation, providing an array of services such as application development and maintenance, and kept in touch to make sure they were happy. Just by getting these basics right when many others didn't, we were able to command enormous margins.

But within just fourteen years, this commendable customer centricity wasn't enough, and IBM was in crisis. Globalization meant lower-cost competitors. Customer consolidation meant professional purchasing departments who were squeezing margins hard, and who were happy to give business to specialists in parts of the product range if IBM wouldn't comply with price demands. The problem with this trajectory, familiar to so many business-to-business executives, is that it's a game of diminishing returns. If we cut our prices, we reduce our margins. If we cut our costs, our competitors will follow.

Incoming CEO Lou Gerstner took a different approach. He saw that IBM's profit growth was dependent not on selling and implementing hardware and software, or even on providing integrated product-service solutions, but on transformation of the customer's business to support and enhance the customer's strategy. That of course had always been part of the sales pitch, but he turned it into a business model, affecting every aspect of IBM from who it hires and how it's structured to how it measures and reports success. That model centres on customer value: value to the customer, and value to the firm. IBM had long been customer-centric. Lou Gerstner made it value-centric.

Customer value is a bit like the tale of the emperor's new clothes that everyone complimented but which didn't actually exist. Talk of value is ubiquitous in mission statements and business plans, but when challenged, very few executives can define it, let alone measure it. I met a vice-president of a billion-dollar firm who had been given the task of measuring the value they created for customers. After a few months, he asked his boss to take it out of his year's objectives, as neither of them could work out how to approach the job.

Mark Davies's book is therefore long overdue. He begins with an insightful analysis of the problems that the world's major goods and service businesses are facing. He precisely delineates the multiple forms of value leakage they exhibit, from a lack of selectivity in targeting key customer segments to a lack of co-creation. He describes the vital but neglected role of demonstrating the value actually created for the client, without which superior margins are impossible.

Mark then unpacks how to create a great value proposition. When I began my career at IBM, Logica CMG and Xerox, we thought a value proposition was about benefits minus costs. But focusing on customer value means starting not with our offer and its benefits, but with the customer's business goals. Mark therefore derives a far more powerful formulation of the value proposition, which can be summarized as impact minus total costs of partnership. And impact in turn involves focusing the analysis on the customer's customer. This of course requires a great relationship and great account managers: but that's only a start.

If the book stopped there, it would have done the world a considerable service. This is the best, most useful and least waffly exposition of how to create a value proposition that I've seen, full of tools and practical insights. But it doesn't stop there. Mark draws on his long experience driving change in BP, as well as his work with Cranfield School of Management over the last decade helping blue chips to transform, in spelling out what is involved in becoming truly value centric. He tackles the role of structure – central in Lou Gerstner's transformation of IBM – with the invaluable concept of the value cell. He outlines how to measure impact. He gives particularly deep attention to the transformation of sales and account management, his core discipline. And of course he discusses people: who we need, what skills they require and how they're motivated.

This, then, is a highly practical book. We all know a great value proposition when we see one. But Mark Davies spells out how to create it – or, rather, how to co-create it with the customer – and vitally, how to make it happen. Along the way, incidentally, the book also helps us think more clearly about another vague term: business solutions. I have observed a difference between how suppliers and customers talk about solutions. To suppliers, a solution is a bundle of products and related services in order to provide a capability which takes pressure off the customer. Useful though that is, to customers, a solution enhances their proposition to their own customers, generally in ways that they hadn't thought of in advance. The book is full of tools and examples that give such clarity. What's more, it rings true to my professional experience working with some of the world's great companies; I'm sure it will ring true to your professional experience, too. Creating value for customers and other stakeholders is why organizations say they exist. This book will help make it happen, so I commend it to you.

Hugh Wilson
Professor Of Strategic Marketing
Cranfield School Of Management,
September 2016

Introduction: Accelerating profitable growth through value-based selling

> One of the only ways to get out of a tight box is to invent your way out.
>
> Jeff Bezos

If you are a senior leader in an enterprise organization, responsible for the delivery of profitable sales and growth of the top line, you may not have an easy job. Disruption from new technologies; global competitors; increasingly savvy consumers; professional buyers; and uncertain economic conditions can all lead to a rough trading environment (and you are in the eye of the storm).

The world is changing for many organizations that are selling products and services to customers in a business-marketing environment. Life is becoming increasingly challenging for sales directors, key account directors, heads of marketing, general managers and those responsible for developing and growing business. Historically, a portfolio of strong brands and products was enough to compete and consistently grow the top line. Today this is not always enough – and if you do have a product or brand advantage, the period of time in which you can enjoy making money before you attract the attention of aggressive competition is greatly diminished. There is nothing new here. Competitive forces have always been a feature of business. But with the seismic shifting macro and industry forces, the pace of disruption is accelerating.

Increasing global competition and ferocious disruption from technology and shifting macro-economic pressures can put suppliers on the back foot as the strength of their offering weakens or becomes obsolete. In addition, the customer procurement function is increasing in capability, power and importance. During the 2008 recession, many organizations relied heavily on procurement to reduce costs as a means of protecting profits. Today, procurement functions have retained a 'seat at the table' of the board, and their elevated status and power remains intact. The internet provides a further transparency for consumers and commercial buyers to compare and contrast virtually any purchase, again placing pressure on suppliers. The net effect of all of these changes potentially puts suppliers on the back foot, and if they have a weaker offering that does not demonstrate unique value to the customer, they can lose bids, lose growth with existing customers or see their offering increasingly commoditize and having to fight with the lowest common denominator: price.

Many organizations recognize this plight and seek a response by trying to improve the offering that they develop and take to the customer. *Infinite Value* was originally going to be a book about just this – a guide to demonstrate how to create a powerful customer value offering. At its heart, it still is. Chapter 6 (Offer development and innovation) is dedicated to this very topic. But in itself, this is not enough.

Organizations wanting to develop a strong competitive advantage that responds to changing market conditions, beating competitor offerings and meeting customer needs should consider doing business in a *different way*. If this business model were to be likened to an iceberg, the customer offering is the part that sits above the surface. It is maybe one eighth of the total business mass. The other seven eighths of the iceberg comprise the supporting elements of the business that make this way of working possible. *Infinite Value* looks at the seven eighths of the organization beneath the surface. In the dark, cold murky depths of an enterprise business that is capable of responding to rapidly changing market conditions and increasingly demanding customers, what does the successful organization look like? How does it function, and what are its core components?

While evidence suggests that organizations that focus on a value-based approach have a sustainable competitive advantage, becoming this type of organization is often a difficult challenge. Organizations that do follow this way of behaving are defined in *Infinite Value* as operating a value-based business model, and the focus is on describing the core components that enable this way of working in a practical 'toolkit' manner.

Infinite Value looks to address a practical question:

Question

What techniques do enterprise organizations adopt in order to develop a competitive advantage by continuously creating, selling and delivering value to their customers?

The book is structured in three parts to provide a blueprint that can help leaders to build an organization that builds value.

Part One discusses the shifting and changing trading environment in which many organizations find themselves. The case for doing business based on delivering customer value is made – along with observations that many organizations do not operate in this way. The seven foundation elements of value-based business are introduced and discussed as a suggested alternative business model.

Part Two describes each of the seven elements (Figure 0.1). This model is the core of *Infinite Value*, and the foundation of a value-based business. Each element is described in a 'toolkit' style, and can be adopted as a series of stand-alone techniques. For example, there is no reason why an organization looking to develop a new customer segmentation model cannot simply look at this one aspect of the customer strategy element. It provides a straightforward model to guide the development of a practical approach to achieve this. Far greater business results are achieved, however, when a more holistic approach to value-based business is adopted – linking the other six elements to customer segmentation and building an organization that balances its resources and ways of working around the customer portfolio.

Each of the elements is intended to focus the organization on co-creating value for the supplier and the customer. The focus is on building an understanding of what the customer needs to achieve by the strategies and activities they are following every day. By understanding this, and by having a clear appreciation of what is important for the customer, a clearer understanding of what they value can be established. This can shift the conversation. If the sale is focused on what you have it will

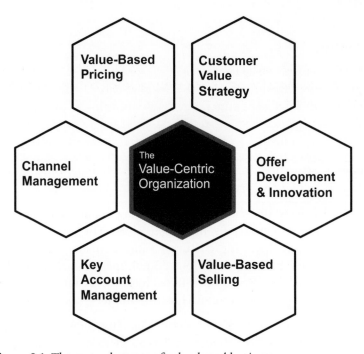

Figure 0.1 The seven elements of value-based business

be compared with other suppliers that have similar 'me-too' offerings. This puts the power with the customer, who can trade based on price. When your value position is determined by the price discount you offer, your value is finite.

However, if your position is based on other aspects that are important and of value to the customer, such as quality, compliance, business security and risk aversion, these can be unique and higher-ticket items. Value becomes Infinite, and will deliver stronger results for both you and the customer. Building an organization that focuses on an Infinite Value model is the focus of Part Two.

Part Three provides very practical techniques and advice to assist organizations in the transformation to a value-based business model, and how to keep working in this different way. Since every organization is different, there are simple tools to help with self-diagnosis and organizational assessments, to enable the application of techniques and equally to eliminate those elements that are not applicable to your business.

The seven elements have been identified, developed and used over a period of some fifteen years. I first identified them when working in a customer management function in BP, operating across different downstream organizations that operated in a global business-to-business environment. I was part of a central team that was tasked with supporting business units to develop the organizational sales capability and effectiveness. This can be a broad church of concepts, and the intention of my in-house research was to ascertain exactly what was critical and what could be de-prioritized. From several quite different business units (involving senior sales, key account directors, marketing and general managers) the seven themes kept coming through as factors that were seen as business critical. This set the direction for our 'internal consulting' activities – the subsequent focus of resources as we looked to build capability in these areas.

To further cement the idea that the seven elements are robust, my consulting work over the last eight years, working with many diverse industries (such as technology, logistics, professional services, pharmaceutical and medical, energy, engineering, industrial, telecoms, facility management, construction, civil engineering, and public sector) indicates that there is a requirement for a deeper understanding of value and value-based selling in order to become more competitive. When organizations have not focused on creating and developing value (or, for example, when they have relied on products and brands to do the value selling for them) a gap in capability occurs. With increasingly competitive commercial trading conditions, this approach may no longer be enough, and a focus on creating value with the customer becomes necessary. If you think you are in this situation, or if you recognize that money is being left on the table, the practical guidelines in this book can help.

As a final thought to introduce Infinite Value, it is worthwhile looking at the future. The seven elements were formed initially to define and build customer management capability. They still do this, but in today's fast-paced economic environment, with intense competition shortening product life cycles, a value-based business model provides more than just a way of developing the skills of front-line sales and accounts managers. It re-defines the way that an organization approaches the fundamentals of business and the strategies it follows. It can define a business model and an approach to the way business is conducted. This is an important point that needs to be stressed. Increasingly today, and in the future, organizations need to align the resources and thinking capability that they have. Sales are already shifting toward becoming more aligned and focused on a smaller portfolio of higher-value customers (key account management) – with the rest of the customer base being served by digital channels and/or third-party distributors. This is the reality of the future, and it aligns with the seven principles of value-based business, as a fundamental organizational capability.

The value-based business model will become essential rather than something that can be considered merely 'nice to have'. The models and techniques presented in this book provide a starting point to build competitive advantage and to thrive in challenging times, but it is a different way of doing business and will stretch advocate organizations that wish to work in this commercially robust way.

PART ONE
THE INFINITE VALUE CONCEPT

Chapter 1

Challenging trends for business markets

Even if you are on the right track, you'll get run over if you just sit there.

Will Rogers

Question
Why is it getting harder for business marketing organizations to keep doing business profitably?

Ever-decreasing circles

Charles Handy makes the analogy of a frog that is placed in a pan of cold water:

> ... it will not bestir itself if that water is slowly heated up gradually, and will in the end let itself be boiled alive, too comfortable with continuity to realize that continuous change at some point may become intolerable and demand a behaviour change.

This story resonates. It captures the idea that organizations sometimes struggle to look outside themselves, so change can creep up on them. Handy made this observation in his excellent book, *The Age of Unreason,* first published in 1989. The 'frog analogy' is one that I often use with Senior Leadership teams when discussing the concepts of value-based business and how it might apply to their worlds. I was recently working with a team of strategic account directors and heads of marketing from an energy technology organization. They pondered for several minutes as I asked them to pause for thought over the question: 'If your company was a frog, would you be in a comfortable place, or should you be hopping out soon?' One strategic account director summed up the team feeling with his reply: 'We can feel the heat and we know that we are starting to lose precious flesh, but frankly the heat is not coming on gradually ... it is being applied as if we are in a pressure cooker ... external change occurs rapidly, regularly and it is intense. It's really not much fun being a frog anymore ...!'

So, Handy really had something with his observation, and he delivered a complicated concept via a simple model. His observations since 1989 are not only robust, they seem to have become a way of life. During this period, computing, the internet, mobile technology, media devices and communications have reduced in price, increased in performance and become part of the mainstays of everyday life. In 1970, Gordon E. Moore, the co-founder of Intel, developed a law of computing power, stating that processor speeds (or overall computer power) would double every two years. That law has largely been found to be correct, with significant impact on technology; the development of the devices driven by these technologies; and, ultimately, significant changes to social and commercial life, as the devices driven by these faster (and cheaper) chips become more sophisticated and accessible.

Describing an overall historical picture of the events that have unfolded during the last twenty-five years is not the purpose of this chapter. Tensions and wars in the middle east, the end of the cold war, 9/11, the recession of 2008, AIDS and a massive trend towards business globalization are but a few of the macro trends that have occurred. The takeaway for those leading businesses is that change happens and it is rampant. Handy captured this idea perfectly. My client who observed his business was not just being boiled to death but 'pressure steamed' also pointed out that change was coming from many directions – and often these disruptive forces overlap: 'Our offers become affected as well – we come out with new products but the length of time they provide a competitive advantage seems to reduce year on year ... our product life cycles are a series of ever decreasing circles.'

Maybe there is an inverse reaction to Moore's Law for business marketing organizations. While the speed of computing power doubles every two years, the effective length of time that organizations can realize enhanced profits from these products and brands halves. I have no concrete evidence or research to back up this apparent correlation (maybe I should call it Davies' Law?) but it seems to capture a challenging scenario for many organizations.

All the macro-economic levers are being pulled

The best way to consider the external macro-economic forces that change and create opportunities and problems for organizations is a STEEP analysis (Social, Technological, Economic, Environmental and Political). This covers the breadth of external factors that subsequently impact on industries, organizations and consumers. According to Richard Dobbs, James Manyika and Jonathan Woetzel, in *No Ordinary Disruption* (2015), the world is now roughly in the middle of a dramatic transformation, and any one of four global forces/disruptions, by itself, would probably rank among the largest economic forces the global economy has ever seen. The four forces that they have identified are:

1 The age of urbanization: by 2025 they predict forty-eight of the largest 200 cities will be in China. This means that there is a shift of economic 'centre of gravity' back to the East.
2 Accelerating technological change: it used to take a very long time for a technology to reach saturation and scale – but now, driven by mobile technology and a greater readiness to adopt technology, an application can grow to fifty million users in less than a year (TV took thirty-eight years to achieve this level of penetration!).
3 Ageing populations: with advancing healthcare and improving living standards, people are living longer. This places pressures on economies, with governments facing a future with fewer workers relative to the number of elderly.
4 Greater (and more complex) interconnectedness: we are all more tightly connected than ever before. This is a benefit for organizations that want to trade and sell products worldwide. The

challenge is that competitors are also global, and may appear from industries and markets that you least expect.

No Ordinary Disruption also describes twelve technologies that have massive potential for disruption in the coming decade (Table 1.1).

All four forces identified in *No Ordinary Disruption* are significant for business marketing organizations. They present a profound impact by changing the background of what is important to customers, and in so doing they shift what suppliers need to do to be regarded as valuable and important.

There are two ways to view the changes. First, to fear them and try to resist the impact they have by trying to keep competing in spite of the new paradigms they present. Second, to stand back and be more proactive. Consider this: if these changing forces are causing you problems and uncertainty, are they also causing similar crises in the boardrooms of your customers, suppliers and other commercial partnerships?

If we are only half way through this storm of change, as suggested in *No Ordinary Disruption*, it can be assumed that there is more ahead: and

Table 1.1 The disruptive dozen: Accelerating technological change

Changing the Building Blocks of Everything	Rethinking Energy Comes of Age	Machines Working for Us	IT and How We Use It
1 Next generation genomics 2 Advanced materials	3 Energy storage 4 Advanced oil and gas exploration and recovery 5 Renewable energy	6 Advanced robotics 7 Autonomous and near-autonomous vehicles 8 3D Printing	9 Mobile internet 10 Internet of things 11 Cloud technology 12 Automation of knowledge work

Source: *No Ordinary Disruption* (2015)

possibly the pace of change will intensify and accelerate. One thing is for sure: these macro-level forces are not going away.

The buyer perspective

An example of where changing forces are altering a social trend is described by I. Simonson and E. Rosen in their book *Absolute Value* (2014). They outline what significantly influences customers in the age of (nearly) perfect information. It is a great example of colliding forces, whereby technology in the shape of the internet, mobile and on-line comparison sites and apps has changed the social behaviour of consumers, especially the way they make buying decisions.

A model called 'The Influence Mix' is presented by Simonson and Rosen, suggesting that consumers can make purchasing decisions with significant information that is gained from the internet and feedback from other consumers. Value becomes transparent and quantifiable.

- Marketing: the information that sellers send to the market in the form of advertising, brand positioning and promotions.
- Prior Preferences: the consumer draws on their own personal history and experiences when buying goods and services.
- Other People: this is an emerging influence, where consumers take the views of other consumers and seek advice (good and bad) about the products they are buying.

Simonson and Rosen propose that these three factors are always considered, but if one influencer is used more, the others will be reduced. The three influencers should make up 100 per cent of any purchasing decision.

Consider the Disruptive Dozen presented in Table 1.1. The trends under the heading 'IT and how we use it' potentially give even more information and power to the consumer. The opportunity to collaborate, share experiences and write reviews fuels the capacity for consumers who seek input from 'other people'. Sites such as TripAdvisor specifically aim to enable these conversations, but most sites have the opportunity for customer feedback, and it is increasingly an important factor to consider when making a purchase. When did you last ignore a string of 1-star reviews on Amazon?

Specific industries are also seeing changes whereby power is shifting to the customer. Eversheds is one of the fifty largest UK-based law firms. In 2010, they wrote and issued a report entitled 'Law Firm of the 21st Century. The Clients' Revolution'. They quote four major forces having an impact on the UK legal profession, with the recession accelerating these changes and intensifying the need to change. The Eversheds disrupting factors are:

- Globalization – the move to the East;
- Increasing professionalism and status of General Counsel (clients' own legal teams);
- Technology;
- The Legal Services Act in the UK.

Of course, some of these factors are unique to legal services, but technology and globalization are aligned with the other generic forces discussed so far. What is interesting with the Eversheds' conclusion is that power has shifted to the client, and the way for law firms to prosper post-recession is to really focus on client needs and provide offerings that they value.

Forrester, a market research organization, claims that we are now in the 'age of the customer': this period started in 2010, and continues to evolve. Previous ages were: (1990–2010) the age of information; (1960–2010) the age of distribution; and (1900–1960) the age of manufacturing.

Forrester claims that we are now in a period whereby empowered buyers demand a new level of customer obsession.

Conversations with senior commercial teams (key account managers, sales directors and marketers) also provide rhetorical evidence that buyers are becoming more savvy, have greater respect in their organizations and generally have the upper hand. In a market that is still fragile post-recession, and where, if suppliers have failed to provide a customer offering that is differentiated and clearly adds value to the customer business, why wouldn't buyers have the power in securing new deals and supply positions?

New norms: New challenges, new rules

We are living in a world where there are new 'norms' (normal situations) occurring at a fast and confusing pace. The basics of business are being turned upside down, with highly disruptive organizations taking advantage of technology and simply 'changing the game'. As Tom Goodwin of TechCrunch.com observes in his blog article, 'Something Interesting Is a Happening':

- Uber, the world's largest taxi company owns no vehicles;
- Facebook, the world's most popular media owner, creates no content;
- Alibaba, the world's most valuable retailer, has no inventory;
- Airbnb, the world's largest accommodation provider, owns no real estate.

If you are a business operator, supplier, employee or associate to any of those industries, your commercial life has recently been turned upside down. Imagine you are a taxi firm owner in London, an advertising agent in New York or a hotel chain operator (just about anywhere in the world) – your business has been disrupted. All parties need to understand what is happening, and they all need to respond. The rules of the game change, and they are altered by organizations that you have never even heard of.

The forces of disruption, however, are available for anybody to observe and utilize. Technology can be embraced by all organizations and new social trends can be observed and acted upon. Handy was right with his observations in *The Age of Unreason*: organizations need to have their antennae permanently outstretched, looking for major changes that are on the horizon as well more immediate short-term changes that may be happening within an industry or customer. Failing to look and anticipate the coming waves of disruption is one issue. Having the courage and organizational intent to respond to these changes is another.

The argument of this book is to centre the way an organization competes by the strength of the customer value propositions they create, develop, sell and deliver. High impact customer value propositions are fuelled by a number of factors:

- Strong insights about the customer business;
- A description of a future state for the customer and supplier;
- Insights about macro trends that are affecting the customer's industry (and your own industry);
- An understanding of the customer's value proposition that they take to their customers.

These insights describe the disruptive forces that are occurring in the customer's business. You need to have a grasp on what is fuelling the heat that is boiling the pan of water the customer swims in.

A shortsighted view on the customer will lead to short-term results. If suppliers maintain a view that the customer is a source of revenue, and sales strategies talk about how much product can be sold in the next month, quarter or year, this opportunity is potentially being undervalued.

Later in Part Two of this book, the case for a value-based business will be explored. There is evidence that this approach leads to organizations enjoying a more superior long-term performance. The secret to this is to focus on developing and delivering value for customers. With the pace of change and dramatic forces that are occurring today, it should be highly compelling for organizations to become very focused on value, collaborating with customers and other alliances in order to respond to disruptive forces and to prosper.

Chapter 2

A faltering response

If the rate of change on the outside exceeds the rate of change on the inside – the end is near.

Jack Welch

Question
What might be the reason(s) that some organizations struggle to compete effectively?

Observations from business marketing organizations

For many organizations in multiple industries, life used to be fairly straightforward. Once established, they could rely on the perceived value and benefits that were baked into their brand, and sell products and services to established customers in stable markets. Conversations with customers centred on understanding their immediate and narrow requirements, and then providing more of what had worked in the past. Business life was good. A career in sales could be lucrative.

Today, things are more challenging for organizations, and especially for account managers and sales people. The disruptive macro forces that are driving change in most industries place the customer in the driving seat, and can put suppliers on the back foot. Brands and products are no longer enough, competitors can change supply positions and buyers take full advantage by boiling purchasing decisions down to the lowest common denominator: price.

Businesses can see a shift in the markets they serve. The life cycle of products that historically might have lasted for years can be reduced significantly, maybe down to months. With this reducing product life cycle, and increasing competitive forces, it can be very difficult to maintain growth and retain profit margins. One of the most consistent and recurring challenges I receive when asking sales leaders in organisations about their biggest challenges reflects these changing pressures. A common request from suppliers is: 'How do we change the conversation that we have with buyers and get the focus away from simply price?'

Value in practice
A feeling of impotence ...

One sales manager working in a global oil and gas services' business described the shifting markets he was serving quite eloquently (but also tinged with a certain amount of desperation): 'Things used to be fairly straightforward ... we have very respected brands and our customers wanted to buy them ... But today ... I feel like a man with a fork in a world of soup ...'

When I first heard this issue, my initial reaction was to try to develop methodologies that enabled stronger negotiation capabilities for accounts managers so that they could defend themselves more effectively with increasingly capable and aggressive buyers. Being able to negotiate is a vital skill, and something that is often under-developed. Negotiation (at a very high level) is discussed later in this book, but it is not the answer in itself to enable organizations to defend themselves in this shifting environment. After much reflection and working with numerous organizations (many of which have very strong products and brands) it became apparent that there was a gap in organizational capability and the basic belief in the way some organizations operate. This gap is concerned with an ability to fully understand the concept of value that could be created and delivered to the customer (and by communicating this value position, being able to justify stronger supply positions and prices routinely).

Value leakage – money that is being left on the table

In order to model the observation that a lack of focus on value (and an over-reliance on product and brand) is a problem for suppliers, the value leakage model (Figure 2.1) describes this idea.

Value leakage is a concept that looks at a supplier when trading with a customer. The model applies to large strategic key account customers, but equally to smaller accounts. It attempts to highlight the fact that organizations often have significant potential value that could be delivered to the customer, but due to a lack of focus on the concept of value in use in the customer's business, this value is not discussed, captured or realized. In many cases, value is actually delivered to the customer, but since there is a lack of discussion regarding this value (the discussion is about the product and/or service) it is not qualified or captured. The value that is created 'leaks' away and is lost. What a waste!

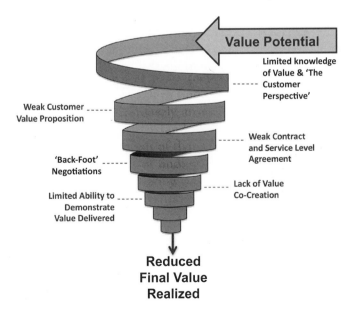

Figure 2.1 Value leakage

At the top of the spiral, like any energy model, there is potential value. This is calculated by considering the impact that the supplier products and services will have on the customer business. This will often be a very significant figure. The problem is that it is often diluted. If the buyer looks at the offer and merely compares it with the next 'equivalent' offering, value will be determined by the price they are paying (the customer sees the offering as a cost – a commodity to be reduced, both in volume and price). So the starting point for any value-based business model is to develop an organization that completely understands the customer business, and deeply understands the impact that the offerings will have on that business. Trusted and proven brands (products and services) help this: but it is no longer enough. In a business-marketing environment, suppliers have to work very hard at developing a strong understanding of how they create an impact on the customer's business – and what that means to them. In short, the bigger the value potential is at the start of the sales cycle, the greater will be the value at the end following the usual activities that chip away at this position.

If there is a reduced understanding of value, it follows that there will be a weaker value proposition. Part Two of *Infinite Value* discusses in a lot more detail the components of a value-based business, but Chapter 6 in particular (Offer development and innovation) goes into the fundamentals of the value proposition and supporting offer. It is this statement that captures the essence of what the customer will get from the supplier as a 'future state' vision. With a lack of focus on the customer's business and the challenges that it faces, the strength of the value proposition will be reduced. And yet, when working with organizations and asking them to describe the customer value proposition, a description of the products and brands frequently features at the front of the business case. An over-dependence on the generic product value proposition is provided. This is a good component, of course, but customers are looking for bespoke offerings that talk to their business needs, not the same offer that goes to their competitors because the supplier is just trying to shift boxes of product. These first two steps set up value potential, understand what the customer values and build a value proposition for the customer.

The spiral tends to accelerate downwards from here on. With a weak customer value proposition and commercial framework, it is logical that a weak service-level agreement and supply contract will follow. In the absence of describing a framework of services and activities that will create value, there can only be a description of the supply of product. This will potentially be limited in impact.

Negotiation will always feature as a critical activity in developing a commercial supply position with a customer. Even if you have done a great job identifying the potential value that you can create for the customer, and wrapped this as a high impact customer value proposition, all of this can still be undone if you fail to negotiate properly. Buyers may or may not understand your value pitch. They may trust or dis-trust you as a strategic supplier. But, if they are skilled negotiators, you can lose all of your potential at this stage. The more ideas and grasp of value creation options that you could deliver, the stronger will be the negotiation that you have. Conversely, with a limited idea of customer value, then your negotiation activity will be weaker.

Customers may want to collaborate with suppliers, in order to work together in seeking ways to develop more effective ways of developing business opportunities for both parties. The shift towards 'servitization/solution'-based business relies heavily on this idea. This way of closer working requires both customer and supplier to recognize that there are potential benefits in exploring and expanding the offering provided by the supplier. But, with a limited view of the customer's world, and what they value, why should this discussion even start? Why would any business collaborate with another business when they do not have a knowledge of what is important to them (and whose principal motivation is to sell more product). Value co-creation relies on both parties collaborating and seeking to build a combined new business model. Focus on value and the customer needs and this will become possible.

The final problem that arises is that, during the supply period, it is hard to demonstrate the value that has been delivered to the customer when these areas have not been explored, developed and described. Even if the supplier has had a reduction in fee (i.e. the customer did not accept the value position), it still pays dividends to track your performance. In two years' time, when it is time to renew the contract, you will be in a much more robust position to discuss future business proposals if you have a body of evidence quantifying the value you add to the customer business. Without this information, and without a focus on value, you are merely another supplier, fighting to win business based on price.

The bottom of the spiral is the 'reduced final value realized'. In reality, this can always be increased. Reducing the gap between this and the initial value potential is the focus of *Infinite Value*; a case is made to work in a different way, to follow a different business model and then capture more value for both the supplier and the customer. This is a different way of working and is a new business model, fundamentally with leadership recognizing that this is the way they need to operate.

Tensions and the headaches they cause

Tensions arise in any business that looks to follow a value-based model. These tensions are always present (even when the organization is clearly working in an established value-based manner). There are, of course, many tensions that can arise in business. Figure 2.2 presents four scenarios that are considered to be core issues.

The tensions are shown as left-hand side (the 'traditional' product-based business model) and the opposing right-hand side (the 'value-based' business model).

First, there is a natural requirement for organizations to be very focused on achieving sales quotas for the next quarter (or similar short-term period). These targets can become an over-riding focus and obsession for leadership and sales employees alike. This drives a short-term approach to business, and certain behaviour with sales people who receive attractive bonus payments based on these sales. The opposite side of the tension is the value-based longer-term view. The longer view of working with customers in a more strategic manner, looking to co-develop new offerings, takes time. If you are developing a bespoke offer for a key customer, the additional effort to deeply understand the customer's business and develop broader relationships

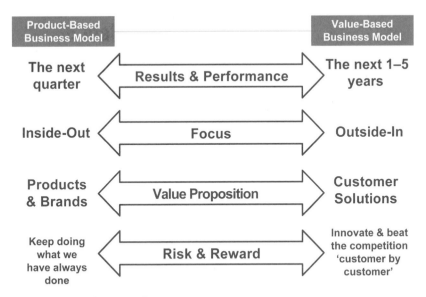

Figure 2.2 Business tensions

can take months, if not years (especially with global customers). This tension arises since they are two very different ways of working.

The tension 'inside-out' and 'outside-in' captures a business attitude. Organizations that look to sell whatever they have to customers take the inside-out approach. They look to find buyers who will take the generic version of their offer. Conversely, an attitude that is 'outside-in' is more focused on looking to understand the customer and to develop a unique offering that fits the needs of that customer. As Philip Kotler states: 'Marketing is not the art of finding clever ways to dispose of what you make. It is the art of creating genuine customer value.' The focus tension embodies this observation precisely, with the exception that it is the entire Value-Based Business that looks to create customer value, not just marketing.

The value proposition tension is linked to both of the preceding tensions. There is a shift toward suppliers providing service packages that enhance the core products that they make. The customer value proposition shifts from products to a more integrated offer that 'steps into the customer value chain'. This is a different business model, requiring different people, processes and commercial thinking.

The final tension is concerned with risk and reward. It is this tension that leadership has to consider very carefully and honestly. Staying in the traditional model, focusing on selling products/core services, can deliver results. Eventually, given the aggressive commercial world that most firms operate in, this may change, so a competitive advantage that worked in the past may erode. A choice has to be made – and the option suggested is to become a value-based business. Of course, there could be new products that are developed. These can be introduced and the same model of selling products maintained. Isn't it better to develop new products based on deep customer insights, and to sell them with a strong understanding of the value they deliver to the customer business? The suggestion carried throughout *Infinite Value* is to take the risks and adapt – and to implement and learn before you are on the back foot and having to change as a competitive response. Be proactive, before it is too late.

In reality, for all of the four tensions described above, it is not a black-and-white decision-making process. Behaviour on the left-hand side is critical (for instance, you have to make money in the next quarter ... otherwise, you will not have an opportunity to even think about planning to grow business with customers in one to three years' time!). There also has to be a blend of selling products, and for some customers it simply isn't viable to build a bespoke solution: they may be too small or perhaps do not want an advanced service offering. This is the challenge. Supplier organizations have to look at maintaining both sides of the tensions. It is not a healthy place to be too far to the left, or too far to the right. But if this tension model helps you to think about where you are today and consequently to apply some effort to shift a few degrees over to the right-hand side, then it has done its job!

As a final thought: organizations must be selfish. The value-based business model talks a lot about focusing on customer needs and satis-fying them. There should also be time spent that looks at the market and asks the question:

> Can we change the market by creating offers that provide value that our customers need but are simply not thinking about today?

Customers often demand that suppliers provide offerings that cater to their immediate needs. As a proactive supplier, you may need to ignore this and change the market. Being customer-centric is good, but developing a business that prospers is more important. As Henry Ford famously said, 'If I had asked my customers what they needed they would have asked for a faster horse.'

In more modern terms, Apple is famous for developing highly disruptive products into markets that did not have anything to compete with it. Consider the iPod, iTunes, iPhone and iPad. There is considerable competition in all of these categories now, but it was Apple that created the market – by bringing something that customers were not even thinking about.

This is a final tension (and a rhetorical question): do you exist for you or your customer to prosper and become wealthy?

There needs to be balance. Work hard to meet customers' needs – but don't get absorbed solely in meeting their needs. It might not be the best pathway for your own prosperity and survival.

Chapter 3

Is value-based business a better way?

The successful man will profit from his mistakes and try again in a different way.

Dale Carnegie

Question
Is there a better way to do business?

Is there a different way to do business?

According to Peter Drucker, 'Because the purpose of a business is to create a customer, the business enterprise has two – and only two – basic functions: Marketing and Innovation. Marketing and Innovation produce results, all the rest are costs.'

I don't know exactly when he said this – he was very active as a management consultant during the 80s and 90s, so it is fair to say that his thinking is established and not new. In fact, the essence of this quote captures everything about business and why some organizations struggle to compete effectively.

When organizations are young and in the 'start-up/entrepreneurial' phase they are totally obsessed about winning new business and customers. Figure 3.1 pictures Drucker's quote, and shows how bringing together innovation and marketing creates business growth. Another way to explain the model is to think of innovation as the means to create, develop and build something that people value and are willing to pay for, while marketing is the science of understanding

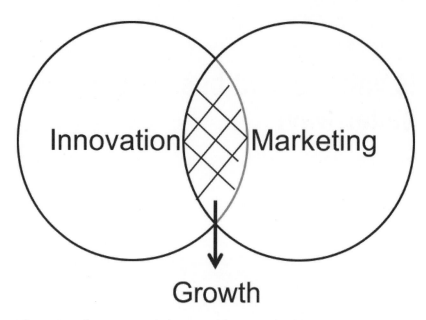

Figure 3.1 The purpose of a business (the two critical functions)

where customers are located and then selling this (product or service) to selected groups of customers.

However, as organizations get bigger, this idea gets weakened. Other functions can start to take primary roles, instead of supportive roles. The initial innovations and customer intensity that started the business can become choked or diluted. As long as the business has some form of competitive advantage (baked into the brand) this is manageable. The problem arises when things change and innovations are required. Speed of response is critical, as well as a huge reliance on innovation and dynamic marketing to re-develop the basis of how the organization competes. This is how things should be. In reality, organizations can sometimes get their priorities wrong. This can be for a number of reasons, including:

- Focus on making short-term profits and failing to look to the future.
- The organization's leadership team is mostly operational and cost-focused. This is typical of organizations when they become larger, since there is an emphasis on running an efficient organization in

a cost-effective way. This is a direct contrast to an innovation- and entrepreneurial-focused approach to business.

- Accountants lead the business – marketers and developers are not sufficiently regarded or valued (marketing is viewed as the people that design brochures and look after the website).

A final reason is that the culture and structure of the business simply do not lend themselves to aligning strategic marketing and innovation. Organizations become very complex structures of divisions and separate business units. Aligning these silos to respond to changes in the market is very difficult and slows down the ability to innovate. And yet, within the construct of silos and business units, most organizations have phenomenal sources of knowledge, resources, brainpower and talent. This collective organizational capability is focused on achieving one set of results, whereas colliding innovation and marketing (as Drucker advises) requires a *different way* of working and thinking.

Organizations should recognize that they could shift the way they behave: a re-alignment back to becoming focused on creating a customer by fusing innovation and marketing. This is easy to say, and hard to do, but a 'sweet spot' potentially exists for any organization that can become entrepreneurial while retaining operational excellence. That is something worth striving for and could be a way to compete in these challenging and changing times.

Will focusing on value improve things?

Professor Malcolm McDonald stated at a Cranfield School of Management sales conference in 2009 that 'There is just one line that focuses on sales on a profit and loss account (income statement), and 500 that subsequently focus on costs.' He built on the simple idea that organizations lose sight of the fact that they have to have a strong capability to develop a 'Top Line' – and this comes from an ability to manage a broad portfolio of customers by delivering high value offerings. The fact that organizations lose sight of this (and focus on the 500 lines of cost) is a huge misalignment of organizational effort and opportunity.

The significance of the talk being in 2009 is important. The conference was themed, 'Selling during a recession', and was looking to help business leaders of several large and varied organizations to deal with a challenging marketplace. Focusing on the top line is solid advice. And yet, during those difficult recessionary years many organizations failed to invest in sales and creating innovative new value propositions, choosing instead to cut costs and be drawn in by the other 500 lines of the profit and loss. What also emerged from this period (and continues today in some cases) is a tendency to simply win business by dropping prices with customers.

If there is a piece of evidence that strongly suggests that a business model should focus on a value basis rather than cost, it is the work conducted by Michael E. Raynor and Mumtaz Ahmed in *The Three Rules – How Exceptional Companies Think* (2013).

> The three rules
>
> 1 Better before cheaper
>   (Don't compete on price, compete on value)
>
> 2 Revenue before cost
>   (Don't drive profits by cutting costs, instead find ways to earn higher prices or higher volume)
>
> 3 There are no other rules, so to change anything you must follow Rules 1 and 2.

Raynor and Ahmed set out to establish whether they could identify what counts as 'exceptional performance' and the behaviours that cause it. Both were employed by Deloitte Consulting, and studied Compustat data for companies on American exchanges, between 1966 and 2010: 25,000 companies from hundreds of industries over a period of forty-five years. This uncovered 344 companies that produced statistically exceptional results. As Raynor and Ahmed state, 'exceptional companies deliver superior levels of performance for longer than anyone has a right to expect'.

The final analysis found that there were only two rules for exceptional long-term performance, with the recipe: better before cheaper, revenue before cost; there is no third rule. They continue with the research today, looking beyond American firms, but this is very solid evidence that there is a better way to do business, and that is to focus on a value-based business model.

Pricing theory also adds to the top-line/value theory. Marn, Roegner and Zawada state in their paper *The Power of Pricing* (2003): that pricing is the fastest and most effective way for managers to increase profits. By advancing one percentage point at a time, the average income statement of an S&P 1500 organization (a price rise of 1 per cent, if volumes remained stable) would generate an 8 per cent increase in operating profit (an impact of nearly 50 per cent).

By focusing on growing the top line, a huge impact in profit can be realized. However, in a similar way, a reduction in the top line will also reduce profits at the same rate. It is a double-edged sword!

So, why is there such a focus on costs and a lack of driving top-line performance, sales and a value approach to business? There is a strong argument to suggest that organizations prosper and deliver healthier business results when value becomes the way of working: so why is it so elusive? Several reasons may be contributing resisting factors:

- It is difficult! There is no question that building strong relationships with customers and subsequently developing and delivering unique value offerings is a more involved way of doing business. Far easier to stick to one set of products and minimize the level of adaption by each customer.
- It conflicts with an integrated business model. When organizations have developed over time to be large-scale, cost-effective production units, it flies in the face of that model to be nimble and responsive to customer needs.
- You need to be brave to change. Many organizations have been successful for long periods. They have established brands and business models. The pharmaceutical industry, for instance, has been hugely successful by developing patent-protected New Chemical Entities for decades. It is a brave leader who claims this model might need to be adapted.
- It is a cultural shift. All organizations have a certain DNA. This can be immensely powerful and defines the business and the leaders who

operate in it. Change is always a cultural challenge, and shifting to a value-based model can be the most difficult.

Refresh your business model

If success comes from having a business that focuses on 'better before cheaper, and revenue before cost' and a focus on top line and value, it would be good to pause and consider exactly what this means.

I suggest the following definition for value-based business:

Defining value-based business

A value-based organization strives to consistently create, develop and deliver offerings that significantly enhance the ability of customers to achieve their strategies, objectives and challenges.

It looks beyond selling a portfolio of products and brands, emphasizing relationship and collaboration with trusted partners.

The value-based business relies on all functions, departments and key individuals to align and support the development of innovative customer value propositions.

Organizations that seek to change and become more focused on value (and not being the cheapest or cost-focused) should recognize that it may require a different way of working and is a different business model.

To consistently develop compelling and innovative customer value propositions that provide value by developing increased results for the customer requires more effort in several areas. Researching, analysing, creating and delivering value propositions cannot lie on the shoulders of sales and account managers alone (though they are vital members of the organization). The value–based business model is more an ethos and a set of standards. Building an organization that behaves this way takes time, focus and energy – but the rewards to remain competitive are significant.

Figure 3.2 Accelerating business

Figure 3.2 takes the original model suggested by Drucker. His idea that 'marketing and innovation' are the only two basic functions is robust. I like to think, however, that adding in a value-based business model to the mix will accelerate this idea. The blueprint that is offered throughout this book to develop such a business can act as this catalyst: it emphasizes the core elements required to make marketing and innovation work effectively alongside each other.

It could be argued that marketing embraces the aspects of the value-based organization. Of course, there is an overlap – but the way that *Infinite Value* describes how these can be achieved is via seven very distinct and tangible functions and ways of working that can be grasped and implemented. They comprise the foundation of the value-based business – and will accelerate growth.

Focus on value co-creation

With a similar (and supporting) proposal, Lemmens, Donaldson and Marcos suggest in their book *From Selling to Co-Creating* (2014) a trend in business that requires a shift from traditional selling to seeking value. The box below provides the definition for value co-creation that they offer.

Defining value co-creation

'Co-creation is about transforming your customer to an active participant, to be able to deliver him/her maximum value.'

The four principles of value co-creation:

1 Focus on ends instead of means

2 Turn your customer into an active partner

3 Develop value propositions based on organizational capabilities

4 Focus on learning through dialogues and building relationships.

Lemmens, Donaldson and Marcos, *From Selling to Co-Creating* (2014)

There is a very strong correlation with the idea of the value-based business model and value co-creation, with a greater emphasis here on the sales function. The four principles they propose really grasp some fundamental issues that help businesses seeking to understand and adopt a value-based approach. Principle no. 2 (Turn your customer into an active partner) is closely aligned and captures the essence of Infinite Value.

When customers *want* to collaborate, and you are in a position to build stronger relationships and dialogue, this can lead to stronger value propositions. The word *want* is important, however. While it makes sense for many suppliers and customers to collaborate, they often choose not to (adopting a more transactional approach to doing business). Segmentation of the customer portfolio addresses this issue (if you are honest about how you and the customer behave).

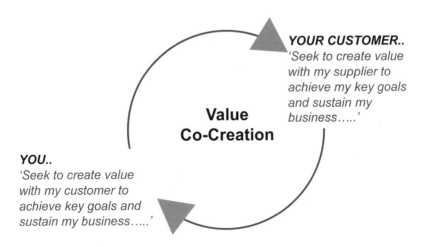

Figure 3.3 Value co-creation (common goals & beliefs)

Value-based business relies on partnerships between organizations that can co-create value 'technically' as well as emotionally and through shared views of business.

Figure 3.3 describes value co-creation as a 'cycle of common goals and beliefs'. When suppliers look to adopt a value-based approach with suppliers (and vice versa) there must be a common understanding that this is the right way to do business. It has to be a belief that business success will result by working in this way – not just for that 'sale or purchase', but also for the wider benefit of the business goals.

Value co-creation fails when there is a tension or lack of understanding between supplier and buyer. If either party maintains traditional trading methods ('I'm going to sell as much product as I can' or 'I'm going to screw you down on price') then trust will be breached and both parties are better off working with a transactional basis. As a commercial director once said, 'It is not always what we want that matters, actually, getting the customer to really consider what they want is more critical!'

Trust is based on understanding the other party, so you need to:

Walk a mile in your customer's shoes

But also …

Walk a mile in your supplier's shoes.

Value-based business needs a longer time perspective for suppliers and customers to establish just how much opportunity is available (or is being missed). If a sale is viewed as a 'one-off' transaction, then the only financial benefit is for that activity. The buyer may try to secure as low a price as possible, whilst the supplier tries to get a higher value.

Real value exists over a longer period. This needs to be estimated and discussed. The two phrases that are used for this view are from the supplier perspective – the customer lifetime value (CLV) – and from the customer perspective – the total cost of ownership (TCO) (Figure 3.4).

CLV:

How the **supplier** estimates the value of a customer over the total life span of relationship & supply

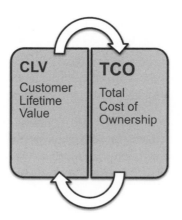

CLV
Customer Lifetime Value

TCO
Total Cost of Ownership

TCO:

How the **customer** estimates the total cost of a purchase over the life time of relationship & usage

Figure 3.4 Value: a two-way perspective

Infinite Value – a value-based business blueprint

To estimate total value opportunity, suppliers should consider exactly what value could be attained from a customer over the length of operation of the product. This will include such things as fees that can be received from maintenance, spares, support and advice, and repeat business. Similarly, customers will look at the supplier and take a longer-term viewpoint: 'How much will it cost to service, operate, support and maintain the product or offering?' CLV and TCO provide an analytical basis to consider a lifetime view of value, for both the buyer and the seller.

There is also a bigger picture that should be considered when looking at value. For instance, if the offering supplied mitigates risk, or enhances other parts of the customer operation, these aspects could overshadow the cost of doing business. Both parties need to really understand

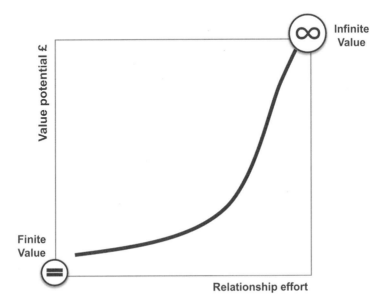

Figure 3.5 Finite or Infinite Value?

each other, and appreciate exactly what value is being created. Value is potentially a broad canvas. Rather than being finite, it could be infinite.

Figure 3.5 is explored more in Chapter 6 (Offer development and innovation). A simple initial diagram can consider the basic idea, however. Finite value occurs when minimal effort is made to co-create. Finite value looks like a 5 per cent saving a buyer achieves by screwing down the supplier price. It is a transaction-based saving and is often a target that many buyers aim to achieve.

Infinite Value is attained over a longer period. Strong collaboration between supplier and customer leads to establishing trust and identifying significant opportunities whereby the customer can make more sales, avoid stoppages, avoid compliance issues and drive quality improvements (to name just a few ideas that drive value). 'Infinite value' helps both parties to succeed by jointly looking at the bigger picture and finding ways to succeed.

Of course, Infinite Value does not occur with just one or two transactions. It can lead to a higher price for a single transaction. There could be value residing in this one purchase for the customer – but this may not be realized in that one transaction. Be realistic. As Louis Rukeyser stated: 'Trees don't grow to the sky.' But if you take a lifetime view, and keep co-creating with customers, value will keep being created. Think of customers as trees – they do keep growing, requiring support, care and attention.

> Trees don't grow to the sky … (… but they do keep growing!).
> Louis Rukeyser
> (my adaptation)

Building a value-based business will enable this way of thinking and collaborating with customers. It will not work for all customers, and not every deal will result in a strong value-enhancing result. But there will always be opportunities to innovate and create new offerings that benefit the supplier and the customer. It is just a different way of doing business.

Chapter 4

The seven elements of the Infinite Value organization

People who say it cannot be done should not interrupt those who are doing it.

George Bernard Shaw

Question

What are the foundation components of a value-based business, and how can they be applied to my organization?

The seven elements of the value-based business

To build a value-based business you need to have an organization that builds capability to focus on developing innovative customer value offerings on a routine basis. Innovation is usually found in new product development and marketing, but in order to be genuinely responsive and have innovation at the forefront of the business, it needs to thrive where interaction with customer relationships is the most active: flowing through the veins of the sales and account management teams.

The function that is sometimes formed to develop this organizational capability is called customer management. When I worked for BP, I was part of a customer management function, looking to develop and consult with global downstream business units and trying to establish what they required to improve their sales performance. In order to gain traction across the business, I spent a nine-month period working

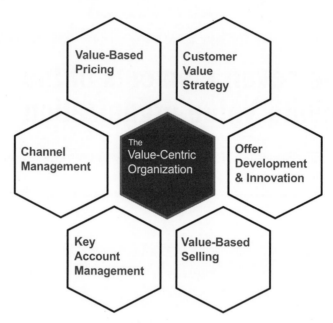

Figure 4.1 The seven elements of value-based business

with several diverse business units in our business, working across Europe, the US and Asia. I was trying to identify and prioritize the most significant areas that the business unit teams felt were crucial to enable them to do business with optimum effectiveness. The result of this study was to identify six core elements – shown in Figure 4.1. These six elements were:

1   The customer value strategy (incorporating a route to market analysis and customer segmentation);
2   Offer development and innovation;
3   Value-based selling;
4   Key account management;
5   Channel management (trading with third-party distributors);
6   Value-based pricing.

I have added a seventh:

7   The value-centric organization.

In an earlier iteration of the model the seventh element was called 'The customer-centric organization', but it has since evolved to be the broader concept of the value-centric organization, which I have found to be a robust model over the last eight years. Briefly, this is how the idea for the value-based business started. As I started my consulting practice, working with a wide variety of business-marketing organizations in technical, engineering, pharmaceutical, logistics, professional services, construction and many others, I have found this seven-element concept to be robust and very relevant. Organizations looking to re-focus on customer or value strategy connect with the model. They find the ideas and simplicity of the model practical and the results it can deliver very powerful.

The model is shown as a hexagon, with the six elements connecting around the central theme of 'value-centric organization', for a reason. Connectivity is very important and key to the success of the model. For example, organizations may embark on key account management programmes, but they struggle because the delegates have a limited understanding of value and value-based selling. In a similar way, most organizations serve key account customers via channels or third-party associates. If this aspect of business is weak, then the key account management programme will fail to deliver robust results. It's the same with value-based pricing. The concepts and ideas are very compelling but without the organizational capability to establish and run value-based relationships and sell based on value it will be a problem trying to implement it.

Everything connects: these seven elements have consistently been found to form the foundation value-cell to enable a solid organizational capability.

Part Two of this book provides more detail around each of the seven elements but, here, each element is briefly explored with reasons why it was identified:

1   **Customer value strategy**
    Customer value strategy enables an organization or business unit to develop a vision, objectives and goals, market analysis and an internal analysis to identify where value-based business gaps exist. It sets out a medium- to long-term plan, so that the organization can start developing new ways of working. As part

of this process, the analysis will look at the six elements of value-based business, and assess if there needs to be development work in these areas.

A critical part of customer value strategy is the development of the segmentation model – classifying the best route to market (channel choice) and customer descriptions (how you look at the customer, as well as how the customer looks at you).

2   **Offer development and innovation**
The ability of an organization to fully understand what value is and then develop offers for customer groups is critical. In many ways, this is the most important of all seven elements (after all, the customer buys the value proposition, they don't buy your KAM programme, channel strategy or pricing systems!).

3   **Value-based selling**
The core skill of sales people in a value-based business is to act as 'value ambassadors' with customers. They need to understand the customer's business, industry, challenges and threats. By having a strong grasp of these issues, the most important aspects of business that the customer values can be discussed. Value-based selling enables the creation and delivery of specific value propositions. This is not traditional selling, and is vital in the transition to become a value-based business.

4   **Key account management**
Many organizations find that they have 80 per cent of their sales and profit coming from 20 per cent of their customers. These larger, more strategically important customers require a more focused and leveraged approach to being managed. Suppliers need to increase the resources and efforts to ensure that business is protected and opportunities grown. Often spanning different countries and regions, and also taking business from several divisions of the suppliers' product base, key account management is a complex activity; it is also vital, as the trend in many industries is for increased consolidation – key account management is a critical organizational capability for many organizations.

5   **Channel management**
Many organizations rely on third-party distributors to manage the supply of products into markets. They offer a cost-effective

mechanism to extend the logistics, commercial, technical and operational reach of suppliers. It is a mistake to think of these channels as an option for purely cost-effective and economic reasons. If they are not selected, developed and managed correctly (and skilled in value-based business themselves), value and brand potential can be destroyed. Channel management considers third parties as essential strategic partnerships, not just as cost-effective (cheap) routes to market.

6 **Value-based pricing**
Value and price are inextricably linked. And yet, pricing is often misunderstood and badly resourced. If supplier organizations do an effective job of value-based selling, KAM (key account management) and offer development and innovation, there should be a good case to have higher prices. The pricing element also considers service-level and contract construct options.

7 **The value-centric organization**
Sitting at the centre of the seven elements is the value-centric organization. This is the way that the business manages itself to be focused on value and to build a value co-creation mindset. The value-based organization looks at all relationships to collaborate, looking at ways of working with suppliers, channels, competitors and associates.

The Infinite Value proposition

This book offers a practical framework for organizations seeking to add more value to their customers and to build a competitive advantage in challenging times. It can be used as a toolkit to aid initial self-analysis and then identify ways to improve performance.

It is more a handbook that guides practitioners and students of customer management, KAM and professional selling. My intention from the early development for the concept of Infinite Value has been to provide the case for doing business by continuously developing and delivering innovative customer value propositions. This has to be an alignment of effort and commitment. The sales-force needs to collaborate with the rest of the organization and become a value-force.

The three rules concept provides a solid rationale for doing business focusing on value, or as Raynor and Ahmed put it: *better before cheaper, revenue before cost*. This is the evidence of the concept. What is missing is a model that explains how to achieve a business that works in this manner. The *Economist* published a review of *The Three Rules* in an article entitled 'Corporate Strategy, Where Thinking is King'. This postulated that while Raynor and Ahmed work hard to provide rigorous data and research to make their conclusions, the difficult question remains: 'How do organizations find a niche to deliver value and to protect this competitive advantage?'

The Three Rules is a well-written piece of research. However, the observation made by the *Economist* is valid.

Infinite Value builds on the ideas that propose that a value-based business is a more sustainable and effective way to compete. It is not intended to provide additional research and data to build the case for value-focused business – this has already been done. Instead, it provides a framework of practical models that will help organizations to understand how to develop a strategy, build relevant foundation capability standards (that apply to the specific organization) and then take the business through a transformation stage to become value-based. It provides guidance for continuously developing innovative customer value propositions – recognizing that this is potentially a *different way of doing business*.

Infinite Value provides a blueprint to *build organizations that build value*. It is strategy: customer-by-customer.

Value matters

1   Life for some business-marketing organizations is becoming challenging as there are new macro trends evolving constantly, with new norms being established just as quickly as previous ones are embraced and mastered. All of the macro forces – social, economic, environmental and political – are highly active, but possibly it is technology that is the most disruptive. All of these factors present opportunities as well as threats, but

organizations need to respond quickly and carefully in order to prosper and grow.

2   To coin a phrase by Doobs et al., we are living in an age where this presents *No Ordinary Disruption*, and this is fuelled by a digital/internet age that if it were a movie would still be 'in the opening credits'.

3   Buyers are tending to have the power. Consumers have access to a wide choice of product and services that they can buy – with the technology providing them the opportunity to select products and services at the push of a button. Business-marketing procurement also has the upper hand, with transparency of data and supplier performance making selection and choice relatively easy.

4   These changes mean that suppliers can be in a situation whereby brands and historical supply position are no longer enough in themselves (although both are very critical). This puts suppliers on the back foot, having to find new ways to compete and continue growing business with customers.

5   There can be a faltering response from suppliers. When they have had an over-reliance by having value that is 'baked' into the brand, it may have been possible to use this to sell to customers. However, in the presence of increasing competition, a constantly shifting trading environment and increasing savvy and capable procurement, suppliers may not get the results that are required. Exasperating this scenario, when suppliers have a weak capability to sell based on adding value to the customer, potential business results can be lost. Customers can gain more value than they are paying for or the supplier provides a weak value proposition. Either way, the supplier can lose out.

6   According to Peter Drucker, the two essential functions in a business are marketing and innovation (all other functions are costs). *Infinite Value* adds to this idea, proposing that if an organization adopts a 'value-based business' model, accelerated growth is possible.

7   Value co-creation is a new trend for suppliers and customers. This concept connects perfectly with the idea of value-based business. In a changing and challenging environment, suppliers

and customers need to work together – collaborating to find new profitable opportunities.

8 There is strong evidence from research conducted by Raynor and Ahmed that the rules to success for organizations come from certain behaviours. These are principles that align with the idea of operating as a value-based business:

- Better before cheaper;
- Revenue before cost.

9 *Infinite Value* recommends seven foundation elements that need to be established for organizations seeking to become a value-based business. These have been used over a sustained period of time (more than fifteen years) with a large number of organizations in a wide variety of industries all over the world.

10 This book provides a 'toolkit' approach that will help practitioners and students to analyse their organization and develop a strategy with supporting capability standards. There is also practical advice to help with the implementation of these potentially different ways of working.

PART TWO

THE SEVEN ELEMENTS OF VALUE-BASED BUSINESS

Chapter 5

The customer value strategy

Manage the top line: your strategy, your people, and your products, and the bottom line will follow.

Steve Jobs

Question

What are the main steps that can be followed to develop an effective customer value management strategy?

Why do you need a customer value strategy (CVS)?

The first of the seven customer value strategy elements is *strategy*. The intent to build an organization that can compete using value-based principles requires leadership focus and effort to stand back and consider what the route forward will be. Building the CVS organization requires two main considerations in order to build an effective organizational capability:

1 **Strategy:** development of an effective value-focused road map to construct a value-based business.
2 **Transformation:** ensuring that the new strategy is adopted and value strategy becomes a reality and the accepted way of doing business.

Being able to continuously deliver a business that develops strong customer value as well as financial results for the supplier is what Infinite Value is all about. However, for some organizations, this can pose a very different way of doing business and it is not difficult to come up with examples of typical issues that arise.

The following are very real examples that have been captured during advisory workshops and consulting assignments when discussing a value-focused way of working:

Discussing the development of two-year plans for key customers

'These ideas to develop strategies over the next two years make sense and we could significantly help our customer ... but our business is set up to record product sales every quarter. We focus on selling boxes of product; it would be very difficult to get our senior leaders to work any other way. They are so focused on selling brands and products.'

Discussing the use of cross-functional teams to support account managers

'We have some great people in our technical functions ... they really understand the business our customers work in and could help the sales teams to come up with new ideas ... but frankly, they have to focus on their own personal performance objectives and they don't talk about customers. Our rewards and recognition systems just don't cater for this: people have to work in their own areas.'

Discussing gathering data about past sales to a major global customer

'Our customer relationship management system is very accurate and timely, so long as our sales guys put data in as required. The problem is we capture data by products and brands ... not by customers. We could modify the system to measure performance by customer, but we have cost controls in place at the moment preventing any changes to our systems. We'll have to make estimates about sales to customers...'

Discussing the use of customer strategy plans

'Our organization has just spent about £250,000 implementing a new sales training programme. It's quite good for some of our smaller customers but there is no strategic planning process for our bigger key accounts. We could really do with a good KAM planning template as these customers represent about 65 per cent of our business ... however we are investing serious money on a "selling by numbers" programme that we really don't need. It's really frustrating.'

Developing a strategy to focus a firm on having a strong customer value-based capability is an essential first stage in order to identify the key steps, activities and investment to be made to become value-based.

When developing a customer value strategy this should align with the overall corporate strategy. Sales strategies can sometimes 'disconnect' from the higher business objectives.

Peter Drucker (2008) identifies the five most important questions that you will ever ask about your organization:

1   What is our mission?
2   Who is our customer?
3   What does the customer value?
4   What are our results?
5   What is our plan?

As Drucker prescribes, strategy starts with the customer: understanding what they value and then planning to compete on that basis. Customer value strategy should align with (in fact it should flow through the veins of!) the higher corporate strategy of an organization. If done correctly, and with strong insights from each customer, an effective customer value strategy will bolster and enhance a business. Strategy and business performance should always start, endure and end with an understanding of who the customer is, what they need and how to compete by providing solutions to meet those needs. In today's constantly changing environment that picture changes very rapidly and frequently: suppliers need to be responsive and change tack in an environment of constant change.

It's a dirty little secret. Collis and Rukstad stated in 'Can You Say What Your Strategy Is?' (2008) that many executives cannot articulate the objective, scope and advantage of their business in a simple statement. They noted that if executives cannot articulate strategy, how can the rest of the organization? The article describes how a well thought out, carefully constructed and defined strategy will make more sense to the people who need to understand it. The other key point in the article describes strategy as being formulated around a clear value proposition, aligning with Drucker's thinking: know your customer and compete by adding value to meet their needs.

Element one of Infinite Value describes how to develop a step-by-step clear and simple customer value strategy.

The customer value strategy cycle

A six-step process is offered to enable the development of a customer value strategy. These six steps are shown as a cycle (Figure 5.1) since the activity should be reviewed and repeated on a routine basis. Reviews should be conducted to ensure that the strategies and actions identified are being implemented, while a repeat of the strategy should occur as set objectives increase and market conditions change to create new opportunities and challenges.

Figure 5.1 The customer strategy cycle

Step 1: Objectives. Initially, setting out objectives (the organizational goals) should be carefully considered and agreed with the input and agreement from the senior leadership team.

Step 2: Market Analysis. New 'norms' are emerging on a regular basis, at a macro-economic level, industry level and with competitors. Standing back and capturing trends today, and projecting to the future, are essential activities to provide the backdrop of future business.

Step 3: Customer Needs. Effective customer value strategies are more effective when the needs of the customer are clearly understood and a focused value proposition developed to help meet those needs. Organizations typically serve many customers, often thousands across many different countries. Step 3 asks the question 'Who is the customer?' and provides a segmentation methodology to help analyse the customer portfolio. Each customer segment is then positioned in ordered to enable a balancing of resources and effort.

Step 4: Value Position. Identifying what is needed for a strong value-adding organization requires the ability to stand back and assess what your internal strengths and weaknesses are. Organizations have a mix of capabilities, but inevitably, as the goals and environment change, the internal elements that enable the development and delivery of really effective customer value propositions can become stretched or misaligned. Step 4 discusses how to balance resources and build organizational capability around the needs of the customer portfolio.

Step 5: Strategies. Analysing the value position in Step 4 will flag up a series of high-level strategies that need to be implemented in order to improve capability. Setting and prioritizing clear strategies establish a pathway towards a better business model.

Step 6: Action Planning: The final step – each strategy is split down into a series of actions. These actions should be detailed with resources, timescales and key deliverables, and ownership identified.

Building an effective customer value strategy

1. Objectives: What do we want to achieve?

Setting out the initial target (and timescale to achieve it) is a critical step for the organization to consider. Too often, not enough time is spent on setting objectives, which is a mistake. If the objective is too soft, the strategy will not be appealing and may not get the attention of leadership. Too stretching and it could be seen as lacking in credibility. If targets are set too high, the organization will fail to achieve them and disillusionment can creep in.

Clear, carefully considered objectives will provide a stronger starting point for the customer value strategy (although remember that this is a circular process and after following all six steps a review of the initial objectives should be conducted).

Ask the question: Is this the right objective to make our business prosper?

Objectives should be described in two ways: words and numbers. Numbers provide clarity about the hard targets that the organization

Table 5.1

Hard Objectives (Numbers)	Soft Objectives (Words)
• Sales (absolute) • Sales (growth %) • Profit (by customer) • Market penetration • Market share • Sales mix (product v. service) • New customers • Shifting customers (direct to channel) • Share of wallet (by customer)	• Be recognized as a category captain with top three key customers • Win new business in Asian region (establish supply position) • Develop case studies in two new target sectors (aerospace and pharmaceutical) • Be recognized as the industry leader providing value-based solutions
Timescale to achieve objectives: e.g. 24 months	

is aiming for, while the words describe how the organization will behave, look and feel. Table 5.1 provides a set of hard and soft targets that have been developed with clients over several years. Note: objectives should be formed by a few components (this is an illustrative generic list).

2. Market analysis: What macro trends do we have to navigate?

In the day-to-day grind of serving customers and delivering business results, organizations can become too focused on today and ignore the future. Customers can force this hand – often procurement will force initiatives with suppliers that are focused on price and efficiency. To

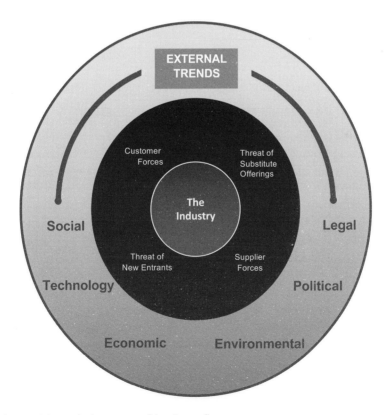

Figure 5.2 Analysing external business forces

remain in business, this has to be managed and respected. However, a focus on emerging new trends and changes in the wider macro-economic world and the corresponding changes that occur within the industry in which you compete should receive time and careful consideration.

A market analysis model is offered that provides a framework for this analysis and structured thinking. It offers a way to start gathering information and data from a wider perspective that will provide a clearer understanding of the external opportunities and threats emerging today and in the future.

Figure 5.2 shows the external analysis model. Analysis should start from the outside inwards, with the wider macro-economic factors being considered first, and then moving in to consider the industry within which you compete.

The industry analysis uses Porter's Five Forces/industry analysis technique:

The first step is the outer circle macro-economic analysis. The factors to consider have the acronym STEEPL:

Social Trends: Involve the cultural and demographic aspects of how people are behaving in target markets. Examples to consider in social trends include health and diet, population growth rates, age distribution, education, wealth status, social behaviour and family dynamics.

Technology Trends: Possibly one of the most active macro factors at the moment is the introduction and adoption of new advancements in software, hardware and engineering-based offers. Typical examples are 3D printing, mobile/wearable technology and cloud computing, The Internet of Things, advances in bio-technology, 5G mobile networks, driverless vehicles, electric/hybrid technology vehicles, robotics and nano-technology/new materials.

Economic Trends: Following the economic recession of 2008, this has become a major area of concern for many organizations (the so-called credit crunch will remain a focal point for all governments for some significant time). Economic trends include interest rates, tax rates, exchange rates, inflation/deflation, bank attitudes to debt, financial stability and stock market performance.[1]

Environmental Trends: Naturally occurring events as well as man-made influences create environmental trends. Naturally occurring examples include drought, flooding, coastal erosion and weather change. Man-made examples include pollution (air, water and soil), rainforest destruction, global warming, oil and fossil fuel extraction and refining, and damage to fish and coral. A big question is to challenge if the naturally occurring environmental trends are due to human/industrial activity.

Political Trends: Governments set policies to stimulate and encourage economic performance and to establish policy on such things as healthcare, social care, industrial policy and control (e.g. banking, pharmaceutical and energy), defence and policing, and financial policy. Changes in government can significantly alter markets and how businesses perform within them.

Legal Trends: Economic and political policy becomes enforceable through legal policy. Examples of legal trends and factors include tax law, employment law, safety law, competition law and industry laws (e.g. the FDA setting policy for food and drug supply in the US).

To analyse the effects of these macro-economic (STEEPL) factors is part science, part art. The scientific activity comes from analysis and gathering data. The art comes from the *interpretation* of what this information indicates about the future. To enable this activity it is always recommended that a cross-functional team work on the customer value strategy – looking at trends and assessing what the impact might be (on the industry and the organization itself).

The second step of the external analysis is to look at the industry within which you operate. Porter's Five Forces is suggested to enable the development of an informed model. All companies operate within an industry (sometimes several if they are diversified) and all companies

---

[1] At the time of writing and editing this book, the British conservative government is going through a major shuffle. On 23 June 2016, the UK voted to exit (BREXIT) the European Union, possibly the biggest economic shift for the UK (and Europe) since the end of World War II. Good or bad, this creates a major level of uncertainty and change for any organization.

Table 5.2

1. Customer (Buyer) Power	2. Supplier Power	3. Threat of New Entrants	4. Threat of Substitution
• Number/size of customers • Price sensitivity • Ease to switch supplier • Buying behaviour	• Number/size of suppliers • Technology/ uniqueness • Cost to change	• Time barriers • Cost barriers • Know-how • Technology • Patents • Labour	• Alternative technology • Alternative business model

5. The Industry (Competitor Rivalry)	
• Number of competitors in the industry • Geographical coverage • People – leadership and talent • Quality/value differentiation	• Customer loyalty • Ability to compete on price • Buying power • Competitor reputation/brand/ positioning

are subject to these Five Forces to a greater or lesser extent. In 'Five Competitive Forces that Shape Stategy' (2008) M. E. Porter offered a number of defensive strategies to counter these forces. In some industries, the Five Forces control the ability to generate profit considerably. The five industry forces are explained in Table 5.2.

Expanding on the Five Forces and suggesting defensive strategies for each:

1 **Customer (buyer) power**

   Customers have power when they have choice to buy similar offerings from multiple suppliers. They can pick and choose, and procure on price.

   To counter customer-buying power, expand the value proposition, offering unique value propositions that stand beyond competitor offerings making switching harder for customers. Understand target customer needs and provide offerings that they value and will pay for.

2 **Supplier power**
The supply of materials, energy, sub-components, people and services is part of any organization's value creation process. If these suppliers are in a strong position (by providing unique or specialized offerings) they can raise prices and reduce your profits.

To neutralize and manage supplier power, standardize specifications for parts so that switching supplier and focusing on price reduction is possible. Additionally, select strategic suppliers and work with them to develop value-enhancing solutions.

3 **Threat of new entrants**
New entrants are other organizations that threaten to move into an industry by offering an alternative (but similar) customer offering. This could be by being more price competitive, or it could be by offering better customer service, stronger quality or a broader and deeper range of products and services.

To defend against new entrants, traditional strategies include elevating fixed costs of competing (e.g. manufacturing processes and/or continually investing in R&D [Research and Development]). A very focused approach to considering whom future competitors might be, and staying close to customers to understand what they truly need and value, will enable you to remain competitive and able to keep changing the game from within the industry (not by being disrupted from outside it).

4 **Threat of substitute offerings**
Industries get disrupted when new offerings are introduced, often negating the industry and removing the need for products and services.

To limit the threat of substitutes, keep close to the customer (and the customer's customer) and stay strategic. Don't be locked into today but balance time between being tactical (serving customers today) and strategic (being disruptive yourself in the future).

5 **The industry (competitor rivalry)**
Competitors collectively form an industry. They create value (products and services) and fight to gain business from target customers. To reduce fighting on price with competitors, invest in products that differentiate and offer enhanced value to the

customer. This requires deep understanding of what customers value, and of how they add value.

Table 5.2 offers a summary of the factors to be considered when trying to understand the five industry forces. The model has been in place since the 1980s. It is a robust methodology that deserves to be adopted in any strategic review. With the pace of change that is occurring today (especially with the adoption of new technologies) an aggressive strategic focus on industry changes and disruption from all five forces should be respected.

The customer value strategy approach to industry analysis is a perfect fit. Understanding how to compete on value and not price lies at the core of how value-based business works. Understanding all of the organizations and forces at play within an industry and responding accordingly is an essential component of being competitive.

3. Customer needs: Who is the customer? What do they need? (Segmentation. Segmentation. Segmentation)

Organizations can supply portfolios of many thousands of customers. These customers have differing requirements from you, but you too will have differing commercial aspirations from each of them. Typically, customers will be attractive as they buy products and services today and continue to do so in the future. Customers are not all created equal, however. Some are smaller consumers and some are larger. Some are proven and have a history of trading with you, while others you suspect could have great potential.

A critical 'keystone' stage of any customer value strategy is to segment the customer portfolio. This will enable balancing/aligning precious resources with opportunities by each customer. Organizations get into problems when they over-serve customers that cannot provide a good return, and under-serve those that can. Segmentation is the process that sets the foundation to build a value-based business. Organizations segment their customer portfolio in many ways.

A methodology is suggested in Figure 5.3 that is practical and has been applied to many organizations in many industries.

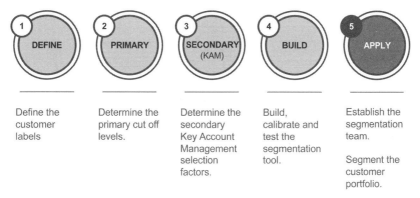

Figure 5.3 Customer segmentation stages

1. Define

A suggested segmentation structure model is provided (other models can be used, but for the purposes of this text this one will be adopted because it is often favoured by many organizations). Organizations need to classify the customer base and 'picture' how they will look. This consists of an initial primary cut, where the customers are put into three tiers: foundation, core and key.

Foundation customers tend to be smaller (by opportunity for the supplier) and have limited scope for future growth. There is typically a larger number of customers in the foundation tier. Core customers are slightly larger, and require a more focused approach from account management teams. They comprise a smaller group of customers, but have a greater opportunity 'per customer'.

The customers that fall into the key classification are a smaller group but also very high value. They are more complex to manage but the potential rewards can be significant. If you lose the business from a key customer it can severely damage overall business performance. Figure 5.4 shows a model that describes the primary segmentation model.

Figure 5.5 illustrates this thinking. The larger key customers represent greater opportunity (and risk, if they are lost to competitors). They also require an increased amount of effort to identify a strong value proposition.

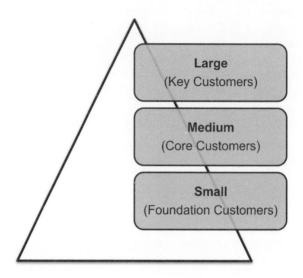

Figure 5.4 Primary customer segmentation model

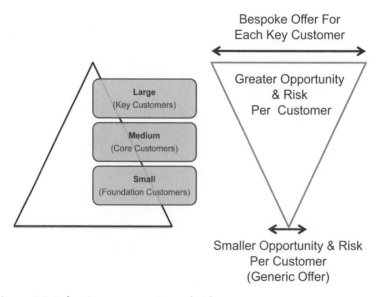

Figure 5.5 Balancing opportunity and risk

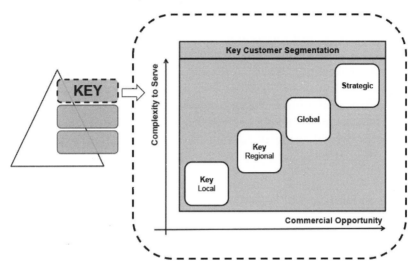

Figure 5.6 Secondary customer segmentation

Foundation and core customers can be managed with a simpler 'generic' offering.

When conducting the primary segmentation exercise, care should be taken to identify high potential customers that fall into the foundation or core segments. Just because a customer is providing low (or even zero) sales today does not mean they will not be key in the future. A system to tag these 'HiPo' customers should be included.

Defining the second part of the segmentation model is provided in Figure 5.6. This is a further classification of key customers. The label 'key' is very wide and covers a range of different customer types with different opportunities (and different management challenges). Four common key sub-types are provided in this model.

1   Key (local): These will be key account customers that reside in a local area/country.
2   Key (regional): These will be key account customers that have operations/touch points in several countries across a region. They require a different approach to management as the expectations of supplier and customer shift between countries (for example, across Europe).

3   Key (global): Moving beyond regional, these are large-scale customers with a requirement to be served across two or more regions (for example US, Europe and Asia).

4   Key (strategic): These customers are different because they take products and services from a number of different supplier business divisions. The co-ordination across these business silos requires increased effort to manage. Alignment of resources can prove very beneficial, however, by leveraging business between different business units of the customer.

These are suggested definitions for key accounts. Of course, every business needs to find definitions that fit their purpose. Some organizations operate within only one country, which would negate the need for a regional or global customer type, but there could still be a strategic classification. It does not really matter what classifications are adopted, the critical aspect is that there should be a review, consideration and acknowledgement that not all key account customers are the same and that the organization needs to manage different classes appropriately.

2. The primary threshold bands

These are usually defined by financial values (typically, annual sales). Once set, this provides an initial 'filtering and positioning' of the customer portfolio. An example from a consulting practice provided an analysis of the primary segmentation, as shown in Table 5.3.

The primary segmentation provided an interesting shape to the business. It also showed a model that the business could discuss

Table 5.3 An example of primary segmentation limits

	Threshold (Sales per Annum per Client)	Number of clients	Total value 2015	Total value anticipated 2020
Key	£(750–2000) k	27	£38m	£78m
Core	£(149–749) k	220	£50m	£63m
Foundation	£(0–149) k	680	£34m	£36m
			£122m	**£177m**

for future analysis of how to deal with an anticipated growth in key account customers (and the organizational challenges that that presents).

Once key customers have been classified (local, regional, global or strategic) there should be further refinement based on the type of relationship and the expectation between both parties. This should be thought of as:

- How important are you to the customer?
- How important is the customer to you?

3. Secondary (KAM) segmentation

This should focus on value creation. This comes from buyer and seller working together. However, regardless of how much you want to work with a customer, if they do not see value in return the relationship could become strained and will not work. The better approach is to analyse each customer and establish what the *mutual* relationship is like. Businesses have relationships. As the saying goes, 'Companies don't buy from companies: People buy from People.' Relationships

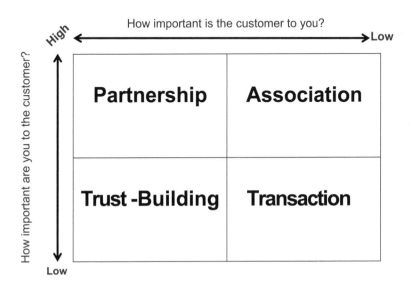

Figure 5.7 Positioning customers by relationship

are important, and analysing customer relationships provides critical insights to trading performance.

Figure 5.7 shows a table that maps mutual relationships. From analysing each key customer, there are four types of relationship:

Partnership KAM: The customer is important to you, and you are important to the customer
These relationships are balanced, mutually beneficial and both parties consider it worthwhile investing time, energy and effort into making things work. There will be open and transparent discussions of how to work together to generate results.

Transaction KAM: The customer is less important to you, and you are less important to the customer
It is doubtful whether either party will see the other as completely unimportant, but their business relationships become necessary and they can focus on a commodity basis (price and adherence to specification tend to become the commercial mechanisms).

Relationships here are based on providing the minimal investment to just 'get the job done'. Investing beyond this level reaps very little reward; indeed over-serving a transactional customer just dents profit margins.

Association KAM: The customer is less important to you, but you are more important to the customer
These relationships need to be managed carefully. Customers that really like your offering but do not have the growth potential, scale or other positioning to be really important can suck in resources if not controlled carefully. Manage carefully – things may change in the future, whereby the customer becomes more attractive!

Trust-building KAM: The customer is important to you, but you are less important to the customer
For any number of reasons, these customers view you as being less important. This could be due to lack of trading history, scale (you just don't register as a big enough supplier, regardless of what you provide), location, or lack of appreciation of what you could provide. Regardless of this position, if the customer is potentially important then you need to build a relationship and establish trust. This takes commitment,

time, effort and focus, but long term, these could be the customers that become partnerships of the future.

All key customers will exhibit a relationship trait. Figure 5.8 shows how the previous segmentation model can be further detailed to capture this analysis. The management and development of these relationships falls into the leadership of the business unit that looks after the customer. Local key accounts will be managed within the country, regional by that leadership, while global and strategic accounts should be discussed at a leadership level.

To provide more detail when asking 'relationship importance' questions, a number of different factors should be used. While the primary selection mode is done very simply using sales, the secondary selection should be more considered and expansive. These factors should be selected and aligned with the nature of your business and the nature of the customer's business.

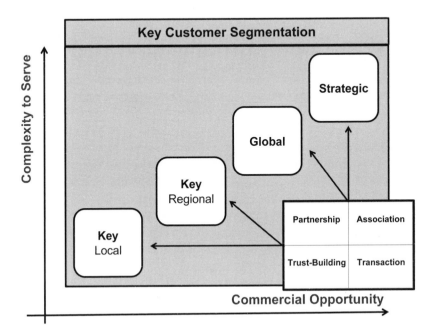

Figure 5.8 Matching relationship to customer type

Factors fall into two categories:

Quantitative: based on hard financial factors. For example, the size of the customer measured by the number of operations they have, or the number of products they produce each year.

Qualitative: based on softer factors. These need to be described and applied to some form of scale to enable comparative positioning in the segmentation process.

A mix of these two is really important and should connect with the overall strategy of the business, the products and services it provides and the value proposition. Why would customer segmentation be developed with misaligned decision-making factors?

When selecting the attractiveness factors, it is a good idea to brainstorm a broad list first. An example of such a list is shown in Table 5.4. The next stage is to brainstorm this list and shortlist two or three from each side. (For example purposes, three have been underlined on each side of the table.)

Table 5.4 Examples of customer and supplier attractiveness factors

Customer Attractiveness Factors: *How attractive is the customer to us?*	Supplier Attractiveness Factors: *How attractive are we to the customer?*
• Trophy name • Aligned with our sector strategy • High spend on our services • Relationship history • Growth opportunities • Interesting work • Geographical alignment • Profitability • Procurement less aggressive • Strong financial health • Realistic opportunity to grow • Large number of operations • Need help with compliance • Good payers!	• Attractive to use 'Top 20' London-based firm • Geography/spend preference • Sector knowledge • Price/value attractive • Reputation and brand • We have connections • Muscle/breadth of expertise • Financial strength • Commerciality/risk share • Intermediary intros • User friendly • Proactive & innovative

4. Build

Weightings can be provided when developing the segmentation tool, for instance growth opportunities might be seen as more important than the number of customer operations. The weightings could be split across the three prioritized factors as 60 per cent, 20 per cent and 20 per cent.

When the attractiveness factors are established, the segmentation model can be developed. This is usually built onto a spreadsheet to capture all of the data and decisions that are made. The model should be calibrated by populating with a small group of customers that you know fall into each category.

The build stage also requires the formation of a KAM selection panel. This is a group of representatives across the organization who will meet and discuss to consider each customer's merit, firstly as a key account and then how they should be segmented. Panel membership will be a mix of commercial sales and marketing, technical, supply chain and business leaders. Individual expertise should be able to provide non-biased but informed knowledge about each customer and realistic ideas regarding potential and effort to manage.

5. Apply

Conducting the primary segmentation is relatively straightforward. Once the threshold levels for each band are set, the identification of the customers that fall into each band can be made by a spreadsheet, especially if a straightforward figure such as annual sales is chosen. More care and attention is required when scanning all customers and establishing which ones in the lower bands have the potential to be key accounts in the future (some of these may have very little or even zero spend today). These high potential (HiPo) customers need to be identified by leaders in the business and put forward to the secondary KAM segmentation stage where they will be reviewed by the KAM segmentation panel.

The secondary segmentation panel should meet over a few sessions to gather data and assess each customer for KAM status. Do not overwhelm the panel with huge numbers of customers; typically thirty to seventy customers should be reviewed and scored using the secondary selection criteria.

A final note on customer segmentation:

Building a segmentation model provides a framework to make better-informed decisions about how to manage and resource customers. While a spreadsheet tool with weightings and descriptions is defined, it should always be seen as *part of the process* that helps the business decide how to position and manage customers.

It is the leaders of the business who decide how to manage customers, not a spreadsheet model.

4. Value position: What do we need to compete?

After considering the external environment and industry and looking at positioning customers by understanding what they need and how you can align with them, a look at the internal strengths and weaknesses of the organization should be considered. Strengths and weaknesses are determined by comparing what you have, along with what the customer needs and how effective competitors are at meeting these needs. This

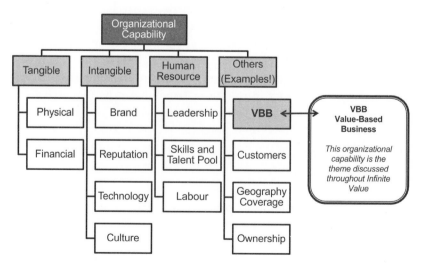

Figure 5.9 Organizational capability tree

analysis provides organizations' value position, and addresses the question, 'What do we need to compete?'

Figure 5.9 is the organizational capability tree. It is a model that helps to assess any organization's ability to operate and compete by creating value for its customers. There are four key categories of organizational capability:

1 Tangible assets. These are tangible assets (such as factories, offices, plant and machinery) and financial assets (cash or access to funding via shareholders and loans). Tangible assets take time to develop. They can be strengths if they are in the right location, are operating with efficient modern technology and are equipped to make the right products. They become weaknesses when they are outdated, inefficient or located in the wrong part of the world. Lack of financial strength can hamper an organization's ability to prosper, hindering expansion or even an ability to stay operational if cash flow becomes challenging.

2 Intangible assets. The 'invisible' assets of organizations are often the most important. These include the brand of the organization (and the brands of products and services they own), reputation, culture and technology. The ability to maintain strong brand equity enables an organization to have stronger dialogues with customers and maintain market share and price positions. Real benefits occur when these assets can be protected with patents, especially technologies.

3 Human resources. '*Clients* do not come first, employees come first. If you take care of your employees, they will take care of your clients' (Sir Richard Branson). It puts a spotlight on this asset, which comprises leadership, employees and talent resources employed within the organization. For many organizations, enhancing the value proposition they provide to customers with services will increase the need for great people.

4 Other resources including capability. Any organization will have a whole host of things they compete with and consider to be resources. Business models attempt to capture and map all options – sometimes it is just easier to have a category called 'other stuff'.

However, 'value-based business' as a capability (and an asset) is included. This is the ability of the organization to compete on value and to be effective at the seven elements of value described in this book. This is a critical capability and a critical asset – organizations will have strengths and weaknesses in this asset area.

Capability can be split down into four components to describe how an organization should be constructed:

i. **Leadership aspects**
   The leadership of an organization set the overall direction, intent and culture of the business. Leadership sets out the right values to make an element work.

ii. **People aspects**
   Sales, account managers and key account managers clearly have to be specified, recruited and developed to manage customers. Value-centric organizations also need the right support teams and alignment across functions.

iii. **Process aspects**
   Ways of working, systems and analysis methods should be in place to provide a blueprint of how to operate. Process aspects should be in place to define the models that the organization has established as being the way that critical activities are managed.

iv. **Planning aspects**
   Every customer should have a customer plan. Key accounts will have more complex documents, setting out a strategy for growth over a number of years, since these customers have larger opportunities but need a bespoke strategy to identify and capture this value. Smaller foundation customers will have a much smaller plan (maybe just a few statements on a CRM system) – but they will have a plan.

Figure 5.10 shows how this capability model should describe each of the seven elements. To assist in this self-analysis, each of the seven elements has a series of questions in Part Three (Chapter 13). The questions link to the content that is provided to describe that particular element of customer value strategy, and enable a simple self-assessment to identify where strengths and weaknesses might be. Where there are weaknesses that are considered to be restricting the

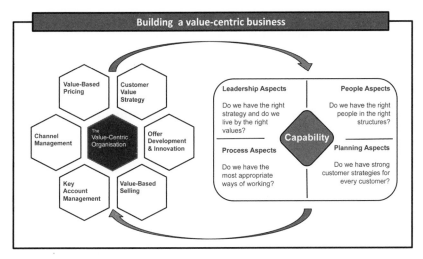

Figure 5.10 Building a value-based business

ability of the organization to be effective at that element, these should be identified as requiring corrective actions. Strategies should be developed to enable these corrective actions to be introduced.

For a complete picture of where these gaps might be, there should be an assessment following the seven elements. There may be occasions when an organization does not need to complete all seven (for instance some organizations do not use third-party channels to serve customers), in which case this element is simply omitted.

To develop a strategy, follow the descriptions in this book and complete the questions at the end of each element. This will provide information that can be pulled back into this stage 4 of the strategy development (remember that the strategy cycle in Figure 5.10 is iterative – you need to go around the various sections to get a full capability picture).

5. Strategies: How do we build our competitive advantage?

The gaps identified in the element analysis will mostly be derived from weaknesses.

Strategies should be worded to correct these issues and to develop a stronger organizational competitive advantage.

Strategy statements should be high level, but clear.

Strategy examples from several different elements are:

From offer development and innovation assessment
- Develop a bespoke value proposition process;
- Create more generic value propositions for transactional customers.

From key account management assessment
- Create a bespoke KAM planning tool;
- Improve the competence of key account managers.

From channel management
- Identify strategic channel partners and other distributor types;
- Increase profitability performance with distributors.

Action planning
- How do we plan to deliver our strategies?

Finally, strategies need to be broken down into smaller bite-sized parts to ensure that they become a reality. These actions should include the following:

- Identify the overarching strategy;
- The right number of actions to make execution clear;
- The action owner;
- A timescale to complete;
- Connections with other actions.

Example of a completed strategy

To demonstrate how the customer value strategy can be combined on a simple two-page model, the final part of this chapter shows a strategy that was developed for a global transport component manufacturer. This was a strategy workshop conducted with the global KAM group. The business makes precision components for global manufacturers of earth moving, agricultural and transport systems. They are an established business, but suffering from changing markets and increasing competition.

The two-page model is provided as a very high-level template. It demonstrates how a lot of complex analysis and strategic thinking can be captured in a logical simple model (from vision to action).

The case study that is described by the model typifies the issues facing many organizations. It also shows how a value-based business approach was critical to help this organization work towards some stretching new targets. Note that the strategies are for year one of transformation only. Other areas to improve were identified, but they were not detailed in this particular instance.

Example of a five-year customer management strategy:

Five- Year Customer Management Strategy
The Earth and Agriculture Components Company
(EAC Company PLC)

Objective	Vision
Grow the overall organization Top Line Sales by 20%	*To be the preferred component supplier to our target Global – Key Account Customers*
Improve gross margin by 5%	
5-Year timescale	*To be recognized as providers of technically excellent components, sub-assemblies and strategic advice*

EXTERNAL ANALYSIS

External Threats	External Opportunities
1 *Agriculture markets suffering – grain and commodity prices are depressed. This has reduced sales in our customer businesses by 10–20%*	1 *Demand for fuel efficient equipment (long term, oil prices will stabilize and increase again)*
2 *Construction markets are slowing in key markets (China, US, Europe)*	2 *Operators are looking for more automation (they seek cost reduction in farming and construction operations)*
3 *Increasing competition from competitors in India and China. They used to be local – now competing on a global basis. Their core products are significantly cheaper than ours*	

Summary and Analysis of External Analysis

The markets and customers that EAC Company serves have been suffering for approximately 18 months. This is a short- to medium-term effect on our customer operations ... and consequently this is impacting our sales.

The increasing competition from manufacturers that were in local markets (e.g. India) but are now seeking to compete in our main markets is compounding the impact on our business. With customers seeing a reduction in their sales and profit margins, it is very attractive for them to take components from suppliers offering much cheaper products (and in many cases very similar base-line quality and performance).

The markets are changing and our traditional supply position is being squeezed.

INTERNAL ANALYSIS OF EAC COMPANY

Our Strengths	Our Weaknesses
Great brand	*Are we a strategic part of the total business?*
Historical trading positions with many key original equipment manufacturers	*High operating costs*
We are part of a global/strong brand organization	*We are inflexible*

Our Value-Based Strengths	Our Value-Based Weaknesses
Our KAM teams have good people	*Weak KAM strategies and plans*
Some good relationships with customers	*Do we know who our Key Customers are?*
Strong intent from leadership team to change and to beat our competitors. We do not want to enter price wars, and there is a desire to 'change the game'	*The local General Managers 'do their own thing'. As a central KAM team we are misaligned.*
	We struggle to define what our customers value. We are not customer-centric!

Prioritized Summary of Internal Assessment

With the external pressures and challenges facing our business, and the stretching long-term goals for growth and improved recognition by customers as the 'Technical Excellence Supplier' we have to start competing based on value and deep customer needs.

Increasing price pressure from competitors (and our customer's willingness to take these offers) means that we must change the way we operate. We need to focus on advanced value-based offerings and develop relationships with the key decision makers in our customer operations. This is not happening sufficiently today.

Year 1 Strategies and Headline Actions
Strategy 1 – Identify our true strategic and key customers
• *Develop a customer segmentation model*
• *Apply to our customer portfolio*
• *Agree with the wider business*
Strategy 2 – Develop a strategic customer planning process
• *Develop a KAM strategy model*
• *Pilot with two customers*
• *Seek approval*
• *Roll out via training workshops*
Strategy 3 – Develop value understanding in our business
• *Seek input from customers – what do they value and need?*
• *Develop value workshops for our KAM teams*
• *Ensure that Customer KAM plans are presented to the board on a regular basis*

Value matters

1 Once an organization determines that it needs to build and follow a value-based business approach, the first step is to develop a strategy. This will enable a review of the organization's ambitions, assess the challenges it faces and then develop set identified activities that it will have to follow in order to transform to a more effective business model.

2 Infinite Value sets out a practical model that turns strategy into activity. There are three main components: strategy, capability standards and transformation. Strategy and capability standards are the subject of Part Two, while transformation is discussed in Part Three.

3 Note that the whole of Part Two (the seven capability standards on value-based business) needs to be understood and utilized in order to identify where internal gaps might exist in your organizational capability. Focusing on Chapter 5 alone will not provide a complete strategy tool (but it will provide a framework).

4 Drucker posited: 'The five most important questions you will ever ask about your organization.' These five questions are covered by the Infinite Value model, but particular focus on the

third question 'What does the customer value?' flows through the veins of this chapter and the rest of the book.

5   To construct a simple but effective strategy, the customer value strategy cycle is provided.

6   Segmentation is a keystone of any customer/value strategy. A simple customer segmentation model is provided – organizations should look to develop their own methodology: the secret to a successful strategy implementation and transformation is that decisions must be made that connect the organization to the segmentation model. You should elevate investment and effort to the higher opportunity customers (and taper off effort for lower opportunity customers). Many organizations fail to make that connection.

7   Setting the objective and purpose of the strategy requires careful consideration and buy-in from senior leaders. Combining hard commercial targets (e.g. increased revenue) as well as softer targets (e.g. to be recognized as a strategic partner of choice with our top ten strategic customers) will really focus and direct all subsequent decisions taken in the strategy.

8   Organizations should look to capture the new external trends and forces that are occurring in both your own industry and your customer's industry. Look for economic trends. The pace of change at a macro-economic, technology and social level is rapid – so be honest and look forward. These new trends disrupt today, and will continue to disrupt in the future, so build to prosper in these new environments.

9   When assessing internal strengths and weaknesses you need to be brutally honest and remember, 'what worked in the past, may not work in the future'. The best way to obtain a measure of your capability is to ask your customer. They are the people paying your invoices.

10   The whole of Infinite Value sets out a strategy and a blueprint for a value-based business model. But it is a *different way* of doing business. Really effective strategy should feel uncomfortable and should challenge current thinking: but keep focused on the objectives and vision to remember that a new business model is required.

Chapter 6

Offer development and innovation

I've been copied so well I've heard people copy my mistakes

Jimi Hendrix

Question
What is value, and how can a supplier develop innovative customer value propositions?

Improving the future state of your customer

Value-based business can look like a series of processes, methodologies and frameworks. In many ways it is, and organizations like and need this approach. A blueprint that shows how to do business in a different way is critical. But the heart of its purpose should not be forgotten.

How do we add value and improve the future state of our customer?

This question lies at the heart of why many sales training, key account management and customer strategy programmes struggle to achieve the results they set out to deliver, because the customer (regardless of the beauty and design of their internal sales systems) does not buy these programmes. The customer buys the value you deliver to help improve the future state of their business.

And there lies a conundrum. What is value? As a concept, value has a very wide field of sight. Warren Buffett famously states that 'Price is what you pay, value is what you get.' He uses this definition when considering the price of buying an organization or investing in its stock. Value in this strategic focus is a consideration of the future profit and cash flows that will come from the organization (with his investment time horizon being 'forever').

The retail industry takes an opposite view when selling to consumers, often adopting the word value to mean low prices. For example, Tesco (a UK-based retailer) has a 'value range' of products, highlighted with blue stripes and meaning that the product within the packaging is a low (or the lowest) price for its category. If the consumer is looking for a cheap product, then the Tesco definition of value is robust. However, if the purchaser considers more criteria (for example taste or shelf-life), this use of the word value becomes confused.

Cost, price and value

Three words – cost, price and value – are often used between suppliers and customers interchangeably and with a lack of clarity. This causes confusion internally when developing sales strategies and offers for the customer, and within the customer decision-making unit (DMU) when deciding to buy.

The suggested definitions in a business-marketing environment are:

- Cost is the supplier's *internal* costs that are required to produce the product/service offering for the customer.
- Price is the financial *external* figure that is presented to the customer (the amount that should be paid to acquire the products and services).
- Value is the cumulative (tangible and intangible) impact that the customer business receives as a result of adopting the supplier offering. It is the amount your customer believes/perceives that your offering is worth.

Focusing on these three terms is critical in a customer value strategy: particularly *value*. A lack of emphasis by both parties (but in particular the supplier) to quantify the potential commercial impact that could be delivered by the offering will slide the discussion back to price. Savvy procurement professionals will go further than bartering over price, often digging into the supplier's costs to manufacture and supply the products and services. This then becomes barter around how much profit the customer will allow the supplier to have on top of the cost to supply the products and services. The challenge is for the supplier to break this cycle and to discuss the value that can be generated for the customer's wider business. Often this number will far outweigh the price tag attached to the procurement of the specific items.

To shift the discussion from this 'fee-wrestling' to 'value-building' a number of things need to happen. These should be led by the supplier, but cooperation and support by the customer is also necessary.

There are six keys to unlocking the value cloud:[1]

1   Make the value clear. Having a vague concept of the value potential will not be enough to win interest. Describing, quantifying, detailing how the value could be released and gaining customer agreement to the concept is critical.
2   Engage with the right people. Procurement has a job to do. Often, the main priority is to control the supplier spend/budget. While procurement needs to be kept in the discussion and can assist in connecting with the rest of their organization, the supplier really needs to speak to the users and benefactors. This could be general managers, supply chain, manufacturing, finance and more. Like beauty, value lies in the eye of the beholder. The beholder is not always procurement.
3   Seek the bigger picture. If the offer enables the customer to achieve bigger strategic goals and targets, it should be met favourably. This requires a deep understanding of what those big picture goals, targets and objectives are. Focus on making big things happen and your fee will seem small in the overall picture.
4   Be a trusted equal. Like in a marriage, long-term relationships last between two parties that respect and trust each other. A value 'promise' is more robust if it is something both parties want, and is delivered as stated. If you keep making and delivering robust promises a foundation to be trusted in the future will start to evolve.

---

[1] The value cloud is discussed in Chapter 7.

5 Be unique and stay unique. If what you offer is the same (or worse!) as your competitor you will offer nothing to the buyer that justifies additional investment (why should they pay more?). If anything destroys value and prompts a price battle it is having a vanilla offering. Know thy customer. Equally, know thy competitors, and then focus on providing a unique and value-adding promise.

6 Think risk averse. Adopting new offerings from suppliers is a risky process (especially if you are new and potentially replacing an incumbent supplier). New ideas and offerings will be more readily accepted when all risk aspects are considered and addressed. Think like the customer. Put their mind at ease by identifying and eliminating the possibility of things going wrong.

Defining value proposition and customer offer

Customers need to understand the potential opportunity and benefits of working with supplying organizations. To have impact with the customer, this can be a difficult task, particularly if the supplier position is weak or not carefully thought out. This is a critical task – competition is often aggressive among firms that are jostling to win business, so establishing a strong offer that clearly meets/exceeds customer business needs is paramount.

There are three levels of value description that organizations work on to engage and communicate with customers. These are the corporate (brand) level; divisional/product level; and the customer level (Figure 6.1).

At the highest level of an organization, this description of value is captured in the corporate branding. It is a general description, shorthand for what the company does and what it stands for. Customers see the brand and there is an immediate understanding of what they can expect to get, both good and bad. Brands evoke perception, and perception is reality. Having a strong brand opens doors with

Figure 6.1 Three levels of value hierarchy

customers and enables entry to tendering processes and the ability to meet with executives.

Brand also provides the communication for organizations at the product and local country level. Strong brands help selling organizations to build trust, improve recognition, attract the best employees and associates, and generate growth with existing and new customers. Brand at the corporate, product and divisional level is a vital starting point for business. As David Ogilvy states:

A BRAND is the intangible sum of a product's attributes: Its name, packaging and price, its reputation and the way it is advertised.

Customer value strategy relies on this brand message being expressed and delivered to a finite selection of customers. It is aimed at individual customers. In this instance, the message becomes the customer value proposition. This is focused toward one customer and their specific requirements:

- A customer value proposition summarizes an improved future scenario offered by a supplier to its target customer.
- It describes products, services and the relationship ethos that will be provided, and it supports this position with evidence to demonstrate

how these value promises will deliver a sustainable competitive performance.

To target a specific customer it is better to develop a bespoke customer value proposition that builds on the supplier brand story. There are 4 main components of a customer value proposition. The opening statement describes a future state that will be received by the customer if the adopt the proposal. This futures state is then supported by details of how the supplier will make this happen, and the evidence that supports why they should be trusted. The final component describes the cost (fee) and its value benefits.

This is far more precise and personal value description for the customer and puts them at the centre of the procurement process.

> The customer offering details all of the components that will be delivered by the supplier to make the value proposition promises become a reality.

Finally, the customer offering is the 'nuts and bolts' of the offering. It is the detail of the offer and describes all of the components that will be delivered by the supplier to the customer. Very often, organizations make the mistake of describing the customer offer as the value proposition. While this is a critical component of what is on offer from the supplier, it is not enough. Customers need to have a commercial description of what they are potentially going to buy. This is captured in the customer value proposition statement, the full detail of which is in the customer offer.

A good way in which to think of this connection is to compare the entire document to a report: the offering is the detailed content. The customer value proposition acts like an executive summary, detailing how the offer will work and the commercial impact it will have on the customer business.

Effective customer value propositions:

- Are written as sharp summaries, usually of three or four paragraphs;
- Are based on a very strong understanding of the customer business;
- Follow a period of development. Like an executive summary, they are written last and follow a significant amount of work;
- Are written in the language that the customer understands – free of jargon (but using terminology that is important to the customer);

- Have a quantified set of criteria to make it clear to the customer exactly what the commercial and business benefits will be;
- Are credible but also compelling (they should be stronger than competitor value propositions).

Weaker customer value propositions do not deliver the above. Perhaps though, the most common error is that they simply describe the components of the offering. Strong customer value propositions talk about the future state of the customer (and not the supplier products and services).

Innovation: 'Today a peacock, tomorrow a feather duster'

The customer value proposition drives the business intent and relationship with the customer. This is what the customer buys and is the promise that they want to be delivered by the supplier. Growth with each customer comes from one or more of the following strategies:

- The customer business expands and your business expands with it (geographically or into new markets);
- You acquire business from your competitors (thus increasing your share of the total 'wallet opportunity');
- Business is taken from the customer (activities that they were doing themselves are handed to you);
- You manage to gain price increases or performance bonuses (these are usually linked to contractual service-level agreements).

All of the above can be attained either by a formal bidding process (the customer specifies what they want from suppliers) or by suppliers working hard to understand the customer business and presenting a new value proposition that will hopefully be bought and implemented. In either situation, suppliers stand a much stronger chance of winning business with a stronger customer value proposition. However, it is very unlikely that in five years' time the customer will be buying the same customer offer as today (Figure 6.2).

It is the job of the supplier to constantly seek these new value propositions and to demonstrate them to the customer. This is an

**Last
Year**   Ask yourself…   **+5
Years**

*Will your customer offering
be the same in 5 years' time?*

Figure 6.2 Innovation *powers* effective customer offers

innovative process, involving value-based selling, account management and innovation techniques to ensure that strong new customer value propositions are always being created and delivered. Failure to foster this focus can result in falling behind competitors and losing business. As the old Wall Street saying goes: 'Today a peacock, tomorrow a feather duster' – you really cannot sit back on your laurels in the highly competitive environment that we operate in today.

The value equation

Question

What is value, and how can a supplier develop innovative customer value propositions?

Value is quantified in any purchasing experience by balancing two components. These are benefits and costs (quantifying what will be received, *less* what has to be paid to obtain it). This can be expressed by the basic value equation (Figure 6.3).

$$\text{Value} = \boxed{\text{Benefits}} - \boxed{\text{Costs}}$$

Figure 6.3 The basic value equation

In consumer-based purchases, a lot of this value equating is captured by the value that is baked into the brand. A Rolex watch costs several thousand pounds versus a swatch watch that costs a hundred (or less).

Both are functional time-keeping products (some people claim that swatch watches actually keep better time than Rolex!) and yet both do very well commercially. Rolex serves other purposes (it is a symbol of status and quality) and, as such, consumers looking for these features will pay the high price tag. Functional 'cost-sensitive' consumers will settle for the swatch – happy to have a watch with a different set of values (good fun, reliable and practical). For consumer purchasing the value equation works quickly, with the brand acting as a shorthand for the consumer to consider, 'Do I want to pay this price for this product?'

In business marketing, brand still plays an important part in the purchasing cycle, but due to the nature of the decision a more involved and considered approach is taken. The customer will look to have a set of needs met in their business. These needs will either be stated very clearly in a bid/request for quotation document, or the supplier will create the list of needs. Benefits become areas of impact that the customer business will receive as a result of purchasing the customer offer.

There are several factors involved in why quantification of the impact side of the equation becomes more difficult in business marketing:

- The decision-making unit. More people are involved in the purchase and usage of the products and services. It is not just the commercial buyer that is involved or impacted, but the people that use them: the specifier of the purchase; customers; and operational/general managers. Understanding the DMU and what each party requires is a critical part of gaining a clear impact statement.
- Strategies and goal alignment. To have strong impact, the supplier needs to offer something that aligns and complements important

things across the customer's business. This means understanding corporate and divisional objectives, strategies and key activities. These are often hard to find and require a close relationship with a wide set of people, and a considerable amount of work. A strong knowledge of the customer's wider business is critical.

- Competitive forces. Customers request competitive bids from suppliers for many reasons, but the over-arching one is to get key suppliers to bid against one another and in so doing drive down the price. Suppliers that do business based on value must offer a stronger, preferably unique value-impacting offer than that of the competition. If several suppliers offer the same thing there will be one winner – the customer – who watches the pack drive down price, working on a commodity basis.

- The procurement process. In business marketing, for complex purchases, procurement takes place over a set period. This will be in a series of defined stages (developing the specification; requesting to bid; bidding; bid reviews; and final awarding of contract). This takes time and at every stage the customer and supplier discuss all aspects of the offering and how it adds value. Suppliers need to work hard at every stage to ensure their offering and value message is not diluted during these stages – focus should be maintained on adding value to the customer business (not the procurement bidding process!).

The procurement function should be focused on considering this split between what the buyer wants and what the business needs and values. Buyers have a major and strategic target that has to be met. They need to control and achieve expenditure budgets. Often there are targets attached to these budgets: for example, it might be making a saving of 5 per cent energy spend on the previous year. These targets can be imposed on the supplier, with simple targets being placed upon them via the competitive bidding process.

Saving 5 per cent on the fee is good for procurement (and could be good for the supplier if they want to take the business at this reduced fee). However, this constant squeezing of prices by procurement with little focus on the value that is added to the wider business operations is shortsighted. It drives suppliers into a stagnant state of simply cutting costs and taking the pain of winning business by price alone.

$$\text{Value} = \boxed{\text{Impact}} - \boxed{\text{Total Cost of Ownership}}$$

Figure 6.4 The value equation (enhanced version)

Many organizations are in the position of fighting for business based on price. This is fine if the supplier value position is to be the lowest-cost supplier in the market. When this is not the case, and the value position is to be a higher value-performing player in the market then either the performance of the value proposition or the value discussion with the customer needs to be improved.

An expanded look at the components of the value equation will help to make this a more detailed discussion: the value equation can be expressed for business marketing as shown in Figure 6.4.

The benefits side of the equation is now described as impact. This is to force the discussion into a more detailed business-wide activity, with the products and services being offered having to be considered by the wider impact they have on the overall customer business.

Costs have changed to total cost of ownership (TCO). Again, this forces deeper thinking and analysis to establish a longer-term set view of value that can be achieved for the customer. Getting under the skin of the customer business and working hard to quantify *both* sides of this equation will get to the heart of a stronger position from which to sell and negotiate. It can change the game (unless the

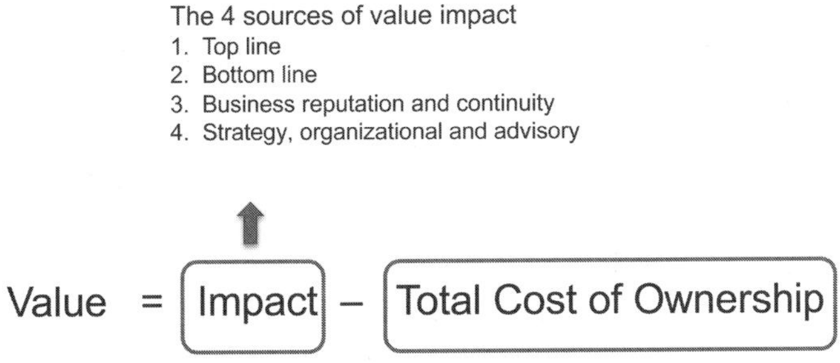

The 4 sources of value impact
1. Top line
2. Bottom line
3. Business reputation and continuity
4. Strategy, organizational and advisory

$$\text{Value} = \boxed{\text{Impact}} - \boxed{\text{Total Cost of Ownership}}$$

Figure 6.5 The four sources of value impact

customer has the DNA, culture and focus to buy only on price) so that the supplier organization gets a fairer price and the customer receives much better collaborative support from suppliers that help them achieve strategies and goals. Focusing on this equation can create a win-win situation.

Building further, Figure 6.5 shows the themes that should be explored to create a strong value calculation. This should be developed by the supplier, but requires mutual cooperation and intent from the customer to work in this value-based manner.

The four sources of value impact

To create an improved future state, a supplier can offer the customer four main sources of value-improving activity:

1 Top line. Adding value to the customer's business by helping them to grow sales and drive the top line of their profit and loss account.
2 Bottom line. Adding value to the customer business by reducing costs in the operation of the way they do business (variable costs) and/or reducing fixed costs. Addressing bottom line value focuses on the way the customer conducts their business and helps to preserve top line performance for stronger final profits.
3 Business reputation and continuity. These are aspects of business that do not feature in the core of the business reporting (sales, costs, fixed and variable assets etc.). Despite being intangible, they have enormous issues for any business. Such things as health, safety, security, environmental and quality are critical to business reputation and the ability for them to keep trading.
4 Strategy, organizational and advisory. Business today is fast-paced and ever changing. Customers have to respond to changing macro-economic new norms, technology advancements and changing competition. Suppliers can offer significant value to them by providing advice and support to help them navigate through difficult and changing conditions.

Table 6.1 Expanding the four sources of value impact

Theme	Customer Future State Options	
Top Line	**Improve market strategy** • Market insights and analysis • Competitor insights • Industry best practice and standards • Future industry trends	**Improve sales performance** • Joint value proposition development • Understanding 'the customer's customer' • Analysing and investing in go to market strategies
Bottom Line	**Improve efficiency and profits** • Cutting operating costs • Improving yield/conversion rates • Improving labor costs/rates • Reducing scrap/introducing recycling methods	**Improve cost structure and balance sheet** • Reducing plant and machinery • Eliminating office/manufacturing space • Improving work in progress (WIP) • Improving the supply of raw materials • Shifting fixed costs to variable costs
Business Reputation & Continuity	**Health, safety and quality aspects** • Focus on brand and market perceptions • Providing safe solutions/advice • Providing quality systems • Assisting with social media/market communications	**Environmental and security aspects** • Advice: Corporate Social Responsibility (CSR) • Ensuring IT systems are secure • Ensuring product supply is robust and secure • Provision (and advice) of robust environmental systems
Strategy, Organizational & Other Advisory	**Strategy and transformation** • Joint strategy planning at board level • Focus on brand and reputation (new and existing markets) • Sharing experiences of business strategy and transformation	**Organizational design and operations** • Advising/providing support functions (HR, supply chain, production & manufacturing, R&D) • Transfer of labor/operations (advanced services & solutions) • Transfer of non-essential activities (e.g. facilities management/outsourcing)

Table 6.1 provides details of the various options that can be considered to detail the four sources of value impact. The table provides ideas and guidance to help consider how impact can be provided for the customer business.

To illustrate the table and demonstrate the breadth of options available when creating innovative customer value propositions, examples of the four sources of value impact (drawn from advisory and observational experiences by the author) are illustrated below.

Top line examples

Improving market strategy

A global supplier of transmission lubricants to a US-based truck and bus gearbox manufacturer provided insights on how to enter new markets. The customer had observed that there was significant market growth in road and off-road markets in emerging markets (India, Brazil, Russia, China) but had little experience of establishing a business to market and sell products in these regions.

The lubricant supplier (being part of a truly global business) had significant and long-established experience of these markets. While this was outside the usual scope of supply (technical fluids products), the customer welcomed the practical advice. This further strengthened the business relationship and led to increased sales at attractive margins.

Improving sales performance

A manufacturer of high-quality process valves and pumps markets to a range of different customer types. Increasingly, the end user (chemical and processing plant) is not the actual economic buyer. The customers for refurbishment and new-build projects are increasingly becoming 'design and build' consulting firms. While expert at specifying the design of turnkey programmes, these organizations are predominantly staffed by mechanical and process design engineers.

The valve supplier recognized that the customer could increase their business with a stronger knowledge of certain industries with very unique requirements (namely the pharmaceutical industry and the nuclear industry). By advising and training these engineering specialists on valve and pump technology for these sectors, as well as value-selling techniques (by quantifying commercial benefits of these more advanced technical solutions), an increase in higher margin solutions was achieved for the valve and pump products. With the increased knowledge of the pharmaceutical and nuclear process industries, additional sales were captured for additional complete design and build programmes.

Bottom line examples

Improving efficiency and profits

A global animal healthcare supplier (manufacturer of vaccine and pharmaceutical products to aquaculture livestock farms) mapped the process that the customer followed when vaccinating and treating animals for health issues. They discovered that on some occasions, farming operators were not administering the correct dosage at the correct frequency (this is a very time-consuming and labour-intensive activity).

Over-treatment of the fish would be expensive and could cause damage to stock as it was handled. Under-treatment would leave the fish susceptible to disease and reduced yield. By providing a simple support system, working with the farming operations team, the exact administration of product could be ensured. As an indication of the value to the customer, a 2–4 per cent improvement in fish conversion (yield) would be equivalent to a year's supply of healthcare products, and eliminating just one treatment cycle could be equivalent to 25 per cent of annual healthcare costs.

Improving cost structures and balance sheet

A maintenance contractor had a long-term contract supplying a plasterboard/building products customer. The steady-state value proposition from the supplier was to improve running efficiency and output in the customer's five manufacturing sites across different countries in Europe. This had seen significant results over several years with commercial success for both parties.

Post-recession, in 2009, saw a downturn in the construction and building industry (the customer's customer was no longer investing and for a period did not require plasterboard products). The customer value proposition therefore needed to change.

Recognizing that five manufacturing sites were not required, a suggestion was made to focus on four sites, applying the usual business solution to make the sites run very efficiently (85–90 per cent). The fifth site could effectively be shut down or 'moth-balled' until the extra capacity was required again by the construction market. This customer value proposition had the potential to save the customer an entire manufacturing site/facility as well as eliminating operational costs for the site. (Note that this value proposition had to be presented to general managers and the board of the customer business, but not the maintenance managers who would be the usual points of contact.)

Business reputation and continuity

Health, safety and quality aspects

There is a growing trend for secondary pharmaceutical organizations to outsource the manufacture, packaging and delivery of their products (tables, ointments, sterile products etc.). Historically, there was a resistance for this contract outsourcing activity, since manufacturing sites and processes had to be licensed by government agencies such as the Food and Drug Administration (FDA) of America.

This has started to change, however, with many contract organizations now having specialist facilities with manufacturing licences, and operating to a very high quality standard. They no longer compete just on price but by providing a cost-effective and higher quality standard. The specialist nature of these operations is often built around increased health, safety and environmental standards for handling complex products.

Environmental and security aspects

A logistics freight-forwarding organization manages the supply of high value electronics components for a major branded consumer electronics device organization. The nature of high-end consumer electronics is that they have short windows of time to get new products to market and to sell these products as efficiently and quickly as possible. Failure to supply can result in lost sales and possible damage to the brand (early adopters of new electronic devices are willing to pay but they 'want it now!'). Additionally, leakage of products onto the black market causes problems for high-impact launch and potentially allows competitors to copy designs.

The logistics supplier developed an entire division dedicated to the customer (a business within a business) with dedicated teams of people and storage/holding spaces. Increased secure warehousing was built and audited/approved (increased investment on security systems and guards was required).

The resulting secure supply solution provided a significant advantage to the customer and ensured a protected commercial position for the supplier as they had created strong barriers to entry.

Strategy, organizational and advisory

Strategy and transformation

Under threat from new entrants from China, a copper-tube mill was looking for alternative strategic options. Frustrated by the advice provided by several large management-consulting firms (they lacked specific knowledge of the challenges and nuances of the industry), one major organization looked to its 'traditional' suppliers.

Among these was a heat treatment firm, designing and manufacturing furnaces and support equipment. Jointly they looked at the market and developed new products (requiring new processes and equipment). They developed a niche offering that was outside the supply of the main Chinese competition.

Organizational design and operations

A software systems company supplying customer relationship management software to a banking group was aware that the bank was trying to downsize its operations. This would involve making employees redundant in countries where the works councils were very powerful.

Having gone through a similar exercise a few years earlier, the software supplier offered to work with the board of the bank and advise on implementing the new structure. This involved collaboration between the HR teams from both organizations.

The examples above demonstrate how suppliers have developed unique value propositions that address the differing business needs of the customers they serve. The four sources of value impact are all effective in differing situations according to the customer's needs at that time.

Table 6.2 The customer's customer (the fifth source of value impact)

Theme	Customer Future State Options	
Meeting consumer needs (Adapted from Maslow)	**Physiological, safety and social** • Hunger and thirst needs met • Security, shelter and safety • Health and well-being • Sense of belonging and community • Environmental (warm, cool, comfortable) • Basic education and development • Communication and understanding	**Self-esteem and self-actualization** • Transportation and movement • Status and brand-association • Cultural and spiritual needs • Joy, pleasure, sport and leisure • Wealth • Advanced education & development • Social class, long-term security

A fifth source of value impact can be identified. Table 6.2 shows a further list of ideas that should be considered when seeking to develop a value future state for the customer. If the customer's customer is the consumer, the things that they look for to add value to their lives differ from a commercial/business-to-business relationship.

Table 6.2 adapts Maslow's hierarchy of needs for an individual, splitting between the foundations of personal needs (physiological, safety and social needs) and the needs that build on these (self-esteem and self-actualization). Think about anything that you buy (or interact with) as a consumer: for yourself, your family and friends. This list will help you to connect the impact of your value proposition/offer with consumers.

Total cost of ownership

On the other side of the value equation, once the impact on the customer business has been estimated and calculated, the total costs of ownership need to be calculated.

The initial purchase price is the first figure that is a cost to the customer. This is the upfront purchase amount or the on-going cost as products and services are consumed. Customers that base purchasing decisions on this value alone (and make decisions on the lowest price supplier) are missing a significant part of the value analysis.

The cost of operating the product needs to be added to this purchase price. These are the on-going costs of operating, and include:

- Energy costs,
- Maintenance costs,
- Labour costs,
- Depreciation costs (consider how long the product will stay in service),
- Updating costs (common with software/IT systems),
- Training costs (if equipment and technology is new to the customer organization),
- Tooling costs (if equipment is required for different product lines),
- Installation and services costs,
- Build and construction/installation time,
- Commissioning and validation.

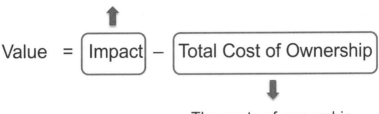

The (4+1) sources of value impact
- Top line
- Bottom line
- Business reputation and continuity
- Strategy, organizational and advisory
- Meeting consumer needs

Value = Impact − Total Cost of Ownership

The costs of ownership
- Initial purchase price
- On-going costs of operating
- On-going costs of 'not operating'

Figure 6.6 The value equation – fully detailed

On-going costs of 'not operating' must also be added as a cost. These costs exist because the product requires periods where operation cannot occur. Examples include:

- Planned maintenance time,
- Unplanned maintenance time,
- Time to conduct changeover (from one product to another),
- Inspection time (health, safety and environmental factors),
- Time to clean/sterilize equipment.

Organizations develop value propositions based around the TCO being more attractive for the customer and better performing than competitor offers. Examples are:

- A dairy processing line – offering an advantage by having sterilize in place (SIP) systems that will automatically clean between batches. This ensures that the operating line is clean and ready to be used with minimal downtime from line changeover and quality checks. Validated evidence and support systems from other installations provide evidence that the systems work and beat competitors. Value is provided by increasing operational uptime and reducing downtime (due to safety issues).
- Aero engines – offering more fuel-efficient technology than previous generations. With fuel being a predominant cost for airline operators, the adoption of engines that are 15 to 20 per cent more fuel-efficient than previous engines offers significant commercial benefits – in some cases it can be the difference between profit and loss.
- Earth moving equipment – can provide systems that monitor the equipment while in operation in construction sites and mines and advise the operator before a machine is due to fail in service. If the service-level package is adopted by the customer, a total service solution can be provided, shipping spare parts and fitting on-site to ensure that the equipment is kept operational at all times.
- Turnkey engineering systems – when customers need to launch a new product/s quickly (for example new car models) the design, construction, installation and commissioning of a new site (or conversion of an existing plant) is critical. The customer values speed of response since delays of a few months will cause lost profits and damage to brand reputation. Engineering organizations

that offer this service provide assured facility development, construction, commissioning, servicing and sometimes operate the equipment.

Total cost of partnership

In professional services firms, TCO does not apply (there are no physical goods to be owned and operated). Law firms, engineering firms and accounting firms provide critical services, but do not incur on-going costs.

A different phrase is suggested for these firms: that of 'total cost of partnership' (Figure 6.7). There may not be ownership of a physical item to maintain, but there will be a relationship that has to be healthy and value adding.

The following is a list of items that can be considered to calculate total costs of partnership:

- The total fee payable for the services;
  +
- Time required to brief the service provider;
- Time required to manage the relationship;
- Physical location (offices and alignment of key people);
- Tension in the relationship or 'do both parties get along?' This is a bit like the saying 'He/she is high maintenance!'

Figure 6.7 The value equation –professional services version

How to write a compelling (customer) value proposition

Over time I have worked with many sales and account management teams. Discussing the day-to-day challenges regarding the development and delivery of customer value propositions is a very effective way for these teams to stand back and reflect on this critical activity, but also enables a consolidation (after many sessions!) of some very effective insights.

The following summary is derived from a list of real quotes in answer to the question: What are the key components of an excellent customer value proposition?

Ten practical ways to develop strong customer value propositions:

1   Use the language of the customer's business: 'We find that a customer value proposition that is written in the language of the customer with no jargon or confusing language gets stronger results. Keep it simple but professional.'

2   Meet the needs of the customer: 'The closer we are to addressing and helping strategically important challenges of our customer, the stronger the impact message is – customers like to know we have listened to them.'

3   Talk to the right people: 'The senior people in the customer organization that will use, and live with, our offering are usually not the buyer (but we must keep them in the loop) – it's a difficult balancing act to manage the egos, but very important.'

4   Be compelling and believable: 'The offer should convince the customer to buy and to show us as the obvious choice. Being believable as well as compelling are two opposing tensions we are always working on ... we want to win business but keep customers for the long term, this comes by our delivering our promises.'

5   Be stronger than competitor offers: 'Our competitors will fight to win this business as well. We have to fight harder and present a stronger business case.'

6   Quantify how good we are: 'Customers look for evidence that we

are the people to trust and can repeat the great work that we have done before. Provide stories, data and if possible endorsements from other customers, especially for new customers that we have a limited trading history with.'

7 Show me the money!: 'Our more sophisticated strategic customers look for us to specify the measures that will be used to capture the results of our programmes. These key performance indicators become really important pivots to winning the business and managing its delivery with some of the more complex offerings.'

8 The devil and the detail: 'Customers want to get a quick flavour of the offering. We find that senior executives are making purchase decisions for lots of items that their company buys, so we have to capture the detail of a complex offer into a short "upfront" summary. Hook them in with the value proposition and they will be more inclined to look at the details of the full offer.'

9 A call to action: 'Our more stretching customer solutions require us to get people across our wider organization involved (beyond sales) ... the value proposition is the only way to build this excitement and gain alignment, from the CEO to supply chain, HR and operations. If we aren't excited, how will we get the customer to be excited and believe us?'

10 Talk about the risky things: 'We need to get the risky stuff on the table ... customers really appreciate that. If a programme needs resources and input from them (and a different way of working) then we have to state that early on in the discussions. We all want to make things better, but some value propositions need the customer to change and they need to be aware of these things ... We don't want to sell a dream and deliver a nightmare.'

The customer value proposition framework

The customer value proposition framework (Figure 6.8) provides a model to pull together all of the thinking presented so far. The customer value proposition sits at the centre of the model, with the customer value state at the top of the pyramid (this is the most important aspect of the proposition).

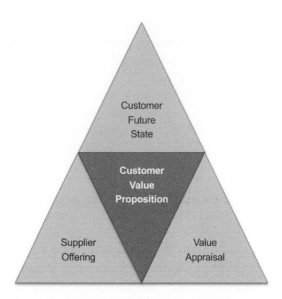

Figure 6.8 Three main components of a value proposition

Table 6.3 Constructing the customer value proposition

What will be the **FUTURE STATE** of the customer business? What customer needs will we meet?
What **OFFERING** do we have that will deliver this future state?
What **EVIDENCE** do we have that we have done this before and that we are **CREDIBLE**?
What **METRICS** will be used to capture **VALUE**?

Table 6.4 The offer navigator

Product	Price	Place	Promotion	Process	People	Physical Evidence
Quality	Fee position	Direct	Joint promotions	Sales processes/account management	Qualified people	Brand
Range	Fee structure (fixed, variable, performance-based)	3rd party distributor channels	Campaigns	Ordering products and services	Experience and attitude	Facilities/offices
Packaging/dispensing sizes	Discounts	Web-based	Fixed-term reduced pricing	Invoicing and billing	Technical expertise	Demonstration of industry expertise
Breadth	Warranty options	Implanted	Social media advice/support	Cost variation and extras handling	Commercial expertise	Transferable expertise from other industries
Flexibility	Rebates	Supply chain management	Conference support	Providing technical support	Aligning leadership teams	Transferable expertise from other technologies and systems
Robustness	Credit options		Article writing and support	Flexibility and responsiveness	Dedicated resourcing	Highly regarded strategic to operational organizational capability
Usability	Service-level agreements			Cost positioning	Industry leading expertise	
User interaction options					Provision of temporary/contract resources	

Supporting the development are the supplier offering and the value appraisal. The framework can also be shown as a table (Table 6.3), which is a good way to complete the thinking of the customer value proposition. The table is structured to ask questions of the supplier in a logical manner (it is ideal for a cross-functional team to work on when developing a new customer value proposition).

The questions flow in the same order that value has been discussed in this section: the customer future state; our offering that will deliver this; evidence and credibility that we can deliver; and finally, capturing and quantifying the proposed value.

To assist in developing each stage, there are additional tables that help to guide the thinking to consider all options. To assist in the development of the customer's future state Tables 6.1 and 6.2 can be referred to in order to align the thinking toward the many opportunities of adding value for customers.

The customer offer table (Table 6.4) provides a way to think across the breadth of the marketing mix, such as drawing on the Seven Ps (Product, Price, Place, Promotion, Process, People and Physical evidence). The table provides a generic list under each heading of the components that can be used to describe which offer the supplier could use in order to deliver the future customer state. Using this is a good way to get supplier teams to think beyond simply describing the products and brands they offer, but to the *collective efforts of the organization*.

The Seven Ps:

1   Product – successful organizations have a business that is built around products that offer something for the customer that they value. Products can be tangible or intangible (increasingly, both). To describe a product, you need to consider how it will be packaged, what its function and position is versus competitive offers (e.g. robust v. disposable) and a list of other factors that can be described.

2   Price – the fee that will be presented to the customer. Attached to this is the full range of commercial constructs such as credit terms, discount mechanisms, rebates, service-level agreements

and contractual terms. In business marketing, price covers all commercial aspects.

3 Place – describes how the customer will be able to access the product. There are usually several available channel choices.

4 Promotion – the ways that value is communicated. This could be a joint activity when developing an offering for one customer in the customer value proposition.

5 Process – dealing with suppliers can be a time-consuming and frustrating activity. Processes that make placing orders or dealing with scope variations, for example, easy to manage can be a big advantage and strengthen your offer.

6 People – if your business is service-based, the statement 'people are our product' is very accurate. Almost any business requires people from across the business – technical, commercial, operational and managerial – to have regular contact with the customer.

7 Physical evidence – a strange phrase! This has been created to help service-based businesses to make their offering more tangible. Physical evidence describes assets and investments that give the business gravitas. Office buildings, websites and published articles are examples.

The best way to demonstrate the customer value proposition framework is by an example. The following is based on an industrial chemical management company bidding to win a contract with an aerospace customer (note the details have been changed, but the intent and content of the proposition remain).

Case study

The supplier organization is Chemco, which supplies and manages industrial grade chemicals, cutting fluids, cleaning fluids, lubricants and associated support services. The case describes Chemco bidding for work with a large aerospace component manufacturer (Air-Frame Co.). The customer is a very large industrial manufacturing operation, developing and supplying air-frame components to various military and domestic aircraft manufacturers.

Chemco has a limited supply history with Air-Frame Co. and limited aerospace business in Europe where this contract bid is being pitched.

They have extensive automotive experience, and also with aerospace products in other parts of the world.

The incumbent chemical management supplier provides a cheaper programme than Chemco can ever supply, but they lack innovation and have had some quality control issues in the past. (It is known that Air-Frame Co. want to improve manufacturing standards and become more efficient – the new manufacturing director's wishes to transfer best practices from other industries, especially the automotive sector.)

The principles of constructing a written customer value proposition (CVP) are as follows:

Step 1: Build the CVP framework with bullet points

What will be the FUTURE STATE of the customer business? What customer needs will we meet?	• Provide a robust aerospace comprehensive management plan • Provide systems and ways of working that will make Air-Frame Co one of the most efficient aerospace manufacturing sites in Europe • Ensure highest standards of quality, environmental and safety across the site
What OFFERING do we have that will deliver this future state?	• Best in class products • Experience in aerospace (outside this region) • Very strong experience in automotive manufacturing • Skilled technical and commercial experts • Processes to drive the implementation of change
What EVIDENCE do we have that we have done this before and that we are CREDIBLE?	• Case studies • Product data sheets
What METRICS will be used to capture VALUE?	• Experience running process benchmarking programmes • Key performance indicator – scrap reduction • Key performance indicator reducing other consumables (cutting wheels and tooling – both more expensive than chemicals) • Safety/mist levels • Payback – 12 to 18 months

This table shows a shortened list of ideas after a brainstorming and fact-finding session. The bullet points in the column on the right are not exhaustive: they capture the key elements that will go into the final executive summary.

Printing the table as a poster and getting a team to work on it is a very effective way to generate ideas. The original thinking of the team could have been locked into 'compete on price', but this would have gone head-to-head with the incumbent supplier and ended in a price war (or simply not winning the business).

Step 2: Convert the bullet points into writing

The final customer value proposition
Chemco will help to enable Air-Frame to become one of the highest performing aerospace manufacturing sites in the world. The comprehensive management plan (CMP) will enable increased manufacturing efficiency, chemical usage cost reduction, significant savings in your tooling and labour activities and total COSHH compliance with your chemical handling activities.

The CMP will help you to improve the delivery reliability of your products to the airline operators.

We have over 500 CMPs operating across the world where there have been significant operational improvements for our clients. In particular, Chemco has a strong heritage working in the demanding automotive sector with clients such as Ford, GM, VW, ZF and GKN. These collaborative partnerships provide us with significant manufacturing knowledge that can be transferred from the automotive sector to your aerospace business.

We have documented programmes showing value improvements with several clients over the last ten years. (Case studies will be provided to support our claims: these show similar performance improvements to this CMP proposed for Air-Frame.)

Globally we have operated with GKN, Volvo, SAAB, Boeing and several other aerospace operators. Chemco has a complete range of aerospace-approved chemical products (data sheets can be provided.)

The CMP will make potential savings of £2.7m per annum. The CMP will potentially increase your machine shop uptime (A and B site) by an estimated 3 per cent p.a.

These will be realized from reductions in your tooling costs, reduced chemical usage and reduced labour costs. Chemco will provide a complete value-tracking system that will measure the exact value that we will deliver. Key performance indicators (KPIs) will include (product costs, tooling costs, chemical air-mist levels, reduced HSSEQ incidents, downtime analysis and cost of labour).

With these hard savings, the CMP will have an anticipated payback period of twelve months.

Notes

It can take a long time to develop a customer value proposition. Many organizations see that it is just one page with a brief description of the intended offering and assume that it will be easy to write. This is not the case! The hard part is the thinking and brainstorming to develop an offer that meets customer expectations (as a minimum) and preferably exceeds them (and the customer offering) in order to win business. This is not an easy task, and requires focus time and energy to produce an effective statement.

Don't forget that the customer value proposition is not the offer – it is an executive summary of the offer, capturing intent in a few short paragraphs. Some organizations never even share these statements with the customer, and this is fine – it is the writing and development of innovative ideas and intent that is important. Ultimately, it is the identification of developing something the customer really values, and winning the sale, that is critical. If this process helps that to be achieved, then it has served its purpose.

Linking customer proposition to the offer

To graphically demonstrate how the value proposition intent connects to the wider offer, an offer wheel can be used. This can be a very useful model to discuss the offer with the customer (as a graphic it holds a lot of information and demonstrates how the details of what the supplier

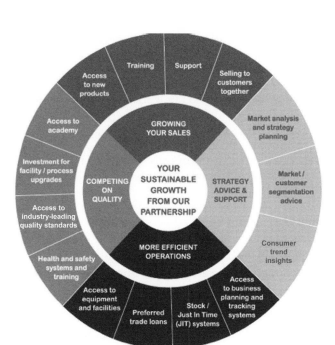

Figure 6.9 Example – the offer wheel

is offering connect with the customer's business). At the centre (the heart of the offer) is the shorthand value proposition statement. This should be a few words stating the value that could be delivered by the offering.

Working out from the centre are the themes of what will be used to deliver this value (use the four sources of value impact in Table 6.1 to help inform these). At the outer circle the elements of the offer or how the supplier will deliver the value are detailed. For these, the Seven Ps can be utilized to inform the content.

Figure 6.9 is an example of the offer wheel that was developed by a global industrial controls/automation manufacturer to propose to selected premier channel partners/distributors. While not the 'end user' of products supplied, many organizations can and should consider channel partners as customers. It is important to have strategic relationships with these channel partners, since they pass value on to the end user customer and in many cases they transfer money back to the original supplier.

In this example, the value proposition was intended to forge a stronger relationship (historically they had not worked together very well). To do this the central offering is all about the distributor ('your sustainable growth'), and we will help that by our partnership.

If this is seen as an attractive proposition by the distributor, further discussion to understand how this will be delivered can be explored from the four themes:

1   Growing the customer sales,
2   Making them more efficient,
3   Assisting to help with quality,
4   Offering strategic advice and supporting business operations.

This came after considerable effort by the controls supplier who wanted to improve relationships with their top-tier ten to fifteen strategic distributors. After many discussions and much research, they concluded that these organizations were often smaller businesses (five to fifty employees) that wanted to grow but lacked the strategy and experience of more established businesses. By focusing on delivering growth of the distributor business (and not just forcing them to sell more product), the relationship changed and became a more solid platform to work together in partnership.

The offer wheel value graphic was often printed out as a large poster, and then the two parties discussed the future relationship, reflecting (good and bad) on the history of the previous trading relationship but focusing on the offer and value proposition to improve the future customer state.

Value matters

1   Hugh MacLeod (gapingvoid.com) describes business as 'The art of getting people to where they need to be faster than they would get there without you'. This aligns perfectly with offer development and innovation since it is also the art of describing a future state for the customer and how you will get them there.

2 The customer value proposition connects an organization's brand to the nuts and bolts of the offering.

3 Value propositions need to be innovative and constantly evolving – customers' needs change and competitors are always looking to take away business.

4 Cost, price and value are three phrases that are often misunderstood and interchanged. To avoid a battle based on price always focus on value delivered for the customer (while ensuring value is created for yourself as well).

5 Strong value propositions take time to develop. They require insights from the customer to capture what is important to them and creative thinking from talented people to generate ideas. Easy-to-*read* value propositions are hard to *write*!

6 The value equation is simple and should be at the forefront of any discussion with the customer. Really understanding the benefits that you will offer (and quantifying this) will provide a bigger number to subtract a higher cost.

7 TCO relevant for product-based offerings. When services are the basis of the offer, total cost of partnership can be substituted.

8 There are four sources of value that a supplier can use to build a strong offering (top line; bottom line; business reputation and continuity; and strategy, organizational and advisory). All four should be considered to stretch out a strong value position.

9 The value proposition framework provides a proven model to enable the development of a strong value proposition. This can be presented to the customer, or the 'ethos' of the offer can be presented (an alternative method is to present an 'offer wheel' graphic). The best way to present is the model that suits the customer's style in the best way.

10 Creating innovative offers sits at the heart of a value-based business. In itself this section provides some useful models to enable a better development of customer value propositions. However, without connecting to the other six elements it is severely weakened.

Chapter 7

Value-based selling

When the trust account is high, communication is easy, instant and effective.

Stephen Covey

Question
Is there a simple and effective sales model that focuses on creating and capturing value for both the customer and supplier?

The value cloud

While we may trust and believe in our brands and product performance, selling is always a requirement. The Infinite Value view is that good value-based selling is an essential activity for any organization and is especially the foundation capability of any key account management programme (one of the early observations in writing this book is that many KAM programmes fail to deliver results because key account managers lack the ability to understand value and how to discuss the concept with customers).

For simple, transactional business, the traditional approach of selling, where the buyer is bombarded with messages about 'product features' and other technical aspects, may be acceptable. But for enterprise relationships, where a more complex delivery of products and services is required and where a long-term partnership between supplier and customer delivers results for both parties, the shift towards a value-based selling model is critical. Shifting the conversation from a price focus to a value focus is beneficial for both parties, and can be simply shown with the value cloud diagram (Figure 7.1).

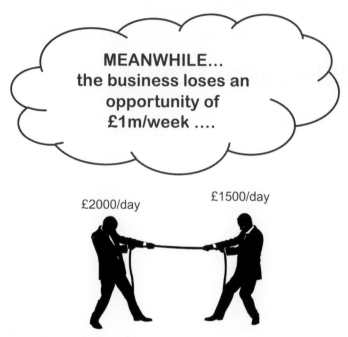

Figure 7.1 The value cloud

The value cloud occurs by default when there is a lack of intent to talk about value and the impact of the supplier and customer working together. The diagram shows buyer and seller fighting in a tug-of-war battle, focused on price (in the example in Figure 7.1, a 'day rate'). This is not untypical of many discussions where professional services providers barter with the client to agree a 'day rate'. The problem exists in that this is a finite spend, and there is a lack of focus on the outcome or impact of the delivery that will be provided by the supplier. The value cloud is an opportunity (or business loss for the client) of £1m/week.

Value in practice

The value cloud example:

This is based on a real example where an engineering services consulting firm was advising a pharmaceutical manufacturing customer.

The customer left the decision making to find a validation/calibration consulting firm to procurement, and they decided to select based on market rates. The specialist nature of the assignment meant that specialists of the required experience, knowledge and leadership were not selected, and start-up of the facility was delayed.

By failing to bring a new facility on stream, validated to the correct standard, a loss of sales (£1m/week) occurred.

Hiring savings were 200 days x £500/day = £100,000

Estimated costs to the pharmaceutical firm delaying the facility start-up date = £30–40m.

And finally:

The customer procurement team was awarded a bonus for saving costs!

When buyers get transfixed on day rates (price) and suppliers fall into the trap of not changing the discussion to the value impact, this price-based tug-of-war will occur (and it occurs often). The outcome of this is that suppliers will provide a service that still tries to make a profit at the reduced fee, but fails to deliver a solution grasping the value cloud issue. Both parties lose.

The four relationship zones

Changing the conversation and re-framing the relationship (and subsequent value discussions) rests with the supplier. Customers will view suppliers as adding value in a transactional manner, or as providing unique value-adding offerings. To enable this discussion requires a focus on relationship, to build trust and depth of understanding to create stronger value discussions. Simply relying on your products and brands is no longer enough (although, with a weak performing set of products you really are on the back foot!).

The essential challenge for suppliers is to re-frame the relationship with the customer, establishing stronger levels of trust and having conversations about value and the impact of your offerings on the customer's business. There are four relationship zones:

1   Product-based,
2   Application-based,
3   Operations-based,
4   Strategy-based.

Discussions between seller and buyer escalate and become broader and deeper as the relationship mode progresses. Organizations initially discuss value with customers by focusing on what they offer – their core products and services. Value is discussed at this specific level, with focus on the features and characteristics of the product. Unless the supplier is offering highly differentiated offerings, this discussion can

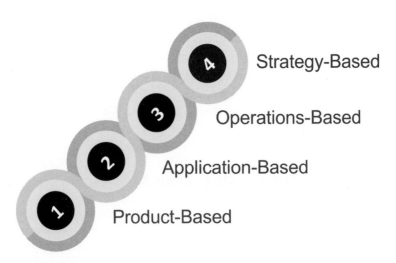

Figure 7.2 Relationship zones

become transactional, with savvy customer buyers forcing suppliers to fight on price to win and maintain supply positions.

Of course, having these discussions creates a platform to start building trust. Table 7.1 expands and details the different facets of each of the four relationship zones. For both parties, increased value opportunities start to emerge as the relationship advances between each zone, but there needs to be increasing co-operation and openness. This comes from a working history, and mutual trust by both parties. The supplier needs to capture an honest appraisal in order to establish exactly where the relationship is today, and where it needs to be in the future. Zone 1 (product-based) is fine as long as both parties recognize that business will be conducted on a transactional basis. It will, however, limit future potential for growth, especially given that this transactional state is

Table 7.1 Comparing the four relationship zones

	1. Product-Based	2. Application-Based	3. Operations-Based	4. Strategy-Based
Value Focus	PRODUCT FEATURES PRICE	PRODUCT/ CATEGORY EXPERT	INDUSTRY & BUSINESS EXPERT	STRATEGY & TRANSFORMATION EXPERT
Customer Connections	Buyer	Buyer + Product user	General managers	Board/senior leadership
Opportunities (Supplier)	Sell product!	Gain value (from products in use)	Provide deeper service-based offering	Establish an intimate understanding of the customer business + Develop broader solutions to capture more value
Opportunities (Customer)	Obtain products at competitive prices	Cost savings and potential improved processes	Significant operational value benefits	Strategic support (coping with disruption and achieving wider business objectives)

susceptible to entry from competitors and a propensity to commoditize and drive down prices.

For most organizations, focus on building Zone 2 (application-
based) and Zone 3 (operations-based) is an essential position to be
in. Suppliers really need to understand the long-term impact of value
realized by the customer as they work with their products and services.
This is where value is generated and has bigger impact, but requires
additional time spent with the customer establishing and capturing
these value benefits.

Value in practice

Key point:

Note that organizations conduct business across relationship zones. It is
unrealistic to think that all business will be at Zones 3 or 4. Indeed for certain
parts of the customer offering, a large proportion of business will be transactional by nature and in Zone 1.

Building relationships and trust at higher levels, however, will pay dividends
– since it will lead to stronger relationships and a deeper understanding of
the customer business.

The value-based selling cycle

All organizations have to sell, although with more complex relationships there is an argument that 'selling' is becoming an 'outdated'
phrase. Consider the four relationship zones described previously. Zone
1 (product-based) is the only one that is concerned with transacting on
product features and (usually) becomes a price-based discussion. This
focus on discussing what the supplier has to offer requires a selling
mentality, but to be really effective a value-based approach can achieve
greater results.

The value-selling cycle (Figure 7.3) is offered as a technique that
enables a set of guiding principles to work with customers, develop

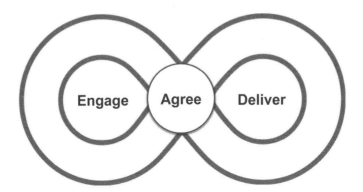

Figure 7.3 The value-based selling cycle

a strong understanding of the customer's business and to create and deliver strong customer value propositions.

There are three main phases:

1 **Phase 1: Engage with the customer**
    To establish what the customer values, a carefully organized approach, to gain an understanding of what is important to the key people in the customer organization, along with a good grasp of the opportunities and challenges in the business that they operate, will provide a solid backdrop to help create a compelling customer value proposition.

2 **Phase 2: Agree the proposed offering and commercial terms**
    Once the customer value proposition is developed, it needs to be demonstrated to the customer for acceptance (this will be more effective if Phase 1 has been conducted properly and key decision makers in the customer organization engaged). If the offer is accepted, negotiating the final fee and deal will be required. Negotiation should focus on the value-adding aspects of the proposal, always attempting to differentiate and shift the focus from price.

3 **Phase 3: Deliver the value promise that is held in the customer offer**
    Once agreed to, and accepted by the customer, the supplier has to deliver the customer value proposition. It is the supplier's job

to ensure that the value promised at the agree phase is obtained. This value delivery should be tracked and routinely reported – seeking customer approval to validate the results.

Value in practice

Trees don't grow to the sky ... (but they do keep growing):

The three phases of the value-selling cycle repeat. By ensuring that value is delivered in Phase 3, continued development of relationship between the customer and supplier will be possible, and can be built upon. Additionally, by focusing on value delivery (within the customer operations) a stronger understanding of the customer business and operations will unfold. This will lead to stronger future customer value propositions (moving back to re-engage in Phase 1).

The value-selling cycle enables a continuous loop (or infinite) approach to value co-creation.

Figure 7.4 expands the value-selling cycle further, splitting the three phases into ten key steps. These help to explain how to make the cycle work, and should be followed as a guide to enable value-focused selling. While the process is aimed principally at the leader of the value-focused selling process (the sales person or account manager), it should also be understood and supported by other key members of the organization that support the delivery of value offerings to the customer, e.g. technical, supply chain and marketing teams.

The cycle is involved and to conduct effectively takes more effort than simply selling products – but this is a fundamental point. Value-focused selling is the methodology that is adopted to deal with customers directly. It can be considered as the foundation activity of key account management. Following these three phases (and ten steps) will provide the organizational capability to manage those significant customer relationships that are deemed sufficiently important to warrant being managed directly, leveraging increased effort and investment since a proportional return from the customer is anticipated.

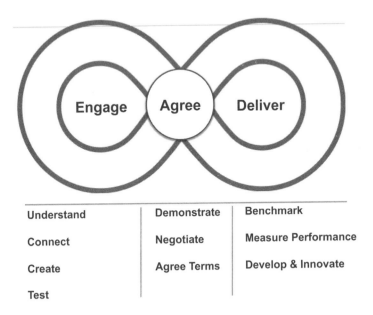

Understand	Demonstrate	Benchmark
Connect	Negotiate	Measure Performance
Create	Agree Terms	Develop & Innovate
Test		

Figure 7.4 Ten steps of value-based selling

Engage with the customer

Expanding on the 'Engage' phase there are four steps, which are detailed below:

1   **Understand** – *The customer's business.*
2   **Connect** – *With the customer decision-making unit.*
3   **Create** – *A compelling customer value proposition/offering.*
4   **Test** – *The customer value proposition for strength and credibility.*

Engage/Step 1: Understand the customer's business

Developing a strong relationship and business with a customer starts by providing an offering that they view as valuable and differing from your competitor's offering. These relationships develop by understanding the customer and the opportunities/challenges of the world they operate within. Understanding the customer first is an observation

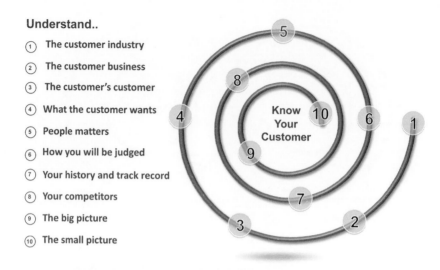

Understand..

① The customer industry

② The customer business

③ The customer's customer

④ What the customer wants

⑤ People matters

⑥ How you will be judged

⑦ Your history and track record

⑧ Your competitors

⑨ The big picture

⑩ The small picture

Figure 7.5 Understanding the customer

of negotiation and innovation (both of which are part of value-focused selling). It is logical to put this thinking at the front of value-focused selling:

Seek first to understand, then to be understood (Stephen Covey)

Figure 7.5 shows the ten steps to enable a review process to capture what is really important for the customer (and the part you can play as a supplier). The analysis starts broad and zooms in to get closer to define the critical points to focus on. Answering these questions helps to think broader and to spot 'new norms' and emerging trends.

Taking each step:

1 The customer industry
  • What markets does the customer serve?
  • Who are the competitors of the customer?
  • Who are the key suppliers?
  • Who are the governing bodies/regulators?

  What is happening with all of these forces, and what impact is it having on your customer?

2   The customer business
    • What is the purpose of the customer's business?
    • What objectives are they trying to achieve?
    • How does the customer create value and make money?
    • What is the customer's value proposition?
    • Are sales growing? Are they winning/losing customers?
    • Are costs under control and are they making a profit?

Top Tip! If your customer is publicly traded, you should be able to access a set of financial accounts. There is a wealth of information in these documents, with commentary about strategy and financial performance. You can download these documents from the customer website and have the information in minutes.

3   The customer's customer
    • If possible, try to establish who your customer's customer is. How do they classify and select key customers themselves?
    • What is happening with these customers?
    • If the customer's customer is the consumer, what are their needs?
    • Consider geographical, cultural and macro-economic challenges facing the customer's customer.

4   What the customer wants
    While we encourage you to research the customer's business to seek strong insights, don't forget to understand the things that they want and state. This can be in the form of a bid request document, or sometimes is even stated by procurement.
    You should challenge what the customer wants. It may not be what they need. As an expert in your field, exploring the gap between what the customer wants and what they need could lead to a rich source of value.

5   People matters
    • Who are the main decision makers that you will deal with?
    • What are the personal objectives of each individual?
    • Can you do anything to help them succeed and make them look good?

6   How you will be judged
    • Where is your organization ranked as a supplier? Are you a Top 100/key supplier? If not in the Top 100, where do you rank?
    • Are you strategically important?
    • Are you a direct or indirect provider of goods/services?
    • What metrics are in place to determine if you will be selected (and retained) as a supplier?

7   Your history and track record
    • Has your organization traded with the customer over a period?
    • What is the view of the customer about this historical relationship/supply position?
    • Is there any bad feeling or history between your organizations?
    • Do bridges need to be mended before you can proceed?

8   Your competitors
    • Who do you compete against?
    • Are there a number of different competitors?
    • How do you think you perform against each competitor?
    • How does your customer think you perform against each competitor?

9   The big picture
    The big picture captures all of the high-level information about the customer and describes the challenges and opportunities that they have. This will be a broad and strategic view. Having this understanding will enable conversations that are more focused on the customer's business – and less on your business/what you are trying to sell.

    This is great – but you still need to sell the products and services that are within your organization's remit. Build the customer big picture. Understand it and adopt the language and nuances within it. Grasp the customer culture and values that they embrace. And then focus on using this to construct your response.

10 The small picture
    Realistically, the offering to your customer is going to impact with a few touch points – but not the entire customer business. Think about the scope of your supply position and the boundaries that

you have in the overall scope of the customer business – but always refer to 'The Big Picture' to articulate the value impact you will provide.

Engage/Step 2: Connect with the customer decision-making unit

An old saying goes that 'Companies don't buy from companies: people buy from people.' It is a very true observation and one that needs to be considered carefully. Connecting with the customer often means connecting with many individuals working in different departments and locations – sometimes in different countries.

If your only point of contact with the customer site is the buyer (a logical relationship to have as they often manage spend with suppliers) then there could be problems with your ability to understand, discuss, sell and deliver your true value. The customer organization creates value by creating their own value proposition – professional services organizations employee talented experts, and manufacturing organizations take raw materials and create products. Procurement is part of the customer value chain, but it is not the sole reason that your customer exists.

You need relationships with more individuals than the buyer. Armstrong Kotler describes the decision-making unit for an organization as having five different roles. These can be five (or more) individuals, or sometimes less than five (in some organizations, one person can adopt more than one role). The essence of the model is to recognize that there are different deciders within the customer operation that need to be identified and understood so that you can discuss and demonstrate your value proposition.

You need to address the following questions for your customer:

- Who is performing each decision-making role?
- How much power do they have in making a decision about the offer I am suggesting?
- How strong is my relationship with this individual – today?
- How strong does the relationship need to be, and by when?
- What do I have to do in order to strengthen the relationship?

Table 7.2 The customer decision-making unit (DMU)

DMU Role	Description	Typical Organizational Position
User	The individual in the customer organization that uses the product/ service over the long term.	• Operators • Facility Managers • Consumers
Influencer	Individuals that affect the opinion of your offering (and you!) towards the customer. They can be employed directly by the customer or be associated (e.g. Non-Exec Directors & Consultants).	• Advisors • Consultants • Professional bodies • Other associates
Buyer	Procurement manage the selection and commercial terms with suppliers. On some occasions they will be the only point of contact with the customer (this can be frustrating!).	• Procurement (Buyers) (Note: can also be external procurement function)
Decider	The member(s) of the customer business that make the final decision about whether to purchase yours or a competitor's offering.	• General Manager • Procurement • Users
Gatekeeper	Accessing senior executives directly (especially in larger customer organizations) is not always possible. They are busy people with full agendas. To help them manage their time, assistants are employed to prioritize who they get to meet.	• Personal Assistants • Executive Assistants

Table 7.2 describes the five roles, indicating 'typical' positions (note that these are guidelines: every organization is different and it is your job to understand who is making decisions about you – and it is not always obvious!).

Meeting the needs of the user
Users are the individuals that have to live with the product over a sustained period. They need assurance that you will make their lives straightforward, trouble free and you will add value and quality to

their output. Spending time with users and really understanding their needs often pays dividends. They are the ultimate 'internal customer': if you take the time to listen and appreciate them, they can become your strongest advocate.

Note also that the user ultimately *could* be the customer's customer, and they are obviously outside the organization. Increasingly, they have a voice through social media and may influence your performance and selection/retention as a supplier.

Meeting the needs of the influencer

Possibly the hardest people to identify – influencers exist within the customer organization and outside it. They are consultants, associates, senior management associates, interim managers and members of professional bodies. Their opinions are often highly respected – in the case of consultants, they have the trust of the customer, so any thoughts they have about your organization will be listened to.

Be acutely aware that influencers exist. Try to identify them and establish a rapport that is favourable towards you. Provide data and knowledge to influencers; often they thrive in the customer organization by being subject matter experts, so help them grow their credibility with more information and knowledge.

Meeting the needs of the buyer

It is easy to assume that procurement is only concerned with getting the lowest price, and in many cases that is correct. However, what buyers do not want to happen is for a purchase that they select to be deemed unfit for use by the wider organization. Buyers need to secure products and services of the most appropriate performance for the best price (the key measure for buyers will be to save money on each category budget).

Manage buyers by working hard with the wider organization and gaining assurance from them that your selection is the right choice for the customer business. Do the hard work for them – and always assure them that the price they are paying is good value (not just the lowest price).

Meeting the needs of the decider

The final decider to purchase your product could be the buyer. With more complex purchases however, it will also involve a more senior operational person. For instance, following the financial crisis, in some organizations even small purchases are signed off by senior general managers, since the focus on cost control has elevated to a high level of strategic importance.

Deciders want assurance and evidence that what they are buying will work and will perform a good job. They want to know that goods and services will be the right quality, specification, delivered on time and the best value. Assurance and performance are the key things to focus on with the decider. Help them to be confident they are making the best decision by choosing you as a supplier and partner.

Meeting the needs of the gatekeeper

These are the people that you have to work with to access very senior people. Their job (in part) is to protect the time of people you need to access (buyers and deciders). Get to know the gatekeeper. Understand and empathize with the jobs they have to do. If they are a personal assistant, provide all the information and background that you can to make it easy for them to explain why they should get you time with the person they are protecting. In the case of executive assistants (these are often high-potential young managers that 'shadow' senior managers), treat them as equals to the executive you are trying to meet.

Be warned! If you patronize or try to by-pass gatekeepers, they can make your life difficult in the future. Respect them, work with them and always give them lots of information. If they are on side with you they can be strong supporters.

Mapping the relationship

Radar diagrams (see Figure 7.6) can be a great way to capture the decision-making unit (DMU) relationship with a customer (Score 5 for an exceptional relationship and Score 0 where there is a terrible 'broken' relationship!). The inner pattern is the relationship today – the outer pattern is the 'required state'.

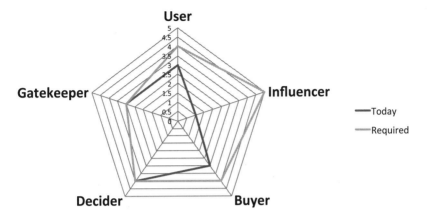

Figure 7.6 The customer DMU (Relationship today v. Relationship Required) (Radar representation of Customer DMU kindly provided by Consalia Limited)

Value in practice

Figure 7.6 shows a customer DMU radar chart for a management-consulting firm that was looking to expand its business with a retail bank. Following several failed attempts to win business they analysed the relationships they had with the client.

Connections were found to be strong with the exception of *influencer*. They discovered that one non-executive director was not agreeing to use their services, stating 'they do not have banking experience, and will take too long to educate on the way we do things here'.

To correct this, the management-consulting firm took time out to explain to the non-executive director that they had banking experience elsewhere in their group – and that expertise could be brought in to serve the client team. They listened to the influencer, accepted his concerns and responded (and consequently won several large consulting assignments).

Engage/Step 3: Create a compelling customer value proposition/offering

The principles and ideas that were presented in Chapter 6 (Offer development and innovation) should all be considered and applied when developing the value proposition for the customer. Value-based selling is the practical mechanism that provides guidance and process to leverage this framework to one customer. The techniques are very complementary, with the value-selling cycle providing a focus on seeking areas of potential impact in the customer business and then creating a value proposition/offering to respond to these needs.

All of the ODI techniques can be used at the engage stage, with a resulting value proposition being the required outcome. However, given that a true focus on being unique and excelling beyond any competitor offering is essential, an additional analysis step is suggested. This draws on a brand analysis technique developed by Kevin Lane Keller and seeks to break your offer down into core component parts and compare these to one or more key competitors.

To develop an offer comparison analysis, draw up a table like that shown in Table 7.3. Note down yourself and the competitor that most aligns with you (or the one that you are most likely to be bidding for business with). Identify the *points of parity* or offer components that you both provide as suppliers to the customer. These could be hygiene factors or areas where you compete on a 'head-to-head' basis. The next

Table 7.3 Offer comparator table

	You	Your Competitor
PoPs (Points of Parity)	Points of Parity are the features and deliverable elements of your offering that are the same as your competitor's offering.	
	With several suppliers offering the seme things, Points of Parity can become expected – 'Hygiene Factors'	
PoDs (Points of Difference)	Things that you offer that your competitor does not (or you significantly excel at)	Things that your competitor offers that you do not (or you significantly under-perform at)

step is to identify the *points of difference* where you clearly have a significant advantage over your competitor (or better still offer something that they cannot). In a similar manner, look at what your competitor offers that you cannot compete on.

As a practical technique this analysis is quite simple to understand but sometimes can be hard to apply. If you have followed the value-selling cycle and used techniques suggested for ODI, you will have a much clearer picture regarding where you stand with the customer and the elements captured within your offering. This final step makes you honest and questions the strength of your offer: after all, your comparative strength and weakness is all relative to how the customer views you and how you compete against your competitor. The secret to an effective offer comparison is being honest, having strong insights and really understanding what is important to the customer.

Table 7.4 shows an example. This was from a consulting assignment conducted with a facilities management (FM) organization, looking to secure business with a number of government customers (these were long-term assignments for the management of several sites and facilities, providing multi-million pound contracts). The table highlights the areas of comparable parity performance between the two organizations. It also highlights where each organization performs differently/more strongly.

Table 7.4 Example

	Supplier (FM Provider)	**Main Competitor**
PoPs (Points of Parity)	• Location to customer operations/sites • Ease of doing business • Transparency of information and costs etc. • Trustworthy/strong track record	
PoDs (Points of Difference)	• Risk and security management • IT systems & management • Flexible approach to business	• Lower priced offer • Location and industry/customer experience

Table 7.5 Constructing a compelling customer proposal

Section	Description
1 Situation appraisal	• Describe your understanding of the customer requirements and situational analysis • Itemize the customer needs that will be addressed
2 Meeting your needs	• What will be the 'Future State' of the customer business if they adopt your value proposition? Describe this scenario. • Describe the full customer value proposition
3 Our capability	• Expand on your capabilities. What are the key components of your offer? • What capabilities do you have? • Why should the customer trust you? What evidence do you have of similar past performance?
4 Outcomes and key deliverables	• What will be the key outcomes and key deliverables? • How will you measure these? • What critical performance indicators (CPIs) will be used? • What broader key performance indicators (KPIs) will be used?
5 Value positioning	• What is the price/fee for the offer? • What is the payback for the customer? • What will be the total cost of ownership? • What are your payment terms and invoice scheduling? • Describe other pricing mechanisms (rebates, discounts)
6 Programme delivery	• When can you start delivery? • What do you need from the customer to start and continue supply?
7 Contact details	• Who is the main contact for the programme? • Who else will be on the team?
8 Terms and conditions	• Provide your standard terms and conditions and any specific amendments for this supply agreement
9 The details of our offer	• Provide full details of the offer – products, services, people, processes etc.

Expanding the creation of the customer value proposition is the development of the customer offer document/proposal (see Table 7.5).

Engage/Step 4: Test the customer value proposition for strength and credibility

Taking the example from Table 7.4 further, initial consideration for the FM provider was bleak. In the highly competitive FM industry, price is often seen to be a deciding factor for winning business: after all, customers outsource these non-value-adding tasks to save money.

Closer examination and measurement of the offer, and providing some scores to each factor, highlighted how a competitive offer should be pitched. By discussing the supply requirements with the client, and by finding the right people to discuss the key points of difference (IT systems, risk and security management and flexible systems), the supplier was able to pitch for the business with a unique and competitive proposition. Fee and costs were still important to the customer, but they took a view to listen and reconsider the way that they would select the supplier based on these discussions. Note that discussions about the differentiating factors were with other people in the customer DMU.

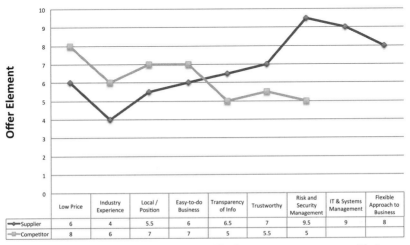

	Low Price	Industry Experience	Local / Position	Easy-to-do Business	Transparency of Info	Trustworthy	Risk and Security Management	IT & Systems Management	Flexible Approach to Business
Supplier	6	4	5.5	6	6.5	7	9.5	9	8
Competitor	8	6	7	7	5	5.5	5		

Figure 7.7 Example – offer comparator (facilities management provider)

Figure 7.7 shows how the offer is mapped and tested to model the offer. This method is based on Blue Ocean Strategy – 'The Strategy Canvas' – it is an excellent way to model, test and evaluate the core elements of any value proposition offering.

Agree/Step 5: Demonstrate

When the value proposition is developed and a potential pitch for competing and winning customer business found, the activity shifts on the value-selling cycle to the 'agree' phase. This is the group of activities that align the selling activity towards seeking customer approval and winning the business.

Demonstrate is the first activity. Two key steps are involved:

1   **Internal: Demonstrate with your own organization that the value proposition is viable and something that the wider organization will commit to. If this is an acceptable commercial offering, then move to Step 2.**
2   **External: Demonstrate the value proposition with the customer and seek approval.**

This two-stage activity is important. Failing to seek internal alignment for new value propositions can cause problems, especially if the offering is slightly different from other activities that have been provided in the past. For example, if additional support will be required from technical departments in delivering the offer, address these questions:

- What will be the time and cost activity commitment?
- Do these support functions have the capacity and the capability to deliver this extra work?
- What profit will be possible by providing this offer?
- What will be the risk profile of the offer?
- Is this something that the organization can deliver?
- Is this something that the organization wants to do?

These are basis questions, but really need to be answered as an 'internal' pitch and selling activity. Does it make sense to provide this offer to this customer?

If the correct people are consulted and a positive response gained, then the next activity is to demonstrate the concept to the customer. This could be firmly dictated by the customer, possibly all responses and bids going through the buyer. If that is the case, you have to comply. However, if the impact and value of the offer is to be appreciated by other members of the customer DMU, present to them, either formally or informally. Discuss and seek feedback. This activity will provide results and is always worth the effort. By gaining alignment from the full DMU, you effectively develop a number of advocates for your value proposition on the inside of the customer business.

In the case of the FM provider in the example (Figure 7.7), the point-of-difference messages of increased risk and security management, IT and systems management, and flexible approach to business had to be discussed with the customer IT manager, HSSEQ managers and general managers. Reaching these conclusions required a far more complex and detailed series of discussions and interactions with a greater number of people across the customer operations. Having this depth of understanding provided reassurance to the buyer however, and he was able to make the decision to purchase this offering (even though it was 20% more expensive than other suppliers) as he had the backing and support from other senior managers within his organisation.

Agree/Step 6: Negotiate

Regardless of how strong your customer value proposition is following the engage stage, it is still likely that you will have to negotiate and agree fees and terms with the buyer. It is not the intention of this book to provide a complete negotiation guide (negotiation books are in the Bibliography section), but the alignment of value-focused selling and negotiation will be made.

As Figure 7.8 shows, there are three areas in which negotiation is enhanced and becomes integrated into the value-based selling process:

1. Negotiation principles

In their book *Getting to Yes* (1982) Roger Fisher and William Ury divide negotiation into two main areas: positional and principled. Positional negotiation is a traditional adversarial approach, with each party looking to win a position over the other. There is little focus on longer-term collaboration and the key to success is winning by making the other party lose.

Figure 7.8 Aligning value-based selling and negotiation

Table 7.6

Negotiation Aspect	Positional-Based Negotiation	Principle-Based Negotiation	Aligning Principle-Based with Value-Based Selling
Style	*Win-Lose*	*Win-Win*	** Win-Win-Win (Also consider the customer's customer!)*
Objectives	*Individual gain*	*Joint and individual gain*	** Value co-creation*
Key interests	*Opposed*	*Possibly opposed Willing to align*	** Strong focus on interest alignment*
Relationship	*Short-term (transactional)*	*Longer term (trust-based)*	** Works better when trust-based*
Outcome (customer offer)	*Factual*	*Open to creative thinking and ideas*	** Highly open to creative thinking and generating solutions*

* Denotes where there is strong alignment (enhancement!) provided to principle-based negotiation by adopting value-focused selling. It can be seen that there is very strong alignment: it could be concluded that better negotiation will naturally result when following a value-based approach to selling.

Principled negotiation seeks to establish a climate where both parties can be creative in searching for mutually beneficial outcomes to a shared problem or opportunity (a very similar framework to value co-creation). The focus seeks a winning outcome for both parties by negotiating over the interests and needs of both parties, not the positions. Table 7.6 contrasts these two negotiation principles with the value-based selling approach.

2. Negotiation key steps

Key steps for any negotiation (but in particular principle negotiation) vary from method to method. Core elements that have been adopted by the author with many clients can be seen in Table 7.7.

Table 7.7

Key Negotiation Step	Enhanced by Value-Based Selling
1. Identify favourable outcomes	*Aims to develop strong customer value proposition.*
	Aims to develop an offering that will also provide attractive returns for the supplier.
2. Create ways to meet needs	*Focus on understanding the customer business, strategy and objectives. Understanding needs is a foundation component of value-focused selling.*
3. Determine who has the power	*Adopting the DMU model helps to assess who has the power to make choices about you.*
4. Set negotiation parameters	*Negotiation theory stipulates that it is critical to ascertain the reservation fee for the buyer (the highest value that they will go to) as well as reservation for the seller (the lowest value that they will go to).*
	While not expressly covered in value-focused selling, having knowledge of the customer and what they need/value will significantly help to determine these key negotiation numbers.
5. Prepare and plan	*The Engage phase focuses on planning to understand the customer and developing a strong value proposition/strategy.*
6. Gain their trust	*Emphasis on capturing value and demonstrating that the value promise has been delivered. Long-term focus: business is built on mutual trust and jointly working to understand and capture value.*

These steps are easier and made stronger if they are part of an overall value-focused selling approach.

3. Core negotiator skills

Table 7.8

Core Skill	Complemented by Value-Based Selling
Being prepared	*Value-based selling is all about planning and understanding.*
	Follow the key steps and you will have clarity about what your customer needs and how you could add value: the foundation of good negotiation.
Understanding the other person	*Walk a mile in your customer's shoes ...*
	Assess who does what in the customer organization.
	Analyse the customer DMU to capture how individuals are personally measured and rewarded. What is important to them personally?
Understanding the other organization	*Follow the ten steps to understand the customer (Figure 7.5).*
	Meet and discuss internal and external key individuals to gain a stronger understanding.
Quantifying the value of trade-off offers	*Describe your value proposition (and offer) in as much detail as possible.*
	By completing the Points of Parity and Difference analysis, and mapping your competitive strengths v. your competition, you will understand your relative value position.
Generating options and offers	*Use the techniques described in the Offer Development and Innovation section to create new ideas.*
	Always look to develop value propositions that meet customer needs and improve the future state of the customer business.
Being a good communicator	*The first rule of communication is listening and understanding.*
	This is a bedrock principle of value-based selling. This is described as a process more than a skill. However, customer-facing people should be coached to be good at listening, questioning and seeking affirmation of the conclusions that they draw about the customer.

Agree supply terms

Agree/Step 7: Agree terms

The final stage of 'agree' is to finalize and capture the terms of supply moving forward. There will possibly have been a lot of discussion to get to this point, especially following the discussion stage, with multiple decision makers and stakeholders on both sides. Agreeing terms formalizes and captures everything that has been discussed to this stage.

There are three main documents to consider:

1   Updated customer proposal;
2   Contract terms and conditions;
3   Project plan and ways of working document.

1. Updated customer proposal

Following negotiations and seeking agreement, the items covered in the customer proposal will possibly need to be updated. Make these changes and seek approval from all concerned parties from your own organization. Return the updated proposal to the customer for sign off.

2. Contract terms and conditions

These should be agreed between the two firms' legal teams. This is for these expert teams to agree. The key components captured in the value proposition and the offer document should be briefed to your legal department, along with any matters that arose from the negotiation phase as a supply position was agreed.

To avoid any delay moving from *engage to deliver*, it is always highly recommended to involve your legal advisers early in the value-selling cycle. It is better that they know you are considering providing a new service package for a customer early on, rather than at the tail end of the sale. This way any concerns or reservations that need to be written in the contract can be dealt with in good time (and your legal counsel will be on-side and happier!)

3. Project plan and ways of working document

Depending on the complexity of your offer, there will be a period of change and activity as you implement your offering. This will be a more dramatic and disruptive period depending on the level of change you are providing. Supplying a customer for the first time, or providing a new portfolio of products and services to an existing customer in a new division, are examples of where this transition period needs to be managed carefully. This is an opportunity to demonstrate value with the customer. Managing this high-risk and high-activity initial 'ramp-up' period effectively, in a well-communicated and trouble-free manner, will be appreciated. Having strong project management capability, and ensuring that the operational members of your team are aligned and clear about what they have to do, will lead to reduced problems at start up.

Project plans and a document that stipulates what you will be doing and what the customer is expected to do will provide a means of discussing implementation and subsequent operating afterwards. Part of this plan should also include working guidelines, for example: how often will meetings be required; what the reporting lines will be; and how to deal with problems and irregularities. Simple guidelines always help to gain clarity regarding programme implementation and operation. As the supplier, take control of this and demonstrate leadership.

Deliver the value promise

Deliver/Step 8: Benchmarking

At the start of implementing the value proposition it is advisable for the supplier to stipulate the measures that will be used to capture the value that is promised in the value proposition. The recommendation is that the supplier takes control of this activity. Identify the factors that need to be measured, set up the current parameters and determine methods that will be used to capture the measurements. Table 7.9 provides some examples of value measurements.

The reasons why the supplier should lead this work are compelling:

- If you don't capture the value that you create for the customer, who will?
- Why would the customer do this?

Table 7.9 Capturing value appraisal

Price (Fee)	Capturing Benefits	Measuring Performance
Quantify the fee and how it will be structured.	Provide / capture the 'value in use'	Detail the key performance indicators (KPIs) that will be used to track performance once the contract commences.
Examples • Cost per annum (£m) • Cost per tonne • Cost per unit • Discounts	**Examples** • Payback (years) • Return on investment • Savings on other consumables (e.g. energy costs, tooling costs) • Savings on labour costs	**Examples** • Saving (cost/tonne) • Reduced labour (labour hours/unit of production) • Reduced scrap rates (yield improvements) • Reduced energy consumption (kWh)

- Why work hard creating value that will simply evaporate away over the course of your supply period?
- How will you defend your good work in the future, when your contract is due for renewal?

To start this process, go back to your customer value proposition. It is the value (and outcomes) of this statement that the customer is buying, so it makes sense to ensure that the measures you benchmark and subsequently track are aligned with this value intent. Benchmarking is a critical activity to consider. For example, if you are supplying a device that saves electrical energy consumption in a manufacturing site (possibly a set of new heavy-duty electrical motors and controllers), you need to measure that amount of electricity being consumed before you provide your solution.

This becomes the benchmark value, and is what you should be working hard to improve (if a 5 per cent electrical energy saving is required to demonstrate a break-even on the investment the customer has used choosing your hardware, 5 per cent is the absolute minimum you want to capture – hopefully a much larger number will be measured, demonstrating that your selection was extremely strong value, a good choice!).

Agreeing the measures with the customer and setting out simple guidelines to agree the results should form part of this activity. Additionally, there may be activities that you need the customer to perform, so seek approval here. For example, if your solution saves the customer spending money on other consumables (bearings and tooling), you may not have access to that information. Try to agree a means whereby the customer will share that information and seek a means where you are given the credit for making the saving.

Deliver/Step 9: Measure performance

Connected to benchmarking is the process of measuring performance. If benchmarking sets out the idea and concept of capturing value, measuring grasps the nettle and identifies what each measure and parameter will be. These parameters are 'performance indicators', and are linked to the value proposition. You should have a range of these measures.

Figure 7.9 shows a performance indicator table to consider and select these indicators. On the left-hand side, CPIs and KPIs capture the value parameters that you will measure as part of the agreed contract. These are measures that you have already agreed to deliver.

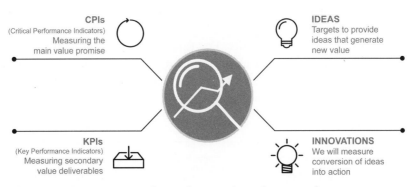

Figure 7.9 Focus on capturing and measuring value created

On the right-hand side, these are measures to ensure that you keep being innovative with the customer, with targets in place to make you bring new concepts and ideas to the customer for review. These measures are provided to accelerate the 'value co-creation' concept – if both parties are working towards creating new sources of value and generating opportunities to improve the customer's business, then there should be a focus on developing these ideas. As a supplier, if you are already integrated into the customer's business delivering value-based solutions, you are perfectly positioned to generate even more ideas to build on your increased knowledge and understanding. To explain in more detail:

Performance Measures – agreed supply position;
Critical Performance Indicators (CPIs) – these are those one or two measures that track your performance delivering the really important value-generating aspects of your value proposition. CPIs are often linked to your points of difference (PoDs).

Some CPI examples include:

- Increasing customer share of market in France by 5 per cent over eighteen months;
- Reducing spend on grinding tools by £500,000 per annum;
- Reducing stock levels by 15 per cent over a twelve-month period (value estimate £10m);
- Reducing scrap rates by 15 per cent (value estimate £5.5m);
- Providing secure transport solutions across Asia (0 theft incidents) within six months (value estimate £250,000 saving/ incident).

CPIs are connected to the heart of the customer value proposition. They should be few in number, harder to achieve and the most important part of the whole contractual position.

KPIs are the measures that track the rest of your performance trading with the customer. They are important and demonstrate value, but are of less importance (since individually they are not generating such critical outcome results for the customer). There might be five to ten KPIs chosen to track a customer offer. KPIs are often linked to your points of parity and include:

- Delivering stock on time as required;
- Packaging quality – scrap rates at 2 per cent/tonne or less;
- Response rate – getting technicians to customer calls within twelve hours or less;
- Just in Time delivery rates;
- Adherence to quality standards.

Ideas and innovation measures are being increasingly adopted in a few industries with great success. Many automotive and manufacturing manufacturers have challenging business models, require fast and regular changes to develop new products, and operate on tight margins. Fostering value co-creation with suppliers is part of the business model that they have developed. To encourage and drive innovation, many suppliers are encouraged to provide a set number of ideas to improve the customer business. These ideas are tracked, and highly valued.

Ideas are measured with one number. Ideas that become useful and are implemented are measured separately (maybe one idea out of every hundred is implemented, but it is the ideas that generate creativity). This is a good conversation to have with your customer. Be proactive and try to establish a mechanism to generate new ideas and develop stronger value propositions in the future.

Deliver/Step 10: Develop and innovate

The final step keeps the Infinite Value-selling cycle active! It is very easy once a value proposition is accepted to stay stuck in the *deliver* side of the value-selling cycle. This happens for a number of reasons: it may be highly lucrative; the effort to deliver may be significant; or challenges elsewhere for the supplier may be pulling them away on to other assignments. Sometimes the account can get forgotten about by business development – why mess with something that generates good income?

A big and frequent occurrence is that the personnel in the supplier business concerned with value delivery love the activity of delivering value, but sometimes lack the skills (and desire) for selling and expanding the supply position. In some ways, this is a good thing – your value delivery needs to be conducted by experts in that field. The customer respects, values and pays for their experience and knowledge. Let that continue, and allow value to be generated for both parties.

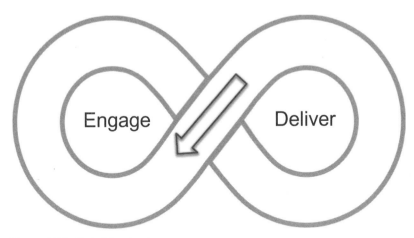

Figure 7.10 Switching back to engage

However, both supplier and the customer need to have a continual and fresh set of new ideas and thinking to generate new sources of value creation. This only comes from changing the value-selling cycle back to the *engage* state (Figure 7.10). This will, of course, be a significantly stronger and more informed activity than the last phase of developing the value proposition. Consider, for instance, the ten steps to understanding the customer (Figure 7.5). Liaise with the people in your organization who have delivered value over the last one to two years: they will have very strong and intimate insights into the customer's business. These insights will greatly help lead to the creation of a stronger *evolved* customer value proposition.

Other aspects that should be considered will have occurred as the trading environment for the customer changes – there may be other competitive factors that they have to operate within, or changes in the customers and markets that they serve. The pace of change is fast and organizations have to respond and navigate new ways of working within them to prosper. Be a highly regarded and value-adding supplier by standing back, re-assessing customer needs and developing new value propositions to add even more value to the customer's business.

The relationship with the customer should also prosper and grow. If you have delivered your value promises and focused on building relationships, you will have a foundation to increase the scope and depth of how you are viewed and ultimately trusted. Reconsider the relationship–trust zone (Figure 7.2). By working hard to deliver value, can you now elevate the zone from two (application-based) to three (operations-based)? Can you have this sort of discussion with the customer? Are they willing to be open and discuss a future trading partnership that is closer and stronger?

The value-selling cycle is iterative by design and purpose. This infinite approach of constantly engaging and creating new value propositions, and then delivering these innovative value promises, will lead to stronger value for the customer and for you as a supplier.

It just takes hard work, focus, investment and commitment. Easy!

Value matters

1   The value-cloud is an image that suppliers and buyers should always keep in mind when discussing the supply of products and services. If the conversation has broken down to a 'haggle' over price (or day rate × number of days) rather than both parties looking upwards to an actual quantifiable value that could be generated by both parties collaborating, then the focus on the big opportunity could be lost. This is a mindset. Both the supplier and the customer need to sign up to the idea and the benefit that can be obtained.

2   A realistic sense of proportion should be maintained. Suppliers can provide extraordinary high-value impact solutions to customers. Realistically, the customer will not pay for all of this value, but failing to identify, quantify and seek agreement from the customer creates a situation whereby value simply evaporates. Be realistic: 'Trees don't grow to the sky – but they do keep growing.' A long-term, trust-based relationship with certain customers will lead to longer value generation.

3   Value-based selling is a technique that helps suppliers to change the conversation with suppliers. A foundation of value-based business, this technique is critical to enable creation, delivery and value-capture of powerful customer value propositions. Organizations that have weak value-selling capability will also

struggle at key account management, channel management and value-based pricing.

4   Trust between supplier and customer cannot be underestimated. It is the bond that holds value-based selling together. Without trust from the customer that you will deliver your value promises, there is a shaky basis for future partnership.

5   The value-selling cycle is offered in infinite value as a three-stage model to enable value-selling: engage, agree and deliver.

6   Essential to value-based selling is a deep understanding of the customer needs and wants. This leads to understanding what they value.

7   Suppliers should work hard to engage and understand a wide base of decision makers in the customer business. While it is essential to have a strong connection with the buyer, connecting and understanding the needs of operations, supply chain, marketing and other functions leads to the true benefactors of the value proposition.

8   All of the principles of offer development and innovation (Chapter 6) should be connected with value-based selling: value-based selling is the dynamic application of ODI.

9   Value-based selling integrates with negotiation perfectly. Strong negotiations should always focus on impact to the customer. Remember that selling and negotiating are different, however. A fantastic job embracing a value-selling approach can lead to the concept of a sale, but a weak negotiation could lose this position. Value-based selling is an approach that works at all times, not just at the point of sale.

10   All members of the organization should understand value-based selling principles. Complex sales activity (the creation and delivery of value to customers) no longer rests solely with the sales-force. Everybody should be considered as members of the 'value-force'.

Chapter 8

Key account management (KAM)

Opportunity is missed by most people because it is dressed in overalls and looks like hard work.

Thomas Edison

Strategy: Customer by customer

Value-based selling is the foundation skill of any organization that wants to focus on higher opportunity 'key account' customers. As described in the customer segmentation section, key account customers are selected based on the opportunity that they present for the supplier and the way that the customer views you as a supplier. In most industries, organizations are finding a natural consolidation of business that is coming from a smaller footprint of bigger, more powerful customers.

Definitions:

Key account customer:

An existing or prospect enterprise customer that has the potential to generate significant commercial opportunity.

Key account management:

The strategic focus of an organization to significantly leverage resources on carefully selected enterprise key customers, in order to enable the development and delivery of unique customer value propositions.

The results that can be obtained from these larger customers can be significant. It is not uncommon to find organizations deriving 60–70 per cent of the profits they make from the top twenty to thirty customers that they manage. However, with this upside there are risks and challenges. The supplier needs to be wary of these challenges, and greater focus on designing the organization to manage these high-opportunity (but high-maintenance!) key account customers is required.

Seven reasons why you might need a KAM programme

There are seven major reasons that key account management is attractive (and highly challenging) for suppliers:

1   **They emerge from within your customer portfolio**
    Even when supplier organizations are not especially looking to have key account customers, they can 'magically' appear. The nature of business is to grow and develop profits for shareholders. This comes from either growing organically or by acquiring other businesses (buying competitor operations). Customers within your portfolio will behave as any other commercial enterprise and will be looking to expand. We have witnessed organizations see a dominant customer acquire several other businesses over a short period.

    Responding to this 'emergent KAM' scenario needs to be considered carefully. While it is great to have business with one customer increase dramatically, failure to recognize that this customer is a different enterprise, probably with new management and new ways of working, could result in partial or total loss of that customer. As these customers increase in number they also draw the attention from your competitors – these bigger customers have attractive prizes attached to them: your long-term customer may suddenly have a number of other suitors looking to steal your cosy supply position!

2 **They are industry leaders, and influential**
Bigger enterprises tend to be industry leaders in technology,
marketing, processes and leadership thinking. If you are an organization that wants to remain at the leading edge of value creation
you will have to develop and deliver effective value propositions
to these main players.

Responding to this scenario means that you have to add
value to the key customer by understanding their business and
complementing it with knowledge, products and services that
complement the industry leading position they hold.

3 **They operate across countries and regions**
As enterprises become larger, they tend to expand outside the
home territory in which they originated (although this can
remain their headquarters). Many key account customers operate
across several countries within one region, and often across two
or more regions. For consistency and sharing good practice,
these regional or global customers can seek suppliers that can
work with them in these countries and regions.[1]

Responding to this opportunity as a supplier can be daunting.
Even if you have operations in the same countries that the
customer is operating, you may not work in a 'joined up manner'.
Organizations often have financial accountability by country or
divisional level. Customers that 'cut across' these boundaries
have a clumsy ownership and accountability.

4 **They seek consistent service everywhere**
As key customers develop and become centralized in the approach
they take with suppliers, there tends to be a requirement to have
a consistent approach to supply. If you have provided good
practice in one division or country, this may need to be repeated
in others.

Responding to this is challenging, especially if it is to be done
in a region/country where you do not have strength of operational support. The key answer to provide this extension to your

---

[1] Not all customers that operate on a global basis do so in a globally 'connected'
manner. Some operate autonomously 'country by country'. Your challenge as a
supplier is to understand how they operate and how they want to be served.

commercial, technical, operational and supply chain is to work with trusted third-party channel partners. Coordinating with your own organization, the customer and channel partners is a complex business, but essential to deal with this KAM challenge.

5 **They seek suppliers that will enable their strategic objectives**
Bigger organizations themselves have challenges. Often they have expanded by acquisition, and are wrestling with the challenges presented by pulling together several organizations (structures, cultures, systems, people etc.).

As a supplier, if you understand these issues and can provide things that help the customer achieve their strategic goals, you can be in a stronger supply position. Of course, this requires leveraged effort on your behalf to understand these customer needs, opportunities and challenges.

6 **They have professional procurement processes**
Procurement is becoming a far more organized and professional function in many organizations, but with larger organizations that typically become 'key customers' the procurement function can become very centralized and strategic.

Remaining a selected key supplier while ensuring that there is clarity around the bidding and tendering process is the first challenge. These larger bids look attractive, but can become difficult to supply profitably, especially when several vendors have fought each other driving down the price. Always stick to the principles of value-based selling and win business based on value not price, if you can.

7 **They are extremely difficult to understand (sometimes they don't even understand themselves)**
Large customers can appear to be organized and efficient organizations. Sometimes, that is not the reality. As organizations become larger, and especially if they operate globally, it takes time for them to develop a consistent strategy with operational ways of working that are understood by everybody.

For a supplier trying to develop key account strategies for a customer, this confusion can become frustrating. Additionally, changes in leadership and management on the customer side lead to further confusion and wasted time as you try to build rapport and understanding. Work hard to research the customer, and build relationships with leadership to try to establish a closer understanding of the strategy they are following.

Strategy. Capability. Transformation

Usually, organizations recognize three to four of the seven reasons listed above as reasons to have to adopt a KAM programme. These are all compelling reasons: on the one hand they offer potentially high commercial rewards, while on the other hand significant business can be lost if they fail to rise to the challenges presented.

The theme of *Infinite Value* is to develop a strategy, build capability and then implement these new business standards via transformation. For key account management, these factors become extremely relevant. The difference between organizations that succeed in KAM and those that fail stems from an understanding that it is a different way to do business and is not merely an 'extension' to the sales organization.

When considering KAM, the three main areas of focus are KAM as:

1 **A strategic issue**

    There is an understanding by the business that KAM is strategically important but is a *different way of doing business*. A strategic review of *what is required to achieve your desired results* and to meet the needs of your key account customers will require a strategy and intent to do these different things well.

2 **An organizational capability**

    Key account *management* is more than just the key account *manager* (although the key account manager is extremely important!). Organizational capability considers the people: how they work; the structure; and the leadership. Organizations that are successful at KAM focus on building an organization that understands who its key customers are, what they need and how the organization should respond *collectively* to create value for both parties.

    Key account management is the leveraging of resources around a selected portfolio of customers – this leveraging comes from your organizational blueprint and KAM programme. Organizations that are great at KAM have a clarity and respect for this way of working. They have confidence in saying *'This is how we manage our key account customers'*.

3   **A transformation issue**
Developing new strategies and capability building inevitably leads to a need to adapt and change. This transformation takes commitment, time and focus. Organizations that are effective at key account management recognize that this is potentially a longer-term transformation. They plan for change and they take time to build momentum by communicating with the wider organization and bringing them along as they learn.

Building KAM capability

A common mistake that many organizations make when developing a KAM programme is to think of all identified KAM customers as being the same. This thinking is flawed for several reasons, since key customers can present opposing challenges in the way that they should be managed. These challenges should be considered for key customers and the way that they are managed developed appropriately. The main considerations are as follows:

Growth v. mature
A key account customer could have zero sales today, but you have selected them to be key since you recognize there will be significant potential sales in the future. Conversely, a customer could have been key for many years and provides a good source of income – but it is now unlikely to grow. Developing a new customer for growth is a different challenge than managing an established large customer that has plateaued (or even is declining), but they warrant strategic focus and consideration of additional resourcing.

Local v. regional v. global
Key customers tend to operate outside the boundary of a country, often having a significant presence within several countries. Customers can also operate across two or more regions (e.g. Europe and Asia). Managing these customers requires a careful focus on

the activity that is required at the strategic customer head-office and how those decisions connect with the local country operations. There is no fixed rule here: each customer KAM team should be designed around the customer and how they work.

Single-division v. multi-division

Customers can take just one of your product/service streams, or they can buy from two or more product streams. Quite often that means the customer is interacting with completely different business units and management teams. Consider this: is it the customer's problem that you are structured this way, or should you adapt to the way they want to buy and interact? ('If only they behaved as One-Supplier Limited!' is often heard by customers when dealing with large suppliers.)

Stable v. under threat

You may have had a great relationship with your key customer over a sustained period. The relationship has reaped rewards for both parties, you understand each other at many levels and there is a mutual trust. Sometimes this can lead to complacency, especially when there are customer management changes, aggressive activity from your competitors or alternative offerings in the market. When key accounts are under threat, a different strategic approach is required. Stay alert and respond when you might lose a key customer!

Transactional v. innovation-'receptive'

All organizations have their own 'value DNA'. This is apparent by the way that they work with suppliers, some being very receptive to innovative and creative value-enhancing offers, and others being very focused on the delivery of a finite offering, meeting tight specifications and meeting a set price-point. Both types of customer can be key accounts – but they need to be managed according to how they 'behave'.

Figure 8.1 is the KAM segmentation model that was described earlier. The complexity to serve increases as each customer type increases (but the opportunity also increases). The factors just described also apply to each key customer type, so it is possible to have a global customer that is under threat and innovation focused. This can be complicated to consider, but this strategic thinking is only for your top ten to thirty

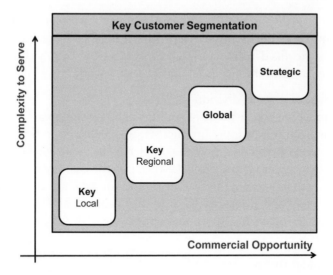

Figure 8.1 Key customer segmentation

key customers. This detailed thinking and understanding of 'how the customer operates and behaves' will pay dividends as you design your organization around them.

Value in practice

Do not over-serve customers that do not justify the effort.

Do not under-serve those customers that do.

However, the critical focus for key account management falls into a few main areas that have been observed as essential for KAM success.

These are:

1 The challenges for the key account manager – what are the main tasks that have to be dealt with?
2 Regional, global and strategic customers – how do you deal with increasing complexity of the customer operational footprint as they expand across borders and business divisions?

3 The need for KAM teams – the required competence of a key account manager is broad and deep. How do organizations build capability around the customer using teams?
4 The KAM plan – what are the constituent parts of a key account strategy? What makes an effective KAM plan?
5 KAM value propositions – how do KAM and service-based offerings complement each other?

After working with many organizations covering multiple industries, we have found the above five capability aspects to be critical, and considerations for high-performing KAM programmes. Of course, the other six elements of value-based business need to be embedded, but following customer segmentation and the identification of your key accounts, the above five areas are essential to address and focus on in order to build a robust and effective KAM capability.

Challenges for the key account manager

Figure 8.2 shows the eight challenges that face key account managers as they look to develop and manage their customers. These are stretching and challenging duties, but all are essential to drive the process of developing and delivering unique customer value propositions. Given that key customers are 'market segments of one', key account management draws on strategy, marketing, project management and selling techniques. Key account managers can be thought of as 'customer-facing general managers', but with the added difficult leadership and network leadership.

Value ambassador: key account managers are at the 'tip of the sword' when it comes to value-based selling. They are accountable for high opportunity, high profit-making customers. It is essential that they understand what these customers value and how to respond to these needs. A strong understanding of value-based selling and offer development and innovation are bedrock skills that need to be developed in order to be a successful key account manager.

This observation is one of the reasons that *Infinite Value* came to be written. It connects several areas of business that are core elements to make a value-centric organization. Many organizations fail at key

Figure 8.2 The key account manager as ...

account management because they have a weak grasp of the fundamentals of value-based selling. Key account managers must act as the ambassadors of this foundation skill, by coaching members of their own organization, the customer and other supporting players.

Strategist: a major difference between selling and key account management is the requirement to develop a strategy that is focused around one customer. This should identify ways of building sustainable value creation for both parties. The difference with key accounts is that these strategies often involve bigger investments and bespoke offerings. With very large key customers, this challenge is like managing a 'business within a business'.

Innovator: ensuring that key customers keep viewing you as a key supplier requires constant regeneration of value-adding offerings. Being creative and innovative can 'fly in the face' of delivering profits today, but the need to look to the future is critical if a long-term partnership is to be maintained.

Rainmaker: it is often said that sales people do not make good key account managers. This is because they lack some of the skills such as project management, strategy and leadership. A skill they do possess, however, is that they can sell. They are good with customers, can handle rejection and they have the energy and motivation to make a sale.

This ability to 'make rain' and win business is a massive skill, and is much underestimated. The view should be taken that sales people can absolutely make excellent key account managers – but they need to be developed with some of the additional skills. Never underestimate the value of good rainmakers. Without sales you have no top line. And with no top line, there is no business.

Team builder: the ability to manage a cross-functional (and sometimes cross-geographical) team of people virtually is a necessary skill. Managing teams when you have no direct reporting line is possibly one of the most difficult leadership challenges. Great key account managers have team-building skills. They gain alignment from people as they follow their energy, passion and vision.

Silo buster: any large organization achieves great things by having smaller divisions and operating units that have financial, functional and operational focus. Organizations have marketing, supply chain, R&D, finance, HR, regional and country leadership and other business units. Great things are achieved by allowing organizations to operate in these carefully controlled 'cells'. Getting things done for the customer often requires connecting with these cells and seeking support. 'Silo busting' may sound like an aggressive approach to business, but this internal selling by gaining resources and support from leadership groups who may well not be focused on the customer is a vital skill. Key account managers bust their own silos (and often have to bust customer silos as well).

Planner: any good strategy is only as good as the detailed planning that gets 'strategy into action'. Being able to detail plan and get innovative concepts developed and implemented is project management and planning.

Change agent: 'If you create a solution for your customer, paradoxically you create a problem for your own organization.' Dealing with these problems and getting your own organization to 'do something different' requires an ability to sell the new idea and to get things done differently. This could be new products, services, data systems, financial reporting or people. All these things are 'different ways of doing business' and require change management.

This mix of unique skills (KAM requirements) highlights the challenge that key account management presents to an organization. It is easy to see why key account managers are highly regarded individuals – and with increasing focus on securing business from a 'smaller more powerful portfolio' of key customers, supplier organizations are increasingly focusing on recruiting, developing and retaining this vital talent pool.

Regional, global and strategic customers

One of the biggest changes that occurs with the relationship architecture of key customers is the geographical footprint that they occupy. Working with large customers that are located within one country is difficult. Working with customers that start to span and operate across several countries within a region gets very difficult, and when they span multiple regions and go global, complexity becomes exceptionally challenging. Add to this the fact that when key customers start to take business from multiple operating 'product' divisions of your business (strategic customers), a recipe of complexity emerges that needs some careful consideration to address.

Following several workshops (with very different organizations) faced with the challenge of managing key customers across several regions and business units, a list of nine factors emerged as common challenges that need to be addressed (Figure 8.3). These issues need to be considered and planned to build a regional/strategic KAM capability standard. Expanding on the nine challenges:

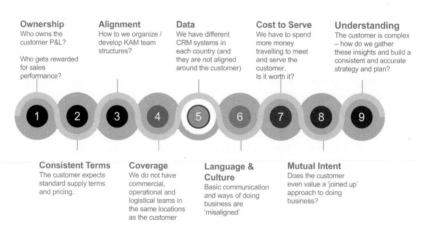

Figure 8.3 Regional and global customer 'typical challenges'

1 Ownership. There are neither priorities nor weighting on the nine factors, but from practical experience this is usually the biggest headache and causes confusion and a lack of progress to execute regional KAM (and especially cross-divisional strategic accounts). The problem of ownership arises when customer operations have been handled by individual business units 'in country' over several years. There may be a great customer relationship in a country leading to strong financial results and performance. Naturally, any customer that produces results (after a period of investment and nurturing) will be very precious to that country.

So, when a corporate 'centralized' view is taken and the local customer is recognized and selected as part of a bigger initiative to be part of a regional/global strategy, releasing the customer to a central team can be emotional. Questions such as 'Who owns the customer relationship? Who owns the financial results? and 'Who discusses initiatives with the customer?' become heated debates.

Staying focused on the overall strategy of managing the customer derives the best solution to the problem of ownership. Relationships at country level should be maintained, and those local units should be rewarded for the results in that country. However, there will be a group customer strategy that will be agreed at the group HQ with the customer. These initiatives should be taken to each local country and implemented.

Tensions arise when the local teams have strategies placed on them with no involvement and no consideration of their experience and knowledge about the customer at a local level. Dealing with this challenge is a critical competence for the key account manager – they need to network, communicate, involve multiple stakeholders within their own organization to best serve the customer and maximize results.

2 Consistent terms. Customers will have different pricing agreements and different commercial terms (rebates, payment periods etc.) in different countries. The supplier and customer agreeing over a period on a 'local basis' often will have derived these. When a centralized view is taken, customers can sometimes (not always) start to look at the most favourable country and request

that those prices and terms be leveraged across all supply points. This presents a risk that should not be ignored. Also, a robust defence position should be taken – in some countries, prices will be higher due to higher costs, taxes and living expenses. Defend these issues on a country-by-country basis.

3   Alignment. This connects with ownership, but is more concerned with getting accountability and structures in place to develop and serve the customer business. The best way to achieve this is to map out the activities that are required to manage each customer on a global/regional/local basis. Reporting lines should be developed with clarity about hard and 'dotted' reporting lines.

Additional resourcing may be required, but this is always subject to separate analysis and business case. You need to consider whether you can justify additional managers and support teams. Will the anticipated incremental business cover these additional expenses and costs?

4   Coverage. Serving a customer in multiple markets is acceptable when there has been material historic business in attractive countries. When a supplier commits to serve a customer as key across multiple countries, a problem can emerge, especially when the supplier does not have offices or representation in those areas. A rapid, cost-effective way to respond to this problem is by selecting third-party channel partners to provide support (additionally, channels can be developed to work in parallel in all countries – but they need to be selected, developed and managed very carefully).

5   Data. Supplier organizations often struggle to capture historical customer sales and supply data around customers when they have legacy systems that have grown and developed in each country. 'Joining the customer dots' is tricky but should not be an excuse to stall transitioning to a regional KAM model.

Overcome this by initially having manual development of data – use students to develop spreadsheet models (they'll appreciate the work experience). It takes far too long to wait for new cross-country/cross-divisional systems to be installed. Get started with some practical 'hands-on' analysis and data crunching.

6   Language and culture. There are two challenges here: firstly aligning your organizational culture with the customer culture

and secondly aligning internally as you start forming the key account team.

Ensuring that your culture aligns with the customer should be considered when you select the customer (at the strategic customer segmentation stage). It makes sense to choose and work with customers that have an aligned view on how you might work together and your shared working ideas.

Aligning your internal teams takes commitment from leadership to establish the principle that each country and business unit should align and focus on the customer. While having a leadership directive to make this happen, hard work is required by the people who will co-ordinate this activity and make it happen. Key account managers have to be mindful that country teams have different ways of working and should consider these nuances. For example, northern Europeans tend to be more direct and action-focused, and work by systems. Southern Europeans tend to work in a more relationship-driven and 'open' style. Neither is wrong, they are just different ways of doing business. Good key account managers understand this and work hard to align these culturally different teams.

7 Cost to serve. Serving customers on a local country level is typically cheaper than having a regional/global team approach. Additional people, team meetings, time spent with the customer and strategic planning sessions are more complex and add to the overall cost to serve the customer. 'Grasping the nettle' and accepting that there will be additional travel, employment and meeting costs is a hurdle that sometimes causes programmes to falter at the very beginning (especially given that it can involve a few years of incremental investment before a return is seen).

A good way to overcome this challenge is to select one target regional/strategic customer. Form a focused team to develop and manage the customer over a set period (say eighteen months). From this, develop your own blueprint for success. If the investment works, it can be replicated with other regional customers.

8 Mutual intent. With regional customers, the mantra *'strategy customer by customer'* is extremely valid. When working with

customers, some will be very receptive to a value-adding agreement that can be rolled out across several of their global operations. They will work with suppliers that provide these benefits.

Other customers are more reticent. They need to be brought on board slowly and carefully over a period.

Neither customer is wrong – they just have different approaches to establish a position of mutual intent and trust. Key account managers need to be mindful of this, and build customer strategies that develop a position of mutual intent for both parties.

9   Understanding. The foundation of value-based selling and key account management is to deeply understand the customer and to build unique value propositions based on the customer needs that emerge from that understanding effort. This is hard to capture for a customer operating in one site/country. If you magnify that by ten countries, with the purchase of several differing product/service lines, then gaining a clear picture of the customer needs and the activity becomes very complicated.

Good key account managers grasp this complexity. They work with global teams and research the global customer footprint. An ability to synthesize the emerging insights and to build a response is critical for the success of KAM and a key skill of the key account manager.

The key account plan

To structure and align a consistent approach to developing and delivering an effective strategy for every key customer a KAM plan is recommended. This should be a standardized model that is adopted across the business. The development and adoption of a common and standard planning process is recommended for several reasons:

It establishes a planning standard: when an organization takes the time to describe the strategic planning model and template, it sets out a stall of the required new ways of working. The KAM plan sets out the required information, analysis, data, communication and strategic thinking that is required for every key customer.

By taking the time to consider and design what goes into your plan it sends out a message: 'This is the standard that we expect for all key account planning.'

Aligning and 'nesting': consider the challenges set out in the previous section discussing the management of regional and global customers. If all of the countries on the supplier side worked with different customer KAM planning models, the alignment and transfer of information would become very clumsy and inefficient. Setting a strategy at the corporate level for the customer, with individual country plans feeding into this 'master' plan is very effective, but only possible if there is a consistent and aligned planning structure at all levels.

Data and reporting: when leadership reviews multiple KAM summaries, there has to be consistent and aligned structure to enable quick and effective reading of the plan. When planning templates are constructed in different formats, reviewing and understanding main messages can become confusing.

Additionally, having a standard KAM planning format is essential if the plan is to be loaded (or connected) to a CRM (customer relationship management) system.

Competence and development: by setting out the strategy and planning standards (captured in the KAM process), competence standards can be established. It takes a capable and experienced key account manager to develop a strategy for a global strategic customer. A competence framework that aligns with the actions required to build the plan can describe the key steps and activities. Once developed, the competence framework can be used for training needs analysis, coaching and career pathway discussions.

The construction of the key account plan should follow on with the same structure of the value-based selling framework. The two models should be aligned seamlessly. Having one model for sales and another for KAM leads to clumsy and disjointed processes and thinking. The advantage of the value-based selling model is that it absolutely aligns with key account management – and making this transition to 'turn up the capability wick' and put more focus on the key customer strategy works very well.

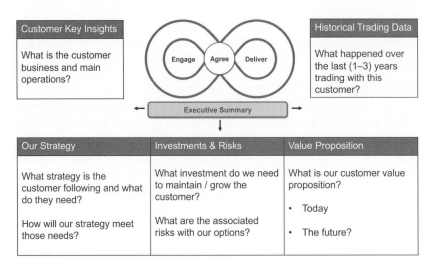

Figure 8.4 The KAM plan (executive summary)

The main addition that adds rigour to the KAM plan is the addition of the executive summary (Figure 8.4). A good executive summary pulls together critical information about the customer, your trading position as a supplier and most importantly the future strategies to grow and protect the customer business.

Five sections enable the construction of the executive summary. These five sections enable the reader of the KAM plan to understand the business that the customer is in. It takes a look backwards at what we have achieved, strategies looking forward and costs plus risks to achieve these growth strategies. Example information that might be included in your KAM plans:

1   Customer key insights
   • What is the customer business?
   • How does the customer create value? (What is the customer value proposition to their customers?)
   • How strong is the customer brand?
   • What are the headline trends in the customer financial report?
   • How important are we to the customer?

2   Historical trading data
   • How important is the customer to you?

- What is our trading history (sales plus profit) in the last two to three years?
- What are the sales trends?
- What is the story behind these trends?
- What value have we added for the customer?
- Critical performance indicators (CPIs)
  - Key performance indicators (KPIs)
  - What is our share of wallet for our products?
- How is our relationship with key decision makers?
- What has gone well, and why?
- What has gone badly, and why?
- Who is on our KAM team? Who do they meet with in the customer business?

3 Our strategy
- What are the customer objectives and strategy?
- What does the customer need to make this happen?
- What do we have to meet these needs?
- What will we do to deliver these value strategies?
- How much can we grow our business with the customer?
- What will be the reaction from our competitors as we introduce these strategies?
- What business might we lose? Why and when?
- Has the customer been introduced to our strategy and ideas? What was the reaction from them?

4 Value proposition(s)
- State the customer value proposition that the customer buys TODAY.
- State the customer value proposition that you will propose to sell to the customer IN THE FUTURE.
- What is different between these two offerings? If they are the same, is that good enough?
- If your short-term KAM plan strategy is the same as your long-term strategy (reflected in the customer value proposition), chances are that you have not been rigorous enough developing a longer-term co-creative analysis.

5   Investments and risks
- Describe what investments you need to achieve future growth targets.
- Describe what investments you need to protect today's business.
- What will be our payback?
- What risks are attached to each investment scenario?
- What will happen if we do not invest?

Blow the socks off your reader.

The people who read the key account plan (and especially the executive summary) are going to be senior executives, board members, country heads and general managers (as well as members of the key account team).

They all need to be impressed and captivated by the plan. As one frustrated business leader once explained:

> I have reviewed many key account plans ... Sadly the last thing that they do is excite, stimulate or blow my socks off.
>   It shouldn't be that way should it? Surely my key account directors should be exhilarated and passionate about their customer? Our KAM plans are 'grey' ... if you dig deep enough there are sometimes nuggets of good news ... but it never jumps out and slaps you across the face. I think we can generate much more exciting strategies and offer for our most important key customers.
>
> CEO of a global technology firm

He was quite right. Things do not have to be drab and dull. While the above framework for a KAM executive summary is stretching and makes for a compelling story, it still has to be written with care, being mindful of the reader. Remember that the people who read your KAM plans are busy, very focused on results and yearn for sound business cases. Focus on these things and you will start to develop stronger KAM plans!

Silo busting (managing virtual teams)

To develop strong key account plans a lot of work has to be conducted to align and leverage the strength and power of your own organization. Remember, KAM is strategy 'customer by customer' and strategy requires a significant amount of investment and time to develop unique sources of competitive advantage. Key account managers have to gain alignment from their own organizations. It is often said that a key account manager spends 70 per cent of their time getting things done in their own organization, and perhaps only 20 per cent of their time with the customer.

In an ideal world where all things in your organization are perfect and pulse around the needs of the customer, data systems provide the right information on time, senior managers share their insights and everybody has an open door to discuss your customer requirements.

Sounds like heaven? It is.

There are very few organizations that spin around the customer. Very often things get done with the aid of a secret organizational weapon: the key account manager.

In the absence of the perfect organization (and usually in organizations where things are pretty good!) the key account manager just 'gets things done' This skill of aligning supplier resources around the needs of the customer is described as 'silo busting'.

Silo busting is an ability to connect the multiple resources in your organization and to make the key account planning cycle come to life. Think about it. Why would a member of your finance team (or others – see Figure 8.5) give up precious time to sit on your 'key customer strategy think tank' session? And yet, a different perspective from finance could provide a spark to your value proposition. They might be able to suggest a new way to discount, price or capture value. They might well help you to win a bid or steal business from a competitor.

Silo busting requires a good knowledge of the organization and how it works. It requires personal skills to see things from the point of view of the 'silo members'. Regardless of the organizational mandate

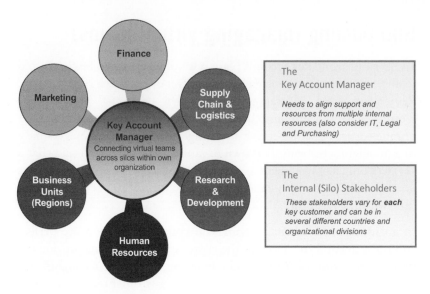

Figure 8.5 Silo busting

to 'support and participate in KAM', it is personal relationships and careful facilitation of those discussions that really make things happen.

Nesting KAM plans with the customer footprint

Building a strategy and a detailed plan around a key account customer takes time and effort and can be challenging. Getting the balance between having sufficient information to understand the customer enough to create a compelling offer and having an overwhelming amount of detail and information that is of no practical use is a skill. It is also paramount to get this balance right: many KAM programmes fail for this reason, with key account managers and their supporting organizations getting frustrated at either a huge administrative task (that produces minimal rewards) or a planning task that is too simple, with equally disappointing results.

This KAM planning challenge becomes hugely amplified when planning for regional, global and strategic customers. This increased complexity arises from a potential misalignment of supplier and customer requirements strategically, tactically and on an individual basis, across different countries' business divisions.

In order to navigate the complexity of this multi-country (and often multi-divisional) challenge, a technique to build a strategy that 'joins the dots' is necessary (Figure 8.6, the concept of 'nesting' plans). While this is a practical method to align the strategy and planning templates at different levels of the customer organization, it is also very effective in aligning teams, resources, strategic planning and operational execution.

The planning changes as the nesting unfolds from top to bottom (following the hierarchy of the plans). Strategic planning is developed and agreed with at the highest level by the global account manager. Consideration should be taken to align with the requirements of the customer. Some customers have very clear centralized strategies and they cascade these down to the various global divisions and operations across the world. Others take a far 'looser' approach.

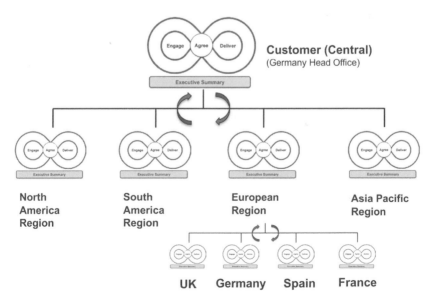

Figure 8.6 'Nesting' customer plans

They establish a high-level strategic direction, but allow regional and country divisions to be far more autonomous in the way that they interpret and implement these strategies.

The skill in setting up customer account nesting is to understand how the customer operates and to align your planning with theirs (it would be pointless to develop a strategy that dictates your central strategy if the customer is not going to enforce this strategy at the local divisions). Nesting works by understanding how the customer works, and aligning. This is initially with the planning template design and structure, but following on from that is the way that you operate and organize your account teams around these plans.

Table 8.1 shows what changes at each level of a KAM planning nest. Strong and effective nested plans work in two ways:

- Top down – a strategic direction is established with the customer from a global headquarters perspective.
- Bottom up – value is created at the local level since this is where the customer uses your products and services.
- It is imperative that feedback is taken from the local businesses and fed back up to inform the over-arching strategic plan. This will inform exactly what is working (and what is not) from the agreed strategy, but also ideas and good practice that operate in the countries can be fed back to the wider group and possibly trans-ferred across the operating sites.

There are inevitably tensions throughout the nesting process. These tensions arise between the various parties and teams that are involved in planning and have to contribute to the development and execution of customer strategies at different levels (Figure 8.7). Tensions arise from differing perspectives and challenges for the individuals managing the customer.

To eradicate these tensions, the leadership of the business should be mindful that these issues will arise, and the key account managers plus local leadership teams should plan and work together in order to build an organization that operates 'in alignment with the customer's regional and global footprint'. Each tension can be explored a little deeper, by understanding what the challenge is and how to introduce ways of working that address the problem.

Table 8.1 Nesting customer plans (what changes at each level?)

	Who is accountable?	Planning requirements
Central (HQ)	Global or Strategic Account Director	Challenge: Strategic planning that considers the customer's highest levels of aspirations for growth and development. Output: An agreed joint plan that establishes a vision, goals, ways of working and key work-streams to achieve value co-creation at the highest level.
Regional	Regional Account Director	Challenge: Strategic planning for the region. This plan should span the global/strategic vision and connect it with individual countries operating in the region. Output: A series of country plans that connect and forge a way to enable the global strategic plan.
Country	Key Account Manager	Challenge: A detailed plan to set detailed strategies and actions that make the agreed global strategy a reality and develop growth at the local level. The country KAM plan should execute the global strategy as well as find sources of value at the local level. These ideas and findings should be communicated back to the Strategic Account Manager to re-inform that plan. Output: A detailed plan to manage the customer on a day-to-day basis.

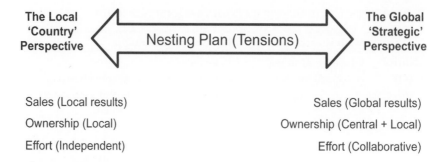

| The Local 'Country' Perspective | Nesting Plan (Tensions) | The Global 'Strategic' Perspective |

Sales (Local results)	Sales (Global results)
Ownership (Local)	Ownership (Central + Local)
Effort (Independent)	Effort (Collaborative)

Figure 8.7 Nesting (tensions)

Sales tensions

What happens? Performance targets are in place for sales with the customer. These sales are usually allocated at a local level in alignment with a country or business unit profit-and-loss account. Accountability for setting the sales target and then delivering this business will be a joint effort, but the global account manager may see their effort being greater than the efforts of the local key account manager (and vice versa of course!). This is a significant challenge, especially when organizations have bonus and reward schemes linked to sales performance. It is not surprising that arguments arise around 'who won the business?' and 'who manages the customer?'.

How can this situation be alleviated? In reality, both the global and the local account managers working together deliver sales performance. Sales should be controlled at the local level and the global account manager rewarded via a 'shadow profit and loss' system. Other measures should also be put into place that will be recognized as effort. Sales results will not come immediately with more complex key account customers: it may take several years to get these results. Careful planning and allocating tasks that will ultimately achieve sales results should be introduced (using a system such as a balanced scorecard).

Ownership tensions

What happens? Due to a lack of clarity compounded by the matrix style of leading a global customer, planning and execution tasks can fall through the cracks and end up having no ownership. This is not surprising. Managing a key account on a local basis has many tasks and functions. This complexity can be made visible and navigated by having a single plan that is managed by one person. When there are multiple plans that 'nest' the allocation of these tasks becomes far more multi-layered and complicated.

How can this situation be alleviated? Once the agreed series of key account plans are identified, the key account management team that looks after each plan needs to be allocated. These 'single points of accountability' should be captured on a central database/table, with a list of tasks and duties against each name. This may sound like a basic and somewhat 'picky' approach to doing business, but failing to allocate responsibilities and duties eventually leads to frustration, failure to execute customer promises and frustration with the customer and the supplier. Plan your customer matrix teams!

Effort tensions

This tension occurs mainly in the local key accounts. It is the result of effort being required from the local country team to support the resulting strategy and also actions from the central/global customer strategy. This effort could be made with little or no results for the local business (or at least a disproportionate amount of effort). A tension arises between the central and local KAM teams when input is requested but not received. This can hamper the overall strategy for the global customer.

How can this situation be alleviated? A leadership perspective is critical. The board/leadership team have to take a stance that says, 'managing our global customers is critical – we all play a part'. This could mean local business units supporting the global/central customer team with no immediate rewards.

All of these tensions are managed by leadership recognizing that there will be problems and taking a stance that there will be a commitment to manage the complexity of larger cross-business-unit/global customers. It is leadership that needs to set the culture and processes in place to manage these tensions.

The key account manager – a competence framework

Building an organization that is able to deliver the stretching objectives of a KAM strategy is difficult. Having the right structures, leadership attitudes, organizational culture, ways of working, customer data and planning systems (such as nesting) are all complex organizational issues. Do many businesses get this organizational design just right and working consistently over several divisions? Yes. But not very many.

The reality is that organizations have intent and a vision to become focused on KAM, but there are always gaps and weaknesses, especially when organizations first set out to build a key account capability. While key account management is not just about the key account manager, your key account managers are still extremely important. They are the transformation change agents and the leaders that really drive this different way of doing business.

Working with many organizations in many industries it becomes apparent that key account managers are critical individuals for a successful value-centric business. This is a trend that is in place today, but is genuinely increasing in focus for future business. It goes without saying that selecting, developing and retaining high performing key account managers is a critical challenge.

In order to plan the competence profile of the key account manager, it is useful to go back to basics and describe what it is that they do. Figure 8.8 provides a list of core activities that key account managers have to perform. These activities are determined by the stages in the KAM planning cycle, emphasizing the breadth and scope of the role of the key account manager. Moving around the cycle, there are four major activities:

Engage (researching, understanding, developing, creating)
Agree (selling, negotiating and establishing terms of business)
Deliver (capturing value, organizing and ensuring operational efficiency)
Leadership (planning, organizing, communicating, leading teams and silo-busting).

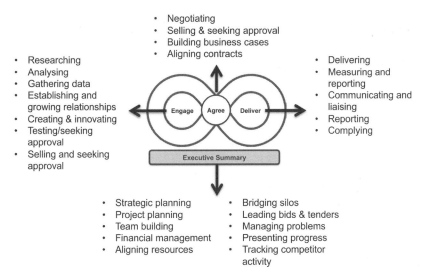

- Negotiating
- Selling & seeking approval
- Building business cases
- Aligning contracts

- Researching
- Analysing
- Gathering data
- Establishing and growing relationships
- Creating & innovating
- Testing/seeking approval
- Selling and seeking approval

Engage Agree Deliver

Executive Summary

- Delivering
- Measuring and reporting
- Communicating and liaising
- Reporting
- Complying

- Strategic planning
- Project planning
- Team building
- Financial management
- Aligning resources

- Bridging silos
- Leading bids & tenders
- Managing problems
- Presenting progress
- Tracking competitor activity

Figure 8.8 Key account manager (core competencies)

These stages are very different modes of leadership and management capability. It is extremely unlikely that any one person possesses all of the skills to perform all of these tasks, but these are the expectations and requirements to effectively manage a key account. The key account manager must have a good understanding of all of these steps, but the emphasis is on making the four stages work and managing a supporting team to provide the skills and resources that align around the customer. Being a key account manager is a very stretching and unique leadership role. It requires a lot of the skill sets of a general manger, blended with the commercial tenacity of a sales person.

The critical partnership: KAM and service-based offerings

One of the main deliverables for KAM is that a unique and bespoke value proposition should be developed. Key customers have significant potential and value, but unlocking this value often requires an enhanced offer to maximize value co-creation.

An emerging approach to develop service-based offerings is called product service systems (PSS). Also known as 'servitization', this is a technique whereby organizations that manufacture products enhance their service offering by wrapping service packages around this core product. Various degrees of service can be provided as shown in Figure 8.9. Think of the offering in two dimensions: the depth that the supplier integrates into the customer business; and the level of complexity that these offer service packages look like in terms of cost

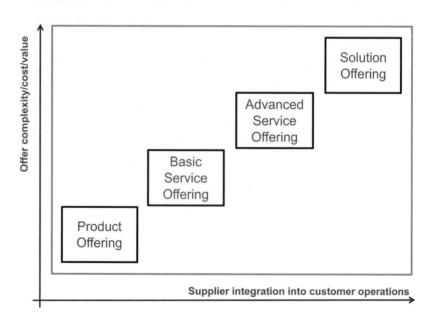

Figure 8.9 Product service solution

to serve and the elements of the offer. There can be multiple levels of offering, but the most common ones can be described as:

Product offering. This is the basic brand/product/service that you can provide the customer.

Basic service offering. The first level of service that supports the product in use with the customer. This option is low risk for both parties and takes a tentative 'first step' into the customer value chain.

Advanced service offering. These packages are more sophisticated and inclusive. More of the activity is handed over from the customer to the supplier (the customer sees the supplier as an expert in delivering this offering – they trust them to take responsibility for the execution of these tasks).

Total solution offering. This final offering sees the supplier taking 100 per cent responsibility for the delivery of the task. The customer buys the output from the offering here; on many occasions the product becomes secondary to the output.

An example comes from the business that I formerly managed in BP Industrial Lubricants. With industrial customers (such as food manufacture and processing) the basic offer provided to the customer was product or 'lubricant' packs of high-performing grease that the customer then applied and controlled with their own technical staff.

The next offering would be a basic service package, or 'lubrication'. Here the control of the *correct* lubricant going into which machine location, control of stock and the actual physical application were provided by us. The customer could relax and let us get on with this activity. The fee to the customer was greater, but there was improved performance for them as their equipment and operations literally ran 'more smoothly'.

Advanced service offerings looked beyond lubrication. We were providing an essential component of equipment rotational and linear movement. Lubrication is only a small part of this activity. Other things go wrong as well: with bearings, bushes and sliders etc. This offering package provided basic maintenance of these components, not just lubrication.

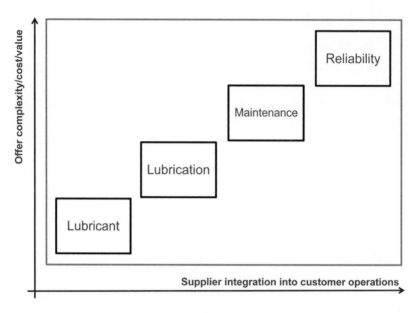

Figure 8.10 Example – industrial lubricants provider

Finally, by considering what the customer really wanted, we could provide a total solution offering. Customers emphatically want a few things from their plant and processing machinery. They want it to run efficiently, smoothly and to have zero unplanned stoppages and breakdowns. Downtime for planned maintenance is OK, but this should be controlled. The total solution offering that we provided placed dedicated teams into the customer operations. We provided vibration analysis equipment, manned by experts who could monitor the condition of the customer site. We could predict when a machine would require a replacement bearing – and schedule in a repair. Eliminating one or two unplanned stoppages for some of our bigger process customers could save them £1–2m/event or more. This total solution package was described as *reliability*. A reliability package could cost £1–2m/annum, employing a team of six dedicated specialists on the customer site and significant off-site support. It is very different from providing tins of grease! The results for the customer could be enormous, however, with payback often achieved in months.

Table 8.2 Simple phrase value statements

	Product (Core) Offering	Basic Service Offering	Advanced Service Offering	Solution Offering
Industrial Lubrication Supplier	Lubricants	Lubrication	Maintenance	Reliability
National Construction Firm	Design	Design and build	Design, build and maintain	Total operational control
Global Elevator Manufacturer	Elevators Travelators	Maintenance *(own products)*	Total maintenance *(own products and competitors)*	People movement *(total care package)*

This concept of providing solutions is not new. Rolls-Royce aero engines make 50 per cent of total revenue from service packages (as opposed to selling engines). They sell the concept of 'power by the hour', recognizing that operators such as American Airlines really want to buy the effects of the engine, not the intricate hassle and activity of managing these complex pieces of machinery.

Other industries that we have worked with can be seen in Table 8.2. A UK national construction firm analysed their customer portfolio and established that a stretched solution offering could be 'total operational control', so that as well as designing and building facilities, some customers might value having the building managed and leased back to them.

Global elevator manufacturers (e.g. Kone, Schindlers Lifts, OTIS) all offer a solution-based package whereby customers (e.g. hotel groups and airport operators) simply want to buy 'people movement'. As a result, this entire industry has shifted towards providing service packages, with very few customers taking on the purchase and management of lifts and 'travelators' themselves.

So, why is there such a strong relationship between KAM and PSS? Successful and profitable PSS programmes occur when the supplier provides a tailored offering that meets customer needs. As shown in Table 8.2 there are always multiple degrees of service package that can be offered. Getting the level of service correctly 'balanced' is critical for true value co-creation to occur.

This 'balancing' is made possible by the supplier having a deep understanding of the customer's strategy, business plans and resulting needs. Strong relationships with senior leaders (on both sides) lead to this strength of understanding. Problems can arise when this relationship and intimate trust is not present. Service packages that are not suitable can be presented and, if accepted, will result in a failure to deliver value for the customer. Compounding this challenge, if the supplier has a weak capability to deliver a PSS package (or if they have stretched resources), failure can also result in delivering the expected future-state scenarios.

Table 8.3 highlights the relationship between KAM and PSS. When KAM is not sufficiently developed, with a lack of customer-focused strategy and customer insights, there is a greatly enhanced possibility for failure.

Conversely, when KAM and a trusted strong relationship is developed, the resulting stronger customer insights lead to a deeper understanding of what matters, how the customer likes to work, how to capture value and (perhaps most importantly) a foundation of trust and intimacy is established to foster a value co-creation partnership.

Table 8.3 The relationship between KAM and PSS

	Weak PSS Capability	Strong PSS Capability
Strong KAM Capability	*High risk of customer benefits not being realized*	*High possibility of mutual success*
Weak KAM Capability	*High risk of total failure*	*High risk of supplier losing money*

Table 8.4 identifies four business challenges that are essential for a successful PSS programme. Against each challenge there is a description of how KAM delivers against the challenge. These four aspects present a case whereby the development of a strong KAM capability is an essential strategy to make PSS work. Given that most key customers

Table 8.4 How KAM enables PSS

	PSS Challenge:	KAM Enables:
Partnership and Relationship	Highly integrated offerings where the supplier 'steps into the customer's value chain'. Focus on collaboration and developing sustainable business offerings with carefully selected customers.	Deep relationship and partnership. Focus on collaboration and developing sustainable business with carefully selected customers.
Complexity	Deeper and more integrated service-based offerings require a deeper understanding of the customer business. Intimate trust-based relationships are essential to make these service offerings work.	KAM is all about 'getting under the skin' of the customer business. KAM focuses on developing strong relationships, trust and seeking value opportunities that are unique and bespoke to that customer.
Resource Challenges	With service offerings it is often stated: 'our people are our product'. Suppliers work hard to deliver strong value propositions – people, equipment and data. This puts a strain on resources.	KAM looks to develop unique customer value propositions. The process carefully considers the financial benefits for the customer and the supplier. Without KAM, service-based offerings can be developed that are unprofitable.
Time and Value Focus	Long term – years to develop and operate. Focus on value co-creation.	Long term – years to develop and operate. Focus on value co-creation.

will need an 'enhanced' bespoke value proposition (some form of service package wrapped around the core product offer), so it can also be said that KAM needs PSS capability.

KAM as the future of value-based business

As a management activity KAM draws on several other activities. It requires strategy, marketing, leadership, team building, project management and organizational change. Key account managers are often thought of as having general management skills and capabilities.

Businesses in the future will find that the direct selling they do will shift away from selling (to a large number of customers) to a KAM model whereby they are seeing a wide saturation of business from a smaller footprint of smaller, more powerful customers. This is already starting to happen in some industries. A prediction is that value-based business will be essential in the very near future, and value-based selling plus KAM will have to take centre stage far more than today.

KAM also has another critical management activity that it needs to embrace. The ability to innovate and develop commercially strong and unique customer value propositions is at the heart of Infinite Value, and is at the heart of KAM. As organizations seek to respond to challenging external changes and disruptive forces, the need to build new offerings for the most valued customers will increase. My prediction is that increasingly these offers will be services and solutions, and the means to create them in a compelling manner will be KAM, as part of a value-based business.

Some organizations are reaching a tipping point. They must embrace and develop a strong KAM capability in order to prosper. It is no longer an activity for one or two customers – it is becoming business critical.

Value matters

A ten-point summary of key account management:

1 The best way to define a key account customer is as a 'market segment of ONE': and the best way to think about key account management is 'strategy: customer by customer'.

2 Most organizations are seeing several reasons why they need to adopt KAM, with this trend looking to continue. KAM is becoming a critical function.

3 In order to build KAM as a competitive advantage, it requires focus in three main leadership-driven areas:
   • KAM strategy
   • KAM capability standards
   • Organizational transformation.

4 Organizational capability standards fall into four main streams: leadership, people, process and customer planning aspects. Key account management is more than just the key account manager (but the key account manager is REALLY important!).

5 Key account managers have commercial general manager skill sets. Recruiting, developing and rewarding them is a critical aspect of building your KAM programme.

6 Value-focused selling is the foundation stage of key account management (many organizations fail to implement KAM because they do not focus on value). The KAM planning template should be a broader and deeper extension to the value-focused selling model.

7 Key account customers often span multiple countries and regions, and they take product and services spanning several different divisions. Organizations have to address this complexity and give key account managers accountability and authority to achieve strategic results.

8 Key account managers should be developed on a career pathway. These pathways can be defined using a competency framework to enable a description of what is required and how individuals can develop into these challenging roles.

9 Expanding the customer value proposition often means adding services to existing core product lines. Known as 'servitization', it

can be seen that key account management works 'hand in hand' with this critical business model.

10 It is anticipated that businesses in the future will look to move traditional sales in one of two ways. Simpler 'transactional'-based sales will be conducted on-line (or via third-party re-sellers), while the more complex value-adding business will shift towards a key account model. This scenario suggests that the need for strong KAM capability will grow still further in the future.

Chapter 9

Channel partnerships

Every collaboration helps you grow.

Brian Eno

Question
How can a value-based business model be extended through third-party channels, so that value is enhanced?

What are third-party channels?

It is very rare for any organization to be able to serve all of its customers *directly* in all of the markets and countries that it operates. A business model whereby the supplier handles all customer interactions alone is unusual. It may occur with some businesses that operate within one country or region, or with some specialist consulting and professional services firms, but even in those circumstances the strategy of collaborating with an extended network is highly beneficial.

Selling organizations need to build an organization that serves target customers *cost effectively* for them while also providing an effective and efficient experience for each customer.

Channels are becoming more varied and (because of technology and digital options) more complex to establish. Typical channel options are:

- Via third-party distributors and wholesalers,
- Logistics and supply-chain providers,
- Technology/specialist application users of your products,
- Other manufacturers,

- Retailers,
- On-line/digital sales.

Note: the purpose of this chapter is not to provide an exhaustive assessment of multi-channel choices or the challenges of channel management. (For this, *The Multichannel Challenge* (2008) by Wilson, Street and Bruce is recommended.) The position adopted by *Infinite Value* is to look at certain channels and consider how to integrate them into a total value-centric business and develop them to conduct business in a 'value-enhancing' manner.

The focus is on the top four of the above list, with consideration of how to select, develop and maintain a long-term strategy that extends the value-centric approach to business with selected third-party channel partners.

Why are third-party channels so important for a value-centric business?

There are several reasons why using a network of third-party providers is important to a selling organization. Possibly the most fundamental reason is that they provide an extended reach into complex and possibly fragmented market places. Organizations that are looking to conduct business in new markets find it highly attractive to find existing distributor organizations and to tap into their network of customers. They will have local knowledge, contacts and a selling history with the customers you are trying to reach, so it makes sound business sense to use this expertise.

They can also respond very quickly. Imagine the time it takes to set up a sales and marketing organization in any country, let alone one where you have limited experience and exposure. Having an established group of companies that are ready and willing to trade is a very quick option, even if you need to make investment to develop the channel members.

A strategy pursued by many organizations is to convert fixed costs into variable costs. It is very expensive to employ a direct sales force, with supporting manufacturing and logistics functions. Using a separate network of third-party providers can provide a platform that is funded mainly by results and activity. Even in situations whereby franchises or investments are required to build the required standard of distributors, it is a far more cost-effective solution than keeping everything in house and serving the customer directly.

A point to consider very carefully that should make channel development a very high priority and strategic matter is to balance the above points with some of the problems that can occur. Gaining a fast, cost-effective reach is attractive, but needs to be balanced with a focus on delivering a robust value proposition to the end customer. Failure to recognize this, and failing to invest in channels, can lead to a poor performance. The value potential that is baked into your brands, products and business reputation should be protected and enhanced by third-party channels, not destroyed.

Figure 9.1 shows these opposing forces as the channel tension, with the corporate viewpoint of what the supply organization requires potentially conflicting with what the third-party distributor needs. Distributors are typically smaller, more nimble organizations, operating like small-to-medium enterprises (SMEs). They are entrepreneurial, customer-focused, nimble and opportunistic. Larger corporations tend to not have these strengths. They are large integrated organizations,

What You Need

What The Distributor Needs

The Channel Tension

A Corporate Viewpoint

- Access to customers in wide market positions

- An extension to your brand values

- A cost-effective and rapid business model

An Entrepreneurial Viewpoint

- Brands and valuable products (to make money)

- Product and commercial support

Figure 9.1 The channel tension

focused on scale and operating by set standards and systems. While opposite business models, it is the fact that they are different that leads one to need the other. This presents a true business tension that should be recognized and embraced.

The many faces of your channel partners

The organizations that operate within your channels exist in many guises. Typically, they are local and smaller businesses, operating independent and highly flexible operations (although some businesses can be global and very large).

Value in action

Henry Scheine Inc. is the world's largest provider of healthcare products and services to office-based dental, animal health and medical practitioners. They had a 2015 turnover of over $10bn. Acting as a distributor and channel partner to some of the world's largest animal health/pharmaceutical providers, they are bigger than some of the organizations they serve.

A question to be considered is: 'What is our relationship with this channel organization?' This sounds straightforward, but is surprisingly tricky, and actually sets the scene for deciding how to manage the relationship moving forwards.

Consider these statements that have been received from commercial directors that I have consulted with:

Commercial director: Precision automotive components

'We supply our products to the distributor. They then sell to our target market. The distributor pays us, so they must be our customer.'

Sales director Northern European: Electrical control panel manufacturer

'This is a large distributor for us in our Northern European markets. While the distributor sells our products, we have also had situations where we have been bidding against them for our target key account customer business. It seems ridiculous, but at the same time as being a customer they are a competitor as well!'

Key account director: Global systems provider

'We build mainframe systems for large global customers. It's very odd because some of our distributors in certain countries are our customers. But at the same time, we sell their products and use their components in our systems in other countries. It's all terribly incestuous! We are competitor, supplier, customer and strategic partner with the same company depending where we operate!'

Figure 9.2 captures this challenging question. It is always useful to have this simple map in your mind when considering the relationship with a distributor. Even if there are multiple 'conflicting' relationships,

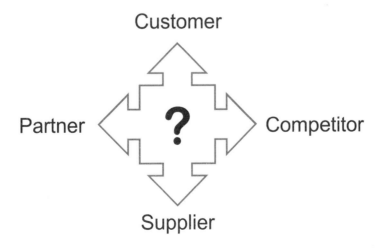

What are you, exactly?!

Figure 9.2 Third-party channel relationships

at least by recognizing that they exist and being aware will help to establish a clearer picture when developing and implementing ways of working together.

A secret competitive advantage?

Getting products to the customer involves going through multiple steps and organizations. This is the supply chain: it will differ across various markets and with the customers that you are trying to serve within those markets. In some circumstances, several steps have to be taken before your product actually reaches (and is used by) the customer that it was designed, developed and built for. It can be easy to lose sight of this fact, with distributors, specifier groups, developers and operating groups all potentially becoming stakeholders and wanting to add value to their own separate customer.

These (value) supply chains can become very complex and present problems. Each step is another mouth to feed, and each step needs to be understood and managed. Figure 9.3 shows a generic model that can be used to model the supply chain.

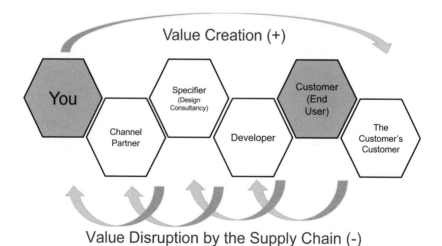

Figure 9.3 Channels and value disruption

When modelling the supply of goods for your customer, follow these steps:

1 Ask yourself: Who is the end-user customer for this product? What do they value, and how does the product meet the customer's needs?
2 Map out each step that is involved from your supply of the product to getting it to the end user (the long-term benefactor of the product when in use or service).
3 Consider how each step of the supply chain behaves and what it is that they do:
   • Who is the customer for each supply chain member?
   • How will they be contracted?
   • How will they be paid?
   • Who will pay them?
   • Does this ADD or SUBTRACT value for you?
4 If the supply chain organization adds value to you, how can you help them to improve this situation? How can your value proposition strengthen their value proposition?
5 If the supply chain organization subtracts (destroys) value for you – why is this? What could you do to improve this situation?

This method of standing back and analysing the supply chain and assessing who is adding value for you and who is destroying value will provide you with a competitive advantage. It is a strategically sensible thing to spend time, energy and focus upon standing back and looking at the bigger picture.

Figure 9.3 was used to analyse a building environment control panel supplier. They make market-leading technically advanced and superior products that are used to control the environmental systems in hotels, offices, retail groups and other major facility buildings. This industry is highly split by work packages and separate suppliers fighting to win bids and tenders. It is not uncommon for these products to go through a specialized control panel builder that is contracted to a mechanical contractor, to a building firm, via an architect, who finally works for the end-user customer. It is easy to see that the supplier value proposition potentially gets diluted at each stage, and value destroyed by the supply chain, not enhanced!

However, by standing back and taking the time to understand the key decision makers at each stage of the supply chain, and getting to understand and build relationships with the end user and specifier, a stronger value proposition could be developed and presented. This approach has to be conducted carefully. Each member of the supply chain is potentially a customer, and working around these organizations can cause friction (they may make less money!). When the end customer/user is a key account this approach is strongly recommended. Stand back and understand the supply chain, and collaborate with members within that chain who want to work towards longer-term value-enhancing targets.

Always consider the following questions when evaluating your customer supply chain:

- Who is the customer?
- What do they value?
- Where is value created? Where is value destroyed?

Extending your business

When selling organizations think too simplistically about the use of third-party channels, they sometimes think of them simply as 'distribution extensions', a means to get products and services to market efficiently and cost effectively.

However, channels serve several functions and can add significant value to the breadth and depth of your business model. Figure 9.4 shows the provision of four key functions as suppliers typically work with channel partners. Distribution is the initial and obvious function that is provided by channel partners.

They can be highly effective extensions to the four areas of your business, with typical activities as highlighted in Table 9.1. This is a brief list: many channels can be developed even further. The major consideration is that channels can be so much more to organizations than just logistics and supply chain operations, provided that they are selected, developed and managed correctly.

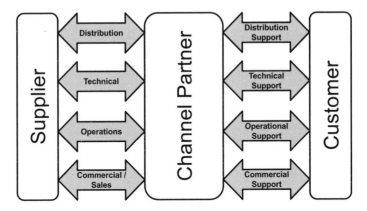

Figure 9.4 The role of channel partners

In contrast to Table 9.1, which is a positive view of how channel partners can add value, Table 9.2 shows how channel partners can sometimes destroy value in these four main areas.

These are two starkly different tables. Operating with a carefully developed network of channel partners will lead to a more productive and effective business model.

Table 9.1 How channel partners add value

Distribution (Logistics)	Technical	Operational	Commercial (Sales)
Holding stock Delivery to point of use Packaging (bulk – discrete)	Adviser Component/ assembly building Support in field post sales	Blending/mixing Final assembly Working and supporting in the end-user customer	Mapping market territory Promotions Advancing sales • New • Existing Market research Joint planning
Operates with an understanding of value-based business			
Works in collaboration and partnership with suppliers			

Table 9.2 How channel partners destroy value

Distribution (Logistics)	Technical	Operational	Commercial (Sales)
Constantly stocking out of products	Lacking knowledge about the brand/ products/service	No interest in providing services or solutions	Sells on volume and price
Damaging goods	Lack of knowledge about the end-user customer industry and application	Operating as simple model that wants to sell goods on at a per centage margin	Total lack of knowledge about value advantages to the end customer in the market
Late delivery			
Expensive delivery			
Bad customer service			Sits back and 'waits for the call' from the customer
Bad/incorrect support documents			Limited knowledge of the market/customer base
			Limited interest to collaborate with suppliers

Operates in a collaborative style
Understands the principles of value-based business

Selecting and appointing channel partners

When third-party distributors take and sell large volumes of product it is easy to see why a supplier might also consider them to be a key account customer. Some channel partners will be more important to your business than others and as such they could be looked at as being key. It is not uncommon for organizations to have 20 per cent or more of sales flowing through one large regional distributor, and of course this will warrant extra care, attention and strategic focus when managing these businesses. Think back to Figure 9.3 and the supply chain map. Distributors are not end-user customers. They do not use your products and services over a period of time, and they are not the focus of your research and development teams when they develop the products that you take to market. Two main differences distinguish between direct and indirect key account management:

1   The value proposition that you establish for direct and indirect organizations is different due to the *needs* of the two businesses being different. The business model that they follow is different so the resultant offering that you take to them will alter.
2   Management requirements. The people and the systems that you use to look after direct and indirect channels are different. End-user direct customers require expertise about their industry and business. They look for knowledge and advice that is focused on the markets that they serve. This is also the case when dealing with channel partners, with the added complexity that you have to understand the wide-reaching challenges that face an entrepreneurial small-to-medium enterprise. It is likely that your commercial people will be dealing with senior leaders/owners of the distributor: this requires an ability to understand wide aspects of running a business (albeit on a smaller scale).

Building a channel strategy should follow the principles of building any customer management strategy (these have already been described in Chapter 5). The selection and segmentation of a channel network is a critical activity: it needs to set the blueprint to ensure there is correct coverage, working with the best channel partners to ensure products and brands reach target customers in the best way possible. This takes some effort and strategic thinking but is essential to commence the building of the distributor capability standard.

Using the segmentation model that was presented in Chapter 5, a decision could be taken to serve small (foundation) and certain medium (core) customers via the indirect/channel approach. This would be established by a cut-off limit (usually annual sales). Making this choice between direct and indirect is to build from a series of considerations:

• Economic: is it cost-effective to serve the customer directly, or is

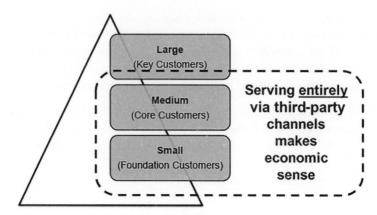

Figure 9.5 Who do you serve via channels?

it more profitable and efficient to serve via an indirect/3rd party channel?

- Potential growth: is there upside potential with the customer that requires a direct model to be adopted?
- Loss risk: is there a danger that the customer will be dissatisfied if a third-party channel serves them? Could they move business elsewhere?
- Channel maturity: is the network of channels to serve the customer developed sufficiently to serve the customers?

These considerations should be developed to enable the right level of channel decision making. For larger key account customers there will be a stronger bias towards a direct relationship with the customer (Figure 9.5).

However, decision making will be informed by two questions:

1 Will the key customer be managed entirely directly?
2 Will the key customer be managed directly and via channels (hybrid)?

Key customers that operate across countries and regions will more likely require a hybrid approach, with head office discussions taking place directly and execution/servicing at a local level being conducted using a combination of direct and channel partner (Figure 9.6).

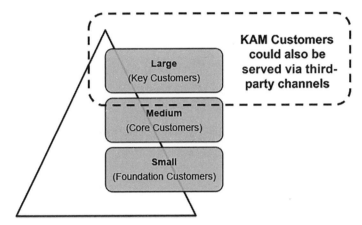

Figure 9.6 Who do you serve via channels?

Establishing this initial model that determines which customers should be served directly, indirectly and via a hybrid (direct and indirect) is a critical step to take when developing any channel (and customer management) strategy. Once the customers are mapped out so that you have an idea about which ones need to be served via channel partners,

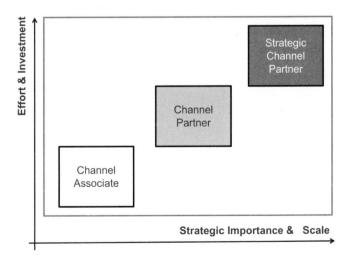

Figure 9.7 Basic channel partner segmentation

Table 9.3 Distributor segmentation criteria – typical (example) selection factors

Coverage	Required Activity	Relationship
District	Distribution	Transactional *(Operate through)*
Countrywide	Technical	
Regional	Operational	Partnership *(Operate with)*
Global	Commercial/Sales	
	All/Part	

the channel network can be developed. A basic model is suggested to present this in Figure 9.7.

In the same way that organizations have different key account customer classifications, there should also be different channel partner classifications. These can be considered by the scale of their strategic importance, balanced with the amount of effort and time that will be required managing the relationship.

Three classifications are suggested:

1 Channel associates. These are likely to be small local organizations, possibly delivering a simple 'sell-through' activity. They will be local to a district within a country, and responsible for smaller total volumes of business.

2 Channel partners. These are bigger organizations, operating across a country and providing a more sophisticated offer to the end customer. Due to the nature of the customers and markets that they serve, they warrant a greater level of investment.

3 Strategic channel partners. These represent the top-tier major distributors in your channel networks. They can operate across an entire country (possibly multiple countries). More importantly, it is agreed between you and the channel partner that you will jointly invest and collaborate to take your products and services into the market and co-operate strategically to develop business.

Table 9.3 shows a list of factors that can be considered when developing a channel partner segmentation model. The selection and development of organizations that will become considered as 'associate, partner or strategic' will be a mixture of quantitative factors (such as location and size) and qualitative (such as willingness to be a partner)

The segmentation model should be developed and built using a mix of these factors, weighting them to enable a focus on selecting by critical factors.

Extending customer value strategy principles with channel partners

Organizations can have typically anything from 5 to 100 per cent of their sales flowing through channels partners. That is a lot of business! And here is a possible threat and an opportunity. You trust these organizations to take your products, brands and services to your end-user customers. They are an extension to your commercial, technical, operational and logistical business reach. If they are not conversant and capable at value-focused selling, KAM and customer strategy, is there a possibility that they will fight and win business based on selling volume and price?

Many distributor organizations evolve and grow from being specialist and SME entrepreneurs. They fight for business and grow on the foundation of their core skills and knowledge. Often they do not possess management skills to develop strategies, and they may well lack value-based business skills. If you want to develop your business fully and create a fully capable business that believes, understands and does business in a value-focused manner, you have to develop your channel partners and help them to build capability that supports you.

This is a big undertaking, and can be a large investment. Failure to invest and prioritize can lead to a situation whereby your channel partners are working in a very different manner to the way that your strategy wants to work. This can confuse your customers and your own customer teams.

Developing and building channel capability

A ten-step approach can be adopted to develop value-based principles with channel partners. This is no easy task! Building organizational capability within your own organization is challenging. Convincing associate organizations that they need to change, and getting them to follow different ways of working, requires considerable upfront engagement, leadership commitment, investment and mutual trust with each selected channel partner.

Figure 9.8 shows the ten-step approach, split into three main stages – strategy, develop and operate – which provide a framework that will help to establish an effective channel value capability.

Strategy Stage

Step 1: Understand what you need

This step should integrate with the Customer Management Strategy that was described in Chapter 5. Ask yourself the following questions to focus on channels:

1. Understand what you need

2. Segment and classify

3. Start a dialogue

4. Agree partnerships

5. Select your team

6. Develop value models

7. Train, coach and develop

8. Build joint strategies

9. Share best practice – the channel partner alumni

10. Reflect

Figure 9.8 Ten steps to build channel capability

- What are the end customers that we need to access?
- Where are they located?
- Do we have the existing commercial, technical, operational and logistical reach/capability to serve these customers?
- What do they need from the relationship with us?
- What do we need?
- What behaviour do we need from our channel partners? Do we get this today?
- What are the gaps in where we are today, versus where we need to get?

Step 2: Segment and classify

As shown previously (selecting and appointing partners), a segmentation model needs to be constructed. The suggestion provided is for three classifications – you can obviously have more or less. Set out the channel partner segmentation model, and allocate criteria to position partners into each segment. This segmentation exercise will provide a first-cut picture indicating how the channel business could be constructed, and the names of partners in each country.

Develop Stage

Step 3: Start a dialogue

The key word in all of this is 'partnership'. In particular, building a common strategy and understanding with the critical Strategic Channel partners requires a discussion. You select them because they seem to have the scale and fit to suit your needs. There has to be a mutual fit for them to work with you as well. This is a conversation that must take place: you need to seek agreement and a commitment to work together.

In situations where the channel partner does not see value in collaboration, you may have to reconsider appointing them as being strategic.

Step 4: Agree partnerships

All partnerships should be agreed upon. This will be a combination of a service-level agreement and more formal legal contracts. These should be drawn up and agreed between both parties. Getting this balance, between a vision of a new relationship and a formal contract, is obviously quite difficult. Try to fall on the side of partnership and be less formal.

Step 5: Select your team

The managers and supporting teams that work with each channel partner should be carefully selected. A channel manager competency profile can be drawn up, and recruitment made against these profiles. Build your organization around each channel type and recognize that managing a strategic channel partner needs more dedicated focus than a channel associate. Establish guidelines: for example, that one full-time equivalent (FTE) channel manager can look after no more than two strategic channel partners, while one FTE could look after ten channel associate partners. Simple guidelines help to build the structure and set up names against each position.

It is also a good idea to develop main contacts and support teams with each channel partner organization. There needs to be a strong consistent relationship that develops over time. Naming teams on both sides of the relationship can help significantly.

Step 6: Develop value models

Value models are the components that will be created and shared with the channel partner to enable them to transition to a value-centric business model. These should be considered and then developed as a series of capability standards that can be shared. When constructing these, it is a good idea to think 'If I was running this channel business, what would I need to have in place to develop the required new ways of working?'

Operate Stage

Step 7: Train, coach and develop

Implementing the new value-based principles means working with each channel partner and implementing ways of transferring the new business models. This could take the form of:

- An agreed series of training modules (direct and web based)
- Training via on-line modules
- Introduction of planning tools and agreeing ways to co-create customer value opportunities with the customer

- Facilitated workshops to help with strategy, segmentation and business plan development
- Leadership coaching.

These are all high-investment and time-consuming activities. It is critical to work with selected strategic channel associates that are committed to the new ways of working and will invest themselves in making the transition.

Step 8: Build joint strategies

Understanding the end-user customer and getting them to buy more products and services at more favourable fees and terms creates real value. This is only realized when you work with your channel partners to establish a stronger understanding of the customers that they reach (especially if they are serving your target key customers). Joint planning where you work with the channel partner team (considering commercial, technical, operational and supply chain aspects) will lead to stronger plans and improved business results for all parties.

Step 9: Share best practice (the channel partner alumni)

Keeping value-based business alive with channel partners takes effort and constant re-energizing. While a series of training programmes and workshops will raise awareness and invigorate excitement, it will soon fall off the agenda if it is not fuelled and reminders provided to enable discussion and sharing of best practice stories.

Alumni organizations work very well for this. Set up a club or group, and once partners have been selected and have been through initial stages of training and development, they can attend conferences and listen to on-line webinars etc. These can be very motivating and will be prized memberships for your channel partners (it can often be a motivational driver to get them to become a club member).

Step 10: Reflect

Situations change in the market, and there is always the possibility that your initial thinking when setting up the channel strategy was not entirely correct. Constant reviewing of your strategy, the segmentation and selection of channel partners and results will highlight areas that you need to focus on the future. Be prepared to repeat the cycle of strategy, develop and operate.

Value matters

1   Channel partners are critical to your business. They provide an extension to your commercial, technical, logistics and operational reach. They provide a flexible, cost-effective and highly responsive business solution.

2   If not managed carefully they can cause severe value leakage. They may not be an extension to your value-centric business model – often channels will destroy value by focusing on price and volume selling. This will potentially damage your profits and brand.

3   They can be multi-faceted. Often channel organizations can be regarded as your customer, while also supplying to you, and occasionally they can also be your competitors.

4   A potential source of competitive advantage can be gained by re-thinking the way you work with third-party channels. Focusing on channels and considering how to transform them to be an extension to your value business models can create a critical extension to your organizational capability and become a competitive advantage.

5   Supply chains by nature create value but can also destroy it. It is always important to map out the supply chains serving your customers and establish stronger value propositions for each participant.

6   Segmentation. Segmentation. Segmentation. Just as you segment your end-user customer portfolio, so you should segment your channel associates. Build capability around each segment type.

7   Key channel partners will potentially exist, potentially taking a larger proportion of business than other smaller organisations. Managing these key channel partners is similar to managing direct key customers, but has some 'commercial and relationship' differences.

8   Build value-based business capability. If you do not invest time and money in building and transforming your channel partners, nothing will change. Build capability with partners that are willing to change.

9   Build your own channel capability. You will need managers with

a particular skill set: They need to have an ability to understand and work with entrepreneurs and small business owners, and to respond to the needs of these dynamic/flexible businesses.

10 A ten-step model to build channel capability. Offered is a proven ten-step model that is split into three stages – strategy, develop and operate. Follow it to build a competitive advantage with your channels.

Chapter 10

Value-based pricing

Nowadays people know the price of everything and the value of nothing

Oscar Wilde

Question
If value and price are inextricably linked, how might value-based pricing capability be developed?

Pricing 'customer by customer'

Oscar Wilde made his very astute observation, 'Nowadays people know the price of everything and the value of nothing', in the late 1800s. I'm not sure what got him so worked up to feel that he had to make this statement (maybe he was a global account director?) but it was extremely insightful and embracing. His thinking that there is a tendency by customers to focus on price, with little connection to the actual value of what they are buying, lies at the core of this book and the ideas that it is built on.

If it were true when Wilde wrote it over 100 years ago, the depth and strength of the meaning is amplified today due to several factors:

- The internet has made pricing more visible and transparent for buyers (they now know the price of everything at the push of a button – usually on a mobile phone).
- Business-marketing procurement specialists have sophisticated systems that can track purchases, prices and supplier performance.
- Globalization creates competition of most products and services to provide a wide selection of choice, specification, supply and price.

This breadth and pace of availability plays to customer demands and needs – but choice naturally leads to price benefits.

This is all affecting the fundamentals of business. Power is shifting to buyers, often forcing suppliers into a position where prices have to be dropped in order to win and secure supply positions. Many organizations complain about this, but in reality if customers can buy cheaper, naturally that is what they will do. Suppliers need to be mindful of three scenarios that lead to prices being driven down for their products and services:

1   The offering is not unique enough to justify a higher price: you are effectively in a commodity/price-driven battle to win business.
2   The offering is unique and delivers value to the customer's business, but you are doing an ineffective job demonstrating and capturing that value.
3   The customer recognizes and understands the value that you can deliver, but cannot justify paying the associated price.

All three scenarios need to be understood and handled appropriately. In particular, scenarios 2 and 3 need a very careful value-based approach.

The connection between value and price needs to be understood and connected into the other principles of value-based business. To explain and position value-based pricing more effectively, an understanding of where it fits in with other aspects of pricing needs to be considered. Figure 10.1 shows a way to present this as three levels of pricing forces (this aligns with the previous model used for strategy development in Chapter 5). The levels start with forces from the wider macro economy. The next level represents price forces that derive within the industry, where supply and demand factors determine prices.

The final level at which price can be determined is with each individual customer. The forces here are affected by the macro and industry factors – but there will be aspects that are pertinent to the customer's business that should be focused upon and the value message carefully examined. This is value-based pricing, and is the focus of this section to enable customer value strategy.

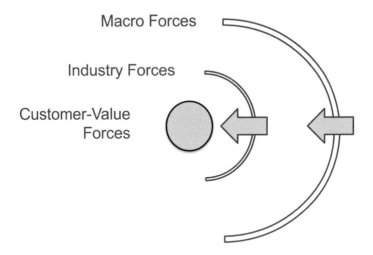

Figure 10.1 The three pricing forces

Table 10.1 expands on these forces. Moving from the outside inwards, the opportunity for suppliers to influence price levels decreases. Macro forces set and establish spot prices: these are fixed. They can be hedged and traded, but these forces set out the price structures. At an industry level, there is more room to differentiate and to be flexible with pricing. In situations where there is strong competition and plentiful supply, customers will compare prices and seek the lowest value.

The final customer-value section is where value-based selling and KAM techniques when applied correctly to develop strong value propositions will pay dividends. This is pricing 'customer by customer', and is in effect a by-product of understanding the customer's business, developing a strong offer to meet needs and a relationship so that the customer trusts you the supplier to deliver your value promise.

Consideration of all three forces should always be considered. It would be naive to think that everything that is presented to the customer can be charged at premium rates – there will always be a blend of commodity pricing and value-add, but work hard at value-based selling and the proportion should shift away from a price/volume discussion.

Table 10.1 The three pricing forces

Macro Forces (Examples)	Industry Forces	Customer-Value Forces
Interest rates	Competitor activity	Specific customer activity
Oil prices	Supply activity	
Energy prices	Customer usage	• Commodity prices
Regulators	Supply and demand	• Value-based prices
	Spot prices	

Price and the marketing mix

Pricing is one of the least understood (and yet most effective) components of the marketing mix. Of the Four Ps (Product, Price, Place and Promotion) price is the least focused on in many businesses and yet is critical to overall performance.

Table 10.2 explores this to examine this claim. Taking product first, most organizations have entire divisions that are focused on designing new products, developing them for markets and then introducing them to customers. While having a new pipeline of innovative new products and services is critical, it is a very costly, lengthy process, often with mixed results (it is rare for organizations to have a 100 per cent strike rate with products that they develop). Compounding this is the fact that competitors can quickly copy new products – often considerably reducing the window to make profit.

Place (establishing direct and indirect selling channels) and promotion are less costly and timely activities, but they also can suffer from mixed results when introduced. They are additionally timely and complex, and can be costly.

Pricing on the other hand is a different matter. Price increases can be formulated and introduced to customers very quickly. Depending on the consumption/acquisition time of what is being sold, this price increase can have a very fast impact on the bottom line of your business.

Table 10.2 Price and the marketing mix

	Cost to Develop	Time to Develop	Risk of Failure	Potential Profit Impact
Product	High	High (years)	High-medium	Varies
Price	Low	Low (days/ weeks)	Low	Very high (can be immediate)
Place	Medium	Medium-high	Medium	Varies
Promotion	Medium	Medium	Varies	Varies

Value in practice

'If I am working with organizations that have severe cash flow problems, one of the first things I suggest is putting up prices. Sometimes this horrifies the client … they say that if we put up prices, they will lose customers …

… my response is always the same: are these the same customers that are forcing you into near bankruptcy? Maybe you should put your prices up – the good customers will stay … the bad ones will go away and help your competitors go bankrupt…?'

VP Consulting Services, Global Strategy Consultancy Firm

And yet, with pricing being such a critical element of the total marketing mix, and the lower risk, high impact effect that it can have on profits, it remains a business activity that is often under-resourced. Organizations have product development groups, sales teams and channels. Marketing departments run promotional campaigns to drive sales and communicate with customers. It is clear who owns these activities and they are usually resourced effectively and have budgets.

It's always an interesting question to consider. Ask who is responsible for setting and managing prices across the organization. And then ask how much effort, analysis and investment goes into making pricing decisions. Very often, there is little focus and missed opportunity.

The top and bottom line leverage effect

Marn, Roegner and Zawada observed in 'The Power of Pricing' (2003) that pricing is the fastest and most effective way for managers to increase profits. They advised to consider the average income statement of an S&P 1500 company, observing that a price rise of just 1 per cent, if volumes remain stable, would generate an 8 per cent increase in operating profits.

This is a staggering phenomenon. There is no magic at play – it is a simple fact regarding the way that income statements are constructed and the connection between 'Top Line' and 'Bottom Line'. Marn, Roegner and Zawada also noted that unfortunately there is a reverse effect. A 1 per cent reduction in price will bring down operating profit by 8 per cent.

This is a basic and yet very effective concept to understand and to put into action. And yet, looking back at the recession when organizations were faced with declining markets and reduced sales, the focus almost immediately went on cost-cutting and downsizing programmes. When taking out costs there is usually an expense to take out that cost (especially fixed costs). Downsizing the workforce takes time, costs money and actually only saves the cost. Of course, cost cutting and 'tightening the belt' is an essential activity when trying to survive a recession or downturn in business, but organizations should also look to grow the top line by focusing on sales strategies and in particular assessing the value-price performance with every customer.

Despite the attractiveness of price leverage, care needs to be taken when analysing pricing points. When organizations review the historical data of large product ranges and the prices that they have charged, anomalies can often be found. Some products and services that you supply may need to be at lower prices, for example when you need a certain volume to make a manufacturing plant meet its fixed cost quota. When supplying multiple ranges of products to customers, it is also typical to find some products that are supplied at a lower price than others: it is the mix of products that are supplied to the customer as a total package that they buy. Some products may be sold at break-even (or even a loss) as part of the total customer value proposition.

Regardless of these considerations, it is nearly always a useful exercise to analyse your portfolio of products and identify areas where price increases can be made. As one general manager that I worked with on a pricing review said: 'I know that we have some situations that we can make a low margin, but not everywhere ... there is nothing strategic about losing money!'

Connecting value-based business and pricing

One of the objectives that professional buyers have is to analyse suppliers and try to achieve as low a price as possible to pay for the goods and services they are procuring. While suppliers may complain about this, why wouldn't their customers adopt this approach? Who pays more than they have to for a product when an equivalent is available that equally satisfies performance requirements? Problems arise for suppliers in two key situations, however:

- When the buyer starts to be overly aggressive on the price that they will accept (by analysing the cost structure of what is being supplied and then dictating the margin).
- When the customer offering provides a strong value impact on their business, but that value has not been clearly described or understood.

These two scenarios are bad for both the customer and the supplier (though obviously the supplier loses more if they are obtaining lower prices than they deserve). Driving down prices to the point that suppliers start to lose money and fail to invest in new products will ultimately lead to a situation where business starts to suffer. A portfolio of suppliers that constantly innovate and bring new ideas to the table will keep business healthy. Running suppliers into the ground will lead to reduced innovation, strained collaboration and a fractured supply chain.

The secret to being able to maximize pricing capability is to make it part of the overall value-based business model. Incorporating pricing into offer development, value-based selling, key account management and channel management, and focusing on the value and price 'customer by customer', creates a better chance to maintain higher prices.

Key points

Value-based pricing can be a very effective technique to establish better prices and profit. It has to be developed and managed in an integrated manner and be part of an overall value-based business model.

Value-based pricing is a close companion of offer development and innovation, value-based selling, key account management and channel management.

In business marketing, focus on value co-creation to realize the true potential of pricing.

This integrated approach to value-based business is a key concept that pumps through the veins of Infinite Value. The concepts challenge customers and ask questions regarding a bigger picture than just purchasing a set of products or services. But it is a different and more demanding way to do business.

Pricing can be a very powerful commercial technique. Value-based pricing 'customer by customer' can create very strong results for the supplier – but the value equation must be in favour of the customer for it to work. Figure 10.2 demonstrates this simple idea, whereby the customer looks at your offering as a cost. As a transaction, this can be very easy: they can compare what you provide with competitor prices and seek immediate savings. To get the discussion 'swinging in your favour' discuss on the other side of the see-saw: have a very firm view about what the value impact will be to the customer and quantify these benefits in hard financial numbers.

These value impact numbers can be large! If you are providing a solution that saves energy, protects the customer brand, or litigation, the 'potential' for upside can be a value that far exceeds what it costs you to provide the service (and what the customer is willing to pay).

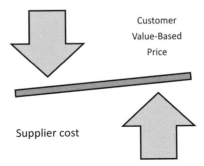

Figure 10.2 The relationship between Supplier cost and customer value impact

Value in practice
The Red Light and The Maintenance Manager …

On one occasion, I was selling a chemical management programme to a large food processing organization. We had a good value proposition, our offering would provide operational savings, health and safety benefits and quality improvements, and we would also manage materials on site to create a cleaner workspace. I was confident that we would add significant 'quantifiable' value to the customer's business. We made out a pitch, and presented our price.

And then the maintenance manager made his observation:

'You know, last week I had a guy trying to sell me a £100 red light that he would install on top of my tall chimney stack. He was claiming that this red light would prevent aircraft from crashing into my building – saving me £millions in fines and lost production … Do you think I should pay £1m for a £100 red light?'

To be fair, he had a very good point.

You have to be realistic, and there is always a limit to what your customer will pay. But the discussion should always be concerned with the value that you create for the customer. This will be different depending who you talk with (the buyer has a different perspective on value to the quality manager) and it is hard work to do all of this analysis, develop relationships and build your value proposition. You may never get the full value that you deliver with your offering, and there will be occasions when you take a hit on your price to win the business.

Maintain perspective: what you need to remember is that 1 per cent price leverage and the impact it has on your bottom line. Failing to get your price higher will only lead to lost profit. And failing to discuss value will lead to a discussion on the buyer's terms (and he/she will focus your price).

Focus on value and use value-based selling techniques and key account management to thoroughly understand your customer's business. Without this, there can be no value pricing opportunity.

If you are faced with a customer questioning your value-based fee and throwing a 'red light challenge' during negotiation, a reflection of the value-price zone (Figure 10.3) can be helpful. At one end, you need to have a very clear analysis of the exact cost of your offering, and your required margin. At the other end of the spectrum is your calculation of maximum value that could be realized for the customer.

Between these two points lies the value-price zone. Both ends of the zone are unrealistic. You don't want to be supplying at cost (or even

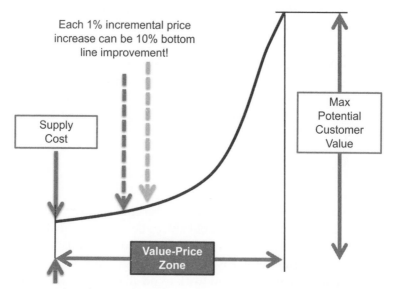

Figure 10.3 The value-price zone

below!). Similarly, the maximum potential customer value figure is unlikely: if you are doing your job properly this should be significant.

So somewhere between those two points is an area that will be acceptable for you and the customer, where a value co-creation assessment is understood and both parties feel they can work to achieve results that satisfy their business objectives. Organizations that operate with a value-based business model understand this. They conduct every customer sales with a thorough understanding of the value potential for the customer, and what it will take for them to enable the offering. They also have an understanding of what every 1 per cent increase (or decrease) in price does to their bottom line.

Figure 10.4 refers back to the value selling cycle, and comments how this foundation model of value-based business aligns with pricing:

> **Engage** – this stage looks at understanding the customer and developing a strong value proposition. The principles of offer development look to capture and quantify the 4 + 1 sources of value. This stage sets the scene to develop the offer for the customer and to quantify what that could mean in the future.
>
> **Agree** – during selling and negotiation, the analysis that is captured in the agree stage is used, setting parameters for cost, customer value and estimates of what happens with each 1 per cent price increase.
>
> **Deliver** – for long-term customer relationships, this stage is critical.

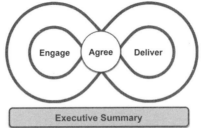

Figure 10.4 Pricing and the value selling cycle

Any value promise that is reached at the agree stage should be quantified and captured. Providing a long-term track record of delivering the value that is promised will give future assurance when agreeing price.

Pricing and contract structure options

When you think about price, it is broader than just price! Other aspects need to be considered to construct a commercial position. To help navigate these pricing construct elements, the customer price framework can be utilized (Figure 10.5). The framework guides price development into five main aspects:

1   Value Aspects
    In reality, not everything that you supply to your customer will be unique and value adding. Assess the components of your offering and split out the transactional elements from the high value-add components.
2   Time Aspects
    Contracts run with customers over set periods. Longer project-based contracts will require staged payments (e.g. design, detail, construct, commission, completion). At the other end of the

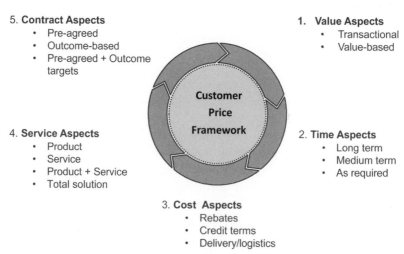

Figure 10.5 Customer price framework

spectrum, completion is on a quick ad hoc basis (e.g. supplying analysis tests for water systems).

3   Cost Aspects

All costs need to be captured and quantified. Costs start with the cost of goods, but should also capture additional elements such as rebates, special deliveries, exchange rate variances and any peculiarities due to the region/country of supply. Credit terms also need to be assessed. What is the impact of your business when a customer pays in 120 days instead of 30 days?

4   Service Aspects

As organizations 'step into the customer's value chain,' there are numerous options available to construct the product/contract. This includes:

- Product-based (the offer is focused on the product, and so is the price);
- Product with separate service fee;
- Service fee absorbed into the product price;
- Total solution.

The options need to be discussed and agreed with the customer. When service costs are absorbed into product costs care needs to be taken. A new buyer in the customer operation might look at your prices and think you are very expensive. They may not realize what is included in the price.)

5   Contract Structure Aspects

There are three main ways that the contract can be structured. The choice between these is influenced by the agreed intent and partnership between the supplier and buyer:

(a) Pre-agreed contracts work on the basis that a fixed or variable fee is established, and the supplier works to provide products and services, invoicing at these pre-agreed prices.

(b) Outcome-based pricing works on the principle that the customer pays the supplier when set targets are achieved. With solution-based offerings becoming more common, these contracts are attractive for customers since the performance of the programmes becomes more complex and the impact of their success (and failure) so significant that it is better to pay when they are confident the job has been done.

> Generally, the supplier can secure higher profits. This truly is a value-based contract!

The most common contract structure is a hybrid of (a) and (b). A basic pre-agreed portion provides the supplier with payment to establish the core of the contract. To ensure that a high level of performance is achieved, targets are agreed and additional outcome-based payments made if they are achieved.

Value in practice

'We like outcome-based price agreements ...

... as much as we trust our suppliers ... it's so much better to put their money where their mouth is ... and not ours!'

Head of Procurement, Global Automotive Group

The customer price framework is a useful model to help establish the basic components of how the contract and resulting fee structure can be developed for any offering. It should be adopted throughout the three stages of the value selling cycle. Unique customer offering requires innovation to create new ideas. Innovation can be derived from new products, services or promotions.

Look at pricing, and everything that is associated by considering these frameworks, and it can become a very useful source of innovative ideas and options.

Five key focus areas to build value-based pricing capability

Building the capability to deliver value-based pricing should be integrated into an overall customer management capability programme. The following guide will help to structure the development of this effort, by focusing on five key areas. (Note that this is not an all-inclusive pricing capability process, since it focuses on developing capability at the customer level.)

1 **Develop a strategy**

Recognition at leadership team level is a very important first stage. With commitment to make investment and focus resources and by developing a purpose, there will be an easier alignment across the organization to make changes happen. This should align and be part of the wider customer value strategy initiative, but recognition of the importance of pricing and its direct connection with value is essential.

A project team should be established: this does not have to be composed of full-time employees (it is a good idea to have part-time members initially), but time should be allocated to allow them to carry out strategy and planning.

2 **Develop capability**

The beauty with value-based pricing is that it can be integrated into the development of the other capability standards. In fact, without an effective execution of value-based selling, KAM, and offer development and innovation, it is nearly impossible to make value-based pricing work.

Additional complementary training programmes can be developed that focus on pricing, providing insights into capturing cost to supply and value for the customer.

3 **Train, develop and coach key people**

The principles of value-based pricing need to be explained and engrained deeply into the way that commercial people think about the way they build customer plans, write proposals, conduct negotiation and capture value delivery to the customer.

4 **Monitor competitor and customer feedback**

The strength of value is relative to how the customer perceives your offering, and also how unique it is compared to competitor offerings. If your offering is a 'me-too' then the price you will be able to achieve will be limited. Monitoring of what the customer thinks, and how competitors respond, provides useful information to maintain the development of stronger value propositions, and subsequently higher prices. Be realistic about the components of your offering; there will always be a mix of transactional (commodity) business and more unique value adding.

5 **Monitor and re-evaluate the strategy**

The pricing steering group should meet and review progress

on a regular basis. As the programme develops it will require adjustment, reinforcement and (occasionally) re-design. The project team should make recommendations to ensure that value-based pricing remains a vibrant and effective focus of the organization.

Value matters

1 Warren Buffet, The CEO of Berkshire Hathaway, famously states that 'Price is what you pay and value is what you get.' This simple idea encapsulates the foundation principle for value-based business. This section discusses pricing aspects.

2 In business markets, there is a trend for the power to shift to the buyer. They are equipped to compare and analyse supplier costs. While this cannot be avoided, suppliers need to shift the focus back to a more even playing field. They can do this by focusing on the potential value they can create.

3 Three forces determine prices: macro/environmental forces; industry (supply and demand) forces; and customer-value forces. The last is the focus of this chapter, whereby value-based business techniques are used to identify opportunities within each customer.

4 In the marketing mix, price is possibly the least understood and utilized. And yet, it offers significant upside potential with lower risk and effort profile.

5 Pricing leverage indicates that a 1 per cent price increase can leverage to the bottom line (if fixed and variable costs remain the same) to provide an 8 per cent improvement in operating profit (it can also work the other way and reduce profit by 8 per cent).

6 Value-based pricing works in parallel with offer development and innovation, value-based selling and KAM. These techniques enable and support each other.

7 While significant upside value can be projected for the customer, it is not always possible to capture this in the price they pay. Having the information through careful analysis is very effective to help at the negotiation stage.

8   The value-price zone is offered as a visual technique to capture the relationship between the costs of the supplier offering the maximum potential for the customer. The final value should be agreed within the zone.

9   Pricing embraces a wide set of commercial parameters. The customer price framework suggests that value, time, cost, service and contract structure aspects also need to be considered.

10 A series of tips is offered to help build value-based pricing capability.

Chapter 11

The value-centric organization

Our highest priority is satisfying customers ... except when it is hard ... or unprofitable ... or we're busy.

Scott Adams (aka Dilbert)

Question
How do I develop my organization so that it focuses its resources and relationships in order to maximize the value that it can create?

The purpose of a business

There is consistently one issue that larger business-marketing organizations identify when I am advising them to implement a value-based business model. This issue occurs in multiple industries and across many countries. When it is a mild problem, it will slow progress and implementation of programmes down. When severe, it derails initiatives, even when they are sound strategies supported by evidence that the changes will drive growth. This issue comes from key account managers, sales people, general managers, marketers and those tasked with developing and implementing customer strategies. The issue can be summarized in a simple statement of frustration: how do I get my wider organization to focus on customer-related matters?

Why this phenomenon happens may seem surprising. But it occurs, and it is a serious challenge for many larger companies. When I discuss this with managers in smaller organizations (fifty employees or fewer) they often find the concepts hard to imagine. After all, when a business is starting up there is a complete obsession about winning and retaining customers. When there are no customers, there is no business. Smaller companies obsess about finding customers and winning business.

They look for market opportunities and develop products and services to meet the needs of the opportunities that they find. If they don't do this, they fail.

With larger organizations that have been trading over a longer period of time, this organization-wide *focus* on the customer becomes diluted. Larger organizations are more formally structured. There are HR, supply chain and logistics, manufacturing, R&D and many other departments. Profit 'centres' are implemented – they manage costs and split the organization into smaller operating units. Global businesses have management structures in different countries and may even have their own functions. All of these organization structures are important. Large organizations create value and they operate across many borders. There has to be a formal connection of divisions and business units. It is how things get done.

However, when organizations become overly corporate, inefficiency can creep in that causes the business to focus on its own issues ahead of those of the customer. It is an exceptionally difficult issue to overcome. On the one hand, there needs to be a focus on running an efficient business that delivers objectives and targets. But on the other hand, the leveraged total impact of the organization's ability to develop new customer offerings and to serve the market should be in place. These are quite different corporate activities, requiring different cultures and ways of working.

A good way to illustrate the tension is when a smaller organization is acquired by a larger more heavily integrated business. I have witnessed this occurring several times when consulting with organizations – the problems that arise can be frustrating for employees in both of the organizations that come together and (in severe instances) can damage customer relationships and business.

Value in action

We were acquired about eighteen months ago. Frankly, our new corporate owner dwarfs us (I think they bought us with loose change from one month's trading profit!).

The reason they bought us was because we do business with customers that they want to do business with. They admire the relationship we have with these customers and the fact that we work closely with them ...

... and yet – we are no longer the company that they bought. We seem to spend our days completing monthly reports and entering data into CRM systems. Everything we do is to report what we are doing to our new owners ... and the customer has had to take a back seat. Whereas we used to spend time talking about our customers and how we could meet their needs ... these days we talk about our owners and how we can meet our own needs. For some of our people, this is not an exciting organization that they want to work for any more. It's very frustrating.

European Sales Director, Medical Devices Organization

The customer-centric mantra

Philip Kotler famously stated: 'The sales department isn't the whole company, but the whole company better be the sales department.' I don't think he meant that everybody should be actively chasing customers and trying to get them to buy products; the intent of his quote is more to address the concerns expressed in the previous section 'the purpose of a business'. He perfectly captures the intent of how organizations should behave, with an instruction that organizations should always be looking to focus on the customer and growing the top line.

This misalignment comes from the way that organizations are structured and organized. Figure 11.1 demonstrates this, by showing how major departments and functions are sometimes established and managed in corporations. There will be a combination of support functions (HR, supply chain, R&D etc.). Business units and functions

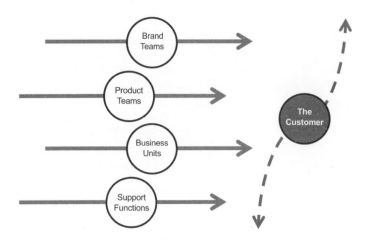

Figure 11.1 Customer misalignment

that control the profit and loss (often by country) and product/brand teams are often of a large scale and become businesses in their own right.

What can happen is that they become disconnected from each other, and appear to be on separate independent trajectories. The customer becomes something that cuts across these 'businesses within a business'. For senior leaders in the organization that are accountable for managing the customer agenda, getting things done and aligning businesses can become a challenge. The following are typical symptoms of trying to get things done in a non-customer-centric organization:

- Data indicating the sales and profitability of customers is hard to obtain, since systems and reporting structures have been developed around internal departments, product lines and brands.
- Establishing cross-functional teams to support KAM initiatives is difficult. Employees that are part of support functions (e.g. supply chain, R&D and finance) do not have any remit or desire to support customer-facing initiatives: 'Isn't that the job of sales?'
- Senior board members have not had any customer-facing experience. Board members tend to have accounting, general management or technical backgrounds.

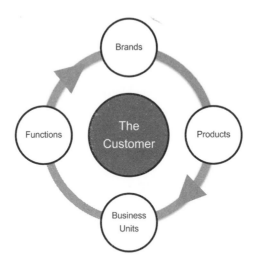

Figure 11.2 The customer-centric business

- Meetings in the organization are focused on internal matters. It is rare to hear any senior managers talking about customer issues. Board meetings are entirely focused on internal targets and cost control issues.

These are just a few of the observations that have been made, working with a wide variety of organizations. As an adviser, it is relatively easy to ascertain if a client has become detached from the customer and if an opportunity might arise to get more people in the organization realigned behind the customer. Many organizations see this problem. Advocates and project leaders who recognize that there is a misalignment with the customer often seek ways to steer the business so that some form of 'customer centricity' is achieved.

Figure 11.2 shows the 'customer-centric' business model. This does not suggest that the organization needs to change the way that it is physically structured. The existing structures of departments and supporting functions should be maintained: this is the most cost-effective and efficient way to achieve things. Organizations should put the customer at the centre of the way that they develop strategies when they are developing specific customer value propositions, however. Customer centricity should be a cultural aspect of business and a philosophical way of working. The customer should be placed at the centre of decision making, with business units and supporting functions providing appropriate support. Getting this balance right is critical – take it too far and you can become a commercial charity!

There are a number of benefits and challenges for organizations that operate in a customer-centric manner. These should be considered and reviewed when developing a transformation programme.

Benefits of being a customer-centric business

- Deeper insights about the customer and markets can be gained, since there are more experts focused on providing data and information. Organizations have a wealth of experience and knowledge, but unless it is channelled and captured, insights can be missed. Customer centricity can provide an organizational culture that captures input from more skilled people (and these people are already part of your business!).
- With deeper insights and a wider skill set from cross-functional customer teams, stronger and more innovative customer value propositions can be developed.
- The customer obtains a more consistent and positive experience. This is critical as offerings stretch from just products to services and solutions. With service-based offerings, a customer-centric business model is essential since 'people become the product'.
- The strength and weakness of each customer value proposition depends on the customer perception of the offering and how well it compares with competitor offerings. The exact details of these offerings can be subtle. Having a wider set of 'eyes and ears' by having more people in the organization aligned behind providing this customer and competitor reconnaissance will provide a much clearer measure of competitiveness.
- Responding to customer and market changes can be quicker and more impactful, since there is a greater focus on what the customer needs and values.

Challenges to working in a customer-centric manner

- The recommended customer-centric model is to have a matrix approach. It is the culture and focus of the organization that puts the customer at the centre of decisions. However, this requires careful communication and careful setting of department and personal objectives.
- When organizations become too customer-centric there is a possibility of over-serving the customer and losing money. Careful tracking of where resources are being applied and the impact on customer profitability can necessitate additional IT systems.
- While cross-functional teams will generate stronger insights and more innovative offerings for customers, bringing these teams together can be costly. Using technology such as Skype and Webex can help, but face-to-face meetings (especially for global teams) will add to costs.

This presents the same challenge for organizations that aspire to become more customer-centric. It could be dangerous to be drawn into the customer's world and to obsess about understanding what they need and how to meet those needs. This puts the supplier at the mercy of the customer. If taken too far, the customer could fail and you will fail with them.

Possibly the biggest challenge is that of focus. Henry Ford stated:

'If I had asked people what they wanted, they would have said faster horses.'

The answer is to be sufficiently customer-centric to maintain near- to medium-term business, but also to be self-centred and look beyond the customer. By not getting caught up in the immediate problems of the customer, and keeping back energy, effort and investment to develop new value propositions to meet customer needs that they have not expressed, there is a chance of changing the market and building considerable competitive advantage.

Is value-celling a better way to do business?

Building on the customer-centricity concern that suggests the supplier exists just to serve the customer (and potentially be in a subservient trading position) means that working in this manner is potentially too restrictive. The principles of value-based business focus on the need to innovate and develop value propositions. There is a requirement to respond to ever-changing market, industry and competitor trends.

In order to fully utilize all of the resources that are available to an organization, it may be better to adopt a broader and less restrictive approach to business relationships. The suggestion for the value-based business is to adopt the concept of being *value-centric*. This maintains the focus on customers, but also suggests that there needs to be an investment in developing relationships with other critical external organizations.

These value relationship types are shown in Table 11.1. Rather than working as an alternative to customer centricity, value-centric business is an extension to these principles (focusing on the customer is one of the essential relationships that are recommended).

The value-centric business looks to develop relationships where there can be benefits to foster value co-creation. While money is created directly by payments from the customer, there is recognition that the pace of change in business, shorter product life cycles, increased costs

Table 11.1 Typical organizational behaviours of customer- and value-centric business models

Customer-Centric	Value-Centric
The organization focuses on the needs of the customer and is responsive to meet these needs if possible.	The organization focuses on value co-creation, and recognizes that collaborative relations beyond customers are critical to ensure new value propositions are created on a regular basis.

to get new offerings to market and the need for expanded solutions require a collaborative approach to business. The critical relationships that form the foundations to value-centric business are shown in Figure 11.3. Collectively, they make up the 'value-cell' organization:

Customers: described already, but still essential in value centricity is a focus and alignment of resources with the customer, in particular strategic/key customers.

Customer's customers: too often suppliers focus on the customer and lock onto their specific demands. Looking beyond the customer and trying to understand what they require can provide very strong knowledge, insights and potentially more powerful value propositions and business models.

Channel partners: this was discussed in Chapter 9, whereby channel partner management was described as a critical component of value-based business. The focus of resources should be maintained on channels; they are an invaluable extension to understanding, developing and delivering value propositions to the market.

Suppliers: suppliers are trying to collaborate with you in the same way that you are trying to collaborate with your customers. They may have access to some new techniques, technologies and processes. Work together and you may develop something revolutionary!

Competitors: obviously you have to be careful regarding anti-competition and monopoly guidelines (some industries strictly forbid collusions between suppliers) but if you are working together to form new products and there is mutual trust and solid business reasons to form alliances, why not go ahead and work together?

Associates: some organizations rely on associates (part-time, interim or consulting-type resources) as flexible resources. They use them on projects and programmes when full-time employees cannot be justified. Associates can bring high levels of skill and immediate impact with minimal levels of support and guidance (in fact, senior associates can be more highly skilled than your own labour force).

At the centre of these associations is your own business. This comprises the many functions and departments in your own organization working together as a 'value-cell'. This is a different model to having a sales force that looks after customers. The value-cell manages all of the above relationships, recognizing that the best way to continuously innovate

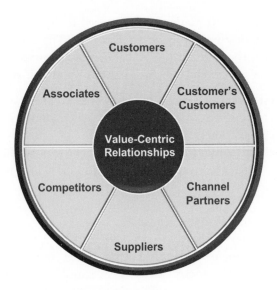

Figure 11.3 The value-cell organization

and create value for all parties is to collaborate and work together in challenging and changing environments.

Table 11.2 highlights the way that relationships shift from a traditional business model to a value-based model. Relationships are not always as 'black-and-white' as shown on the table, but it does indicate the principal intent and focus between the two approaches.

The best way to illustrate the shift in business benefits by developing the relationship behaviour for each type; examples can be described across a number of industries and organizations:

Developing the customer value relationship
A law firm recognized that the nature of legal services is changing. One particular trend is that some of the major clients they serve now look to bring legal advice in-house and stop using external law firms for support. They recognized that the legal industry for business-marketing customers was in a state of change, with the recession of 2008–10 accelerating this change.

To respond, they set up a panel of eight to ten key clients from different sectors (banking, retail, technology, transport). Senior

Table 11.2 Behaviours of the value-cell organization

Customers	Customer's Customers	Channel Partners	Suppliers	Competitors	Associates
Product-based	Target: Low value alignment	Transactional	Commodity	Competitive	Hired-hands
Value partnerships	Target: High value alignment	Strategic partner	Strategic	Potential alliances	Scarce resource 'experts'

members from these clients meet on a regular basis and discuss all matters of legal services. In particular, the question is asked, 'What do you want us to be as a legal services provider in the future?'

Developing the customer's customer value relationship
Consumer packaged goods industries (Unilever, Mars, P&G) focus on the customer's customer (the consumer) as a deeply rooted way of doing business. Having deep insights about consumer buying behaviours and market trends give them a competitive advantage when selling their products into those markets. The customers that they sell to (retailers such as Wal-Mart, Aldi, Tesco) value these consumer insights as they help them to sell more products. Often, the customer selects a supplier to act as 'category captain' to assist in driving sales across an entire range of products (including competitor products). This is possible by having deep insights about the customer's customer.

Developing channel partner value relationship
A global supplier of automotive lubricants looked to provide products to certain markets with an increased focus on using third-party channel partners. This required the selection, development and investment of several new channel partners in many countries.

They built trust by carefully selecting channel partners and conducting joint planning sessions. Channel partners were selected carefully, and then considerable effort made to collaborate and demonstrate the focus on partnership. This was achieved by regular conferences, making awards and providing training.

To make this work, they identified that some channel partners did not trust the historical ways of working. A focus on listening to partner concerns and building relationships set the foundation to improve performance with channel partners.

Developing supplier value relationship

The automotive manufacturing industry often develops supplier partnerships to assist them in building their vehicles. All large manufacturing sites have suppliers integrated into their operations. This approach to letting key suppliers 'step into the value operations' is built on co-operation between both parties and drives a culture to improve efficiency and improve processes. It is common to see suppliers operating entire parts of processes such as tooling management, paint-booth operations, electrical component supply and fitting and fluid/lubrication management.

These relationships work on the basis that the suppliers have expertise and knowledge on the components and services they supply – the customer embraces this expertise and allows them to create more value by becoming part of the process.

Developing competitor strategic alliances

The *Economist* described the need for 'Managing Partners' in a Schumpeter article (23 May 2015). Four reasons are put forward that make it necessary for competing organizations to collaborate:

- The cost of new technologies is crippling – cost sharing helps this;
- Momentum – the window to introduce new products is ever reducing, so there is a need to reduce time to market;
- Cross-border ties;
- The consumer – as consumers become more equipped to select what they buy, pressure is placed on suppliers to find strong value solutions.

Schumpeter raises car-makers as exemplars of competitors that form alliances to counter these shifts in the market. Toyota and BMW are working on hybrid and fuel-cell technologies, while Ford and GM (two arch-rivals!) are collaborating on high-efficiency gear boxes.

There are commercial reasons to form these alliances, but there also has to be considerable effort at all levels of the organization to make these potentially uncomfortable partnerships work.

Developing the associate value relationships

A niche UK-based management consulting firm changed their business model. Historically, they had trained and consulted with large blue-chip organizations but on a small niche scale. The new business model offered global organizations the means to train senior leaders and offer them professional certificates and qualifications.

The concept was well received but required a large increase in the number of qualified trainers and coaches that they had. Historically, the firm had used associates but on a transactional ad hoc basis. This new venture would require more associates operating in more countries than before.

The organization had to adapt the approach they took with associate consultants. This was not a problem of day rate fees or associate development. These things were already in place. The main obstacle to overcome was attitude to a network of associates and treating them as part of the business (not a variable cost).

Treat others as you would like to be treated yourself

At the time of writing this section, I have been working with a large global healthcare company. I was running a workshop with a team of account managers that look after hospital trusts. The workshop was a great success, with lots of discussion and agreement that the organization should work with its customers and focus on value co-creation and developing customer-specific value propositions.

One challenge that this team of fifteen or so senior managers faced was that their customers should work harder to spend time with them as a supplier and to see them as more than just a transactional provider of products. They felt aggrieved and wondered how to address this problem. They wanted to be seen as a trusted provider of value-based service packages.

I think I can speak as a supplier to my client, and I can definitely speak as a small consulting practice. Some three months after this workshop took place, I have an (ironic) issue. They have yet to pay me. In fact, they have yet to advise when I will be paid. Thankfully, I am not dependent or financially exposed by this invoice in order to sustain my business since I have a wide portfolio of clients, but if I were I would be in trouble. This is hardly the behaviour of an organization that treats all of its value relationships fairly. They are certainly not treating others 'as they would like to be treated themselves'.

It is like the advice your parents give you when you are a kid: 'Treat others as you would like to be treated yourself.' If you don't, you create a lopsided and selfish approach to business ... and you will find collaborative relationships very difficult. Why should you be trusted when you breach the basics of business and force terms of ninety days before payment on suppliers? Think about it.

Value relationships work by treating relationships with suppliers, associates, consultants and channel partners fairly and with respect. Figure 11.4 shows how this balance can become skewed.

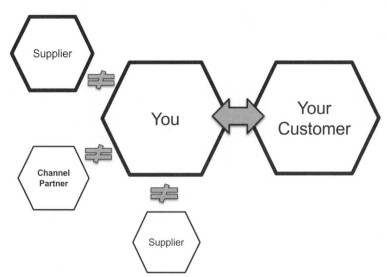

Figure 11.4 Value – it works both ways ...

Organizations aspire to have value-based relationships with their customers (because there are commercial benefits from doing this). It is hypocritical to not allow your suppliers and other value providers to enjoy a similar business experience with you. Value-based businesses build relationship with a wide variety of organizations, not just customers.

Challenges and tensions

Figure 11.5 captures some of the comments that are typically heard within organizations when discussing the idea of developing value relationships. This may appear to be a blunt instrument, with the comments potentially being harsh (on the 'traditional' view side), but they do capture the thinking that is in the minds of many people when reviewing the need to move to value-based relationships. By focusing on a few of these relationships (suppliers, channel partners and associates), these tensions and challenges can be explored a little deeper.

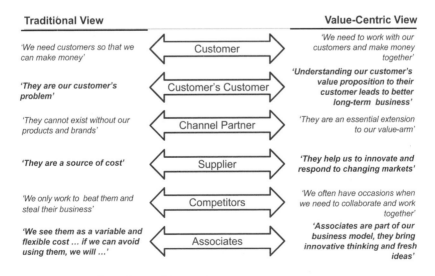

Figure 11.5 Value relationship tensions

Suppliers

Taking a traditional view, suppliers can be seen as providing products and services that have to adhere to a specification. If these relationships are viewed as having to comply and deliver as instructed, the relationship can become very focused on cost.

For some suppliers, where the goods and services that they provide are commodities, that may be the best relationship. The challenge is that some suppliers may have innovative and unique technologies, ideas and experiences that will add real value to your business. Opening the door to suppliers and providing an environment of collaboration in challenging markets is a different way of thinking and behaving.

Tensions will arise in the business when looking to work more closely with suppliers. Balancing cost control on transactional business against collaborating with more innovative value offerings takes some controlling, especially when the same supplier provides a mix of commodity and unique value-adding components to their offer. The secret is to foster open and honest dialogue with suppliers. If the suppliers do not want to work with you and focus on value co-creation, maybe they should be treated as commodity suppliers.

Channel partners

In Chapter 9, the many faces of channel partners were presented. They can be regarded as customers, suppliers and competitors. They can be flexible and highly adaptive partners that add a logistical, commercial, operational and technical extension to your business in markets where you have no presence. And yet, it is rare that channel partners are described as providing a significant competitive advantage to organizations. This is a missed opportunity!

Part of the reason for this is the attitude of organizations towards their channel partners. As Figure 11.5 shows, if there is a view that you have the upper hand and channel partners 'only exist because of our brands and products' then an unhealthy approach to business will develop. Adopting a more collaborative stance and viewing channel partners as an essential part of your business will lead to a stronger value-based business.

Associates

Many organizations rely on associate employees to supplement their expertise. In financial terms, associates are a great way to get employees as a variable cost and not fixed. They can be paid for with project budgets, and avoid adding costs to the profit and loss account. Financially, there are many great reasons to have interim, consulting, contractors and self-employed staff members. But that is where the possible full benefits get strangled. While associates are a flexible resource, they are also very often experts in their field of working. The tension with associates resides with attitude. If you view them as an accounting exercise and only use them when it suits you for financial reasons (the analogy used by some associates is being a 'broom in a cupboard', brought out only when it suits the customer) then opportunities will be missed. In value-based businesses, associates are regarded as critical members of the team. They are consulted on regarding strategy, policy and advice with the management of the business. Associates that are looking beyond billing 'every hour of work done' will contribute to this approach of working. There will be long-term potential benefits for them.

Relationship tensions always exist in organizations. You may recognize the comments provided in Figure 11.5 and get a glimpse of possible issues that occur in your own business. The secret to managing a change in these tensions lies in the mindset of leadership and management. This is all part of building a value-based strategy and business. Figure 11.6 describes the 'heart' of this thinking. If each business unit and function becomes too focused on achieving the objectives that have been set, then a focus on the bigger picture with external relationships

'My job is to achieve my department objectives. What has the customer and sales got to do with me?'

Your Leadership Teams and Employees

'I am clear about my role to create value for customers with multiple relationships that our organization manages'

Figure 11.6 Internal tensions

will result. Leadership needs to drive an agenda whereby supporting sales and account management teams, and the supporting value functions (channels, suppliers etc.), are encouraged and are part of business.

The secret of changing to a value-based business is to change opinions and stay focused on becoming a value-based business.

Tips and ideas to build a value-centric business

Part Three of this book will describe in more detail a methodology to implement a transformation programme and build a value-based business. Organizations often want a few simple tips and ideas in order to gain some traction as they try to re-focus the way that people think and behave. There are a number of simple-to-adopt techniques that can be used, often with very little investment. The beauty of applying some of these ideas is that they prompt a discussion and start members of organizations speaking about value matters, something that they possibly would never do as they remain locked in their individual business units and job roles.

The following list of ideas can be used to start prompting a shift towards value centricity in any organization. These are ideas 'in brief' and provide sufficient information for you to consider introducing into your own business.

1 **Value-moments**
   If your organization has grown very inward looking, with very little discussion about external relationships that are essential to drive a value agenda, it is important as a first step to get senior leaders and employees talking. Value-moments are a simple technique that can be introduced. The idea is that every internal meeting should start with a member of the meeting spending five minutes discussing a real and recent example where value has been created (or destroyed) with customers, suppliers, associates, channel partners or competitors. These discussions should be at

the start of any meeting. For example, an HR meeting could be taking place: it should start with a value-moment. The advantage of this is that it gets people that would possibly talk about internal matters talking about external relationships. Value-moments should be short and never judged. They can be positive or negative issues: the over-arching principle is to get people talking about value and for the organization to learn.

2 **Celebrating success**

It can be very easy for business to become focused on its results and achieving its targets. Of course, this is the right way to operate. When shifting towards a value-centric business however, there will be lots of smaller projects where results and initiatives unlock new ideas and results. Celebrating success recognizes that the organization should be open to discussing these findings, sharing good practice and rewarding (by recognition) the effort that has been made to achieve these results.

3 **Value pilot studies**

Organizations learn by applying and developing ideas that are grown in their own business. Pilot studies work by taking small steps and building strategies 'case by case'. For example, a channel partner could be selected in a country. The channel partner could exhibit the characteristics of a strategic partner but require development and training. Focusing on just one partner and building a pilot study can reveal a significant amount of information (for both parties).

4 **Value partner ambassadors**

Any transformation initiatives in organizations struggle to gain traction without board-level/senior sponsorship. Value-based business programmes are no different. It always helps to have a senior-level sponsor that can advise and coach the project team to build a programme that will resonate with the strategic direction of the wider business. It is always better to align with corporate initiatives than fight against them.

5 **Build a value academy and support alumni**

Academies are usually constructed from a suite of training and coaching products, and membership is for the internal members of an organization. A value academy should be open to those organization members, but also should have members from customer businesses, channel partners, associates and suppliers. Of course, these forums and meetings have to be managed very carefully, but to foster real value discussions some form of discussion and sharing of information will be useful. These conferences, webinars and meetings require some organizational effort and investment, but the resulting benefits often pay dividends.

These five ideas are not exhaustive. Many techniques can be used to start a value-based business campaign. They are representative of the effort that is required and indicate why organizations sometimes do not grasp the nettle to work in this different manner: while it requires time and effort, it does not have to involve significant investment.

Value matters

1 A common question that arises in many larger organizations from those that are trying to implement a value-based business is: 'How do I develop my organization so that it focuses its resources and relationships in order to maximize the value that it can create?'

2 Larger organizations can lose sight of the need to focus on customers and developing value. They achieve a lot by having separate silos and profit centres but, for those with a customer-agenda, getting alignment from these departmental silos can be difficult.

3 A customer-centric organization still has functional departments and profit centres, but in addition there is an alignment and focus on supporting and delivering customer initiatives. As customer value propositions become more complex and innovative, there is an absolute requirement for the whole organization to support the customer agenda.

4 Organizations should not get locked into being overly customer-centric. Time and effort needs to be balanced so that initiatives to enhance the supplier business are achieved.

5 Infinite Value suggests that while customer centricity is an essential way of working, recognition and focus on other

external relationships is necessary. These include customers, customer's customers, channel partners, suppliers, competitors and associates. Managing these relationships is phrased 'value centricity' and an organization that works in this way is a 'value-cell'.

6   Examples are provided that show why and how organizations conduct value-centric relationships.

7   Suppliers should practice what they preach. If they require a customer to value co-create with them, there is a compelling reason to work with their suppliers (and other value relationships) in the same way.

8   A number of tensions can exist in organizations that prevent the shift to become value-centric.

9   Shifting to become value-centric takes time and some investment. Most importantly, it is a cultural belief and mindset that exists in the organization. This is perhaps the hardest (but most important) aspect to change.

10 Five practical ideas are described that can enable the transition to become value-centric.

PART THREE

TRANSFORMING TO A VALUE-BASED ORGANIZATION

Chapter 12

The value management team

In times of change, learners inherit the earth, while the learned find themselves beautifully equipped to deal with a world that no longer exists.

Eric Hoffer

Question
How do I organize my teams and resources to build a value-based business?

Transforming to become a value-based business

The transition to become a value-based business requires a significant amount of effort, planning and commitment. The development of a strategy, building capability standards and the implementation of these new ways of working need to be a recognized management priority for your business. This challenge is often underestimated. Building a value-based business is a different way of doing things. Success comes from somebody initially recognizing that there is a better way to do things and re-building the organization around a new value-based blueprint business model. In large organizations, this can be difficult.

When organizations have reached a level of success and scale by having a focus on developing products, services or expertise there is naturally a culture that evolves around this business model. Organizations can become successful and achieve scale by being quite inwardly focused: as long as they keep producing customer offerings that offer value, they can grow and prosper. As markets shift, customer demands increase and competition becomes more aggressive. This situation can change. Organizations can find themselves on the back foot, and start looking for different ways to compete. When organizations are in this situation, and there is a perceived 'burning bridge', introducing a value-based approach to business can be easier to discussed since leadership is looking for new ways of working. The champions of value-based business need to understand the challenges of their organization, and to carefully develop a case for change. With all of the other noise and activity that occurs within organizations, 'getting value on the agenda' may be a tough job.

There are some practical techniques that can be applied, however, that enable the alignment of resources and to start momentum to become a value-based organization. These techniques have been used with good effect with a number of organizations. This part of the book will describe how they are constructed and can be used. Infinite Value provides a framework for organizations in adopting a value-based business model. It focuses on strategy, capability standards and trans-formation. Although they are connected, the most challenging of these three activities is transformation. However, it is only transformation that will make a difference. As Charles Handy states: 'Change is only another word for growth, and another synonym for learning.'

The benchmark model for organizational transformation is John Kotter's 'Eight Steps to Transforming Your Organization'. Kotter describes this model (and why organizations fail to implement change) in 'Leading Change – Why Transformation Efforts Fail' (2007).

Table 12.1 adapts Kotter's model, and applies it to assist in a programme where transitioning towards a value-based business is required.

There are a number of practical guiding principles that I use when advising organizations when they want to develop change. These principles align naturally with the models and thinking that have been described throughout this book. Taking Kotter's eight-step model and applying the techniques to this proven framework can be essential to help organizations introduce these new ways of working. Taking each of the eight steps (and clustering them into three phases), the ideas and tips are as follows:

Table 12.1 Value-based business transformation (adapted from Kotter)

Establish a 'Call to Action'		
1. Establish a sense of urgency	**2. Form a powerful guiding coalition**	**3. Create a vision**
Build a business case that identifies the need to improve value based business.	Establish a guiding team of cross-functional experts.	Let the guiding team develop a value strategy and vision.
Engage and Enable the Wider Organization		
4. Communicate the vision	**5. Empower others to act**	**6. Plan and create quick wins**
Share the vision and seek buy-in	Build project sub-teams. Start to develop the strategy	Select pilots and build your own good practice
Build a Sustainable Value-Based Culture		
7. Consolidate wins and build a case for change	**8. Make it stick (institutionalize a new business model)**	
Collate and build the case for doing things in a different way	Keep it going! Keep investing and value co-creating!	

Step 1: Establish a sense of urgency

This is the step that Kotter claims causes most transformation programmes to fail. From experience after working with many organizations in many countries, I totally agree with him. When organizations do not believe there is a need to focus on value (or the customer, or KAM), there will be a lack of leadership support, investment and effort. Other initiatives will become favoured and supported. Establishing a sense of urgency and getting 'a chair at the table of the board' is vital. Activities that help:

- Look at your results. If there are trends for sales or profits to be diminishing, or new product introduction failing to deliver the required results, are these trends a concern to leadership?

- Voice of the customer. It is always useful to get the thoughts of the customer right at the start of a value-based programme. Surveys, interviews and invitations to speak at meetings and conferences always provide useful insights. Make sure you capture a good cross-section of customers with the right level of seniority to comment on your supply position.
- Look at your competitors. If competitors are very active and building relationships with your customers, why is this happening? They could be winning business by reducing prices or, more worryingly, they could be focusing on value. Try to piece together a snap-shot of who your competitors are and what they are doing.
- Look outside. Other industries will possibly have best practice systems in place that you can learn from. Consumer packaged goods, automotive and some technology industries are more advanced than other industries. If you can gain insights from them it provides valuable knowledge of 'what could be'.

Step 2: Form a powerful guiding coalition

Transformation usually starts with a few like-minded visionaries in an organization who realize that 'things could be done in a better way'. If they are board-level/senior people this helps, since they can make the programme a priority and make a start. When the visionary is not very senior, there are a few things that they should consider:

- Gaining a leadership sponsor – no investment or serious commitment is required in the early stages, just permission to look into the concept.
- Selecting a leader – the leader needs to be a person who is respected in the organization, understands business (especially sales) and can facilitate workgroups.
- Selecting the team – the initial 'steering group' needs to be a small but representative selection of knowledgeable people in the organization. A blend of sales (commercial), marketing, product and general managers will provide the core of the coalition team. The secret is to get a mix of members who can influence, will be positive about value-based business and can roll up their sleeves to be involved in developing a new strategy.

Step 3: Create a vision

Chapter 5 describes how to establish a vision and build a strategy. As a process, the steering group can follow these steps. Additional advice when building the vision is:

- Make it exciting! The vision should be graphic and show a pathway to greater things. It should be seen as an essential pillar that will deliver the wider organizational vision and objectives.
- Make it worthwhile. You will be fighting to get the value-based business initiative preferred against other projects (supply chain, HR, IT etc.). If your vision lacks commercial impact, or is not seen to be beneficial, you will not gain attention. Typically, you want the value-based business initiative to be a Top 5 management project (anything below the Top 5 may be placed on hold).

Step 4: Communicate the vision

Because this could be a new initiative, communicating the vision (and the whole concept of value) needs to be carefully considered. A simple ABCDE model can help with this communication strategy.

A. Think about who the **Audience** will be. Think like a senior leader.
B. What **Behaviour** do you want them to exhibit after the communication?
C. What should be the **Content** of your communication?
D. How and when will you **Deliver** the vision?
E. What do you **Expect** to happen? Plan for success with advocates and sceptics alike.

You should try to build a simple but impactful communication plan to share your vision. Be clear about what you want ... and even clearer about what your audience wants (they will make or break the programme!)

Step 5: Empower others to act

The strategy will highlight a number of activities that need to be developed. For instance, there could be a need to develop a new key account management planning process. This will require a sub-group to start working on this activity. Select a mixed team of non-customer and customer-facing experts.

Select the sub-team members carefully. A good way to achieve this is to develop a feeling around the programme that it is a unique and highly valued initiative. Having a respected team of leaders on the coalition will help this: 'Get involved and see your career advance!'

Step 6: Plan and create quick wins

This is the step that aligns Kotter's eight steps and my own model to introduce value-based business into organizations. The approach of *Strategy: Customer By Customer*[1] captures this perfectly. This is because organizations start to engage and connect with initiatives when they witness examples of success happening in their own business.

To achieve this, carefully select a number of customers and then build strategies around them. Use the value-based selling, KAM, channel, value-based pricing and ODI techniques. In short, build your own library of case studies. These examples of best practice 'customer by customer' will create a compelling case to apply these techniques in more parts of the organization.

Step 7: Consolidate wins and build a case for change

It is time to start getting serious. By this step, there should be a momentum in the organization to justify investment. The steering group will probably be feeling stretched. There should be investment in the following areas:

- Building a value management team (covered in the next section);
- Investing in KAM teams;
- Reviewing investments in other areas.

Making investments and ramping up change should come from recommendations that the value management team make. As stated earlier, all investments should be made on the basis that value-based business supports and enables the wider business initiatives. It needs to be developed as providing a significant competitive advantage.

---

[1] The strap line for my consulting firm, Segment Pulse.

Step 8: Make it stick (institutionalize a new business models)

Culture has been described as 'just the way we do things around here'. For value-based business, this is a very good description of what you are aiming for. The value management team should be kept in place and constantly look to develop capability and support the business in the way that it creates and delivers value solutions to its customers.

When the culture of the business is aligned with this mantra, life is a lot easier. The goal of any programme should be: 'Our business is built on co-creating and delivering value. It is just the way that we do things around here.'

The missing function: The customer management team

To maintain momentum and build organizational capability, there is a requirement to have a function that focuses on building and implementing the ways of working for customer management. This is an activity that could be integrated into existing teams. These might be:

Sales teams
This makes some sense, since the sales and account management teams are the main operational users of the value techniques. The main challenge is that sales teams are pre-occupied with managing customers, building value propositions and securing business. While they are the recipients and main users of value management techniques, they may not be in the best situation to stand back and focus on building capability. They lead busy and often fast-paced business lives – this does not lend itself to being strategic and building new operational standards.

Marketing
An organization requires marketing to look after brands, new product introductions, campaigns and promotions, and develop sector strategies. They have a longer time horizon and tend to be

Figure 12.1 Critical organization functions

less operational, but value management is not usually part of the marketing remit.

Support functions
Other teams create value, but are not always equipped to develop and focus on value management. Supply chain, HR, R&D and technical functions all participate, but they do not have a remit to develop a value model.

It could be argued that there is a missing function in many organizations. Figure 12.1 shows how sales, marketing and other functions exist, but do not always provide content and effort to build customer and value-based management. This could lead to a loss of focus and progress in developing customer business. There could be several projects that are identified as a result of the value strategy being developed, resulting in questions:

- Who is responsible to develop an innovation and customer proposition capability standard for the organization?
- Who develops a value-based selling model that is tailored for our organization?
- Who develops the KAM planning model?
- Who establishes a channel strategy that can be adopted by our businesses?

These are just a few questions that can arise from a strategic review that highlights gaps in an organization's capability. Developing the new ways of working requires focus and investment. Some organizations have customer management teams/functions. They might be a part of marketing, or independent, but organizations that are successful in this area have formal teams and allocate experts to be responsible.

When these functions are in place, and if customer value becomes an essential part of an organizations culture, these teams can take more of a central role.

Confusingly, these teams often have different names. I have seen:

Customer management team,
Customer standards,
Customer model effectiveness,
Customer academy team,
Customer operations.

Actually, it does not matter what they are called, as long as the organization understands what their remit and role is. One challenge that may be useful is to broaden the function and remit from customer management to value management. Consider all of the aspects that this book covers. Is the development of just customer relationships enough, or should a wider view be adopted?

Do you need a customer or value management team?

Figure 12.2 shows how having a value management team can operate at the centre of the organization. The main goal is to build a business that co-creates value. There is a wide remit (beyond the customer) and the team can draw support from sales, marketing, other support functions, learning and development, and business units.

Widening the remit of the team from customer to value establishes intent to create an organization that builds relationships and collaborates with multiple parties (customers, suppliers, competitors, associates, channel partners and customer's customers). This is a natural extension to the customer management team concept, but places value at the centre of the business.

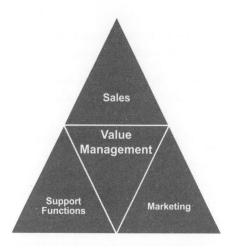

Figure 12.2 The missing function

What does the value management team do?

As a central function, the value management team is intended to work with the business and then develop new ways of working that will enable a better focus on value co-creation. There are four main areas of work that the team focuses on in order to develop and advance a value business model. These are:

1 Setting a vision and strategy;
2 Developing organization-wide capability standards;
3 Developing individual competency standards;
4 Supporting implementation and adoption of these new standards.

It is important to distinguish between capability and competence (Figure 12.3). Organizational capability considers several factors and is concerned with the full organizational construct. Capability includes leadership, structure, planning, data and IT systems, processes, culture and people. It recognizes that an organization needs to have a wide range of things to be in place, designed appropriately to meet the needs of that organization trading with the markets it serves.

Competence is focused on the individuals that operate in the organization. It sets the guidelines and standards for the background,

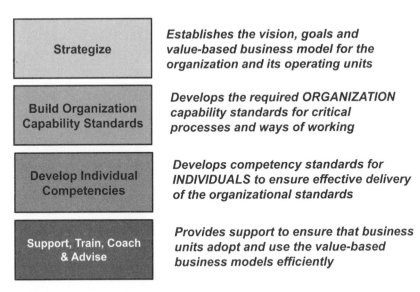

Figure 12.3 What does the value management team do?

experience, skill set, attitude and training that individual people require. These standards should be developed for customer-facing and any value relationship managers. Coaching, training and rewards systems should all be built around these competence standards.

The value management team potentially looks after a wide remit! It covers setting the strategy, building the standards that establish an organizational blueprint, defining the profile and development pathways for individuals, and finally supporting the organization to adopt these new ways of working.

How to structure the value management team

The structure of the value management team can evolve as the programme develops. There are obviously a wide number of options: three basic structures are described here (Figure 12.4) to demonstrate how the team can build.

In the pre-stage (when developing the vision and starting to gain traction) the 'guiding coalition' as adopted by Kotter can be used. This is a network of members that initially seeks to establish value-based business as a strategy and concept the organization should adopt.

The development stage involves bringing in some dedicated resources. The guiding coalition is still in place, but there is justification to bring in a few full-time members to focus on developing the standards and gathering information.

The final advanced stage, assuming that there is widespread acceptance to adopt value-based business, is to have several full-time members. These could be based in regions around the world, acting as specialists (for example KAM and channel specialists) or a mixture of both.

These three models have been developed simply to show how the value management team can evolve. Investment and commitment to full-time employees can be added as and when the programme requires effort and support.

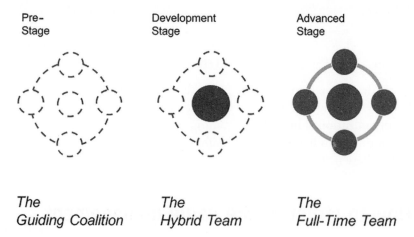

Figure 12.4 Building the value management team

Tips: How to work as a central consulting function

The value management team operates like an internal consulting group. Team members can engage with business units in three ways:

Directive mode: 'We have a new set of standards and you have to adopt them and comply.'

Hands-off mode: 'Here is a set of standards and tools. There is a set of instructions ... good luck implementing them ... I'll see you in two years.'

Consultative mode: 'We have a blueprint and a set of standards that can help you drive growth and meet your targets. Can we work with you and try to adapt these new techniques to best effect for your business needs?'

Even if you have a remit from your senior leadership team to implement the value-based methodology, when you are engaging with business unit leaders it is always best to listen to them, understand their needs and seek to provide a solution that they agree with. Internal consulting requires strong sales and negotiation skills. It is leadership by example and ability, possibly one of the toughest leadership challenges that there is.

The success of the value-based team depends on the ability of the team members to engage, connect and consult with individual business units. The following are a set of ten tips that I have found to be essential when establishing and running an internal value consulting team:

1   Select credible team members. You need ex-sales directors, KAM directors, general managers or business unit leaders. Why would senior business unit leaders, with whom you are trying to engage, respect less experienced executives?

2   Build transformation toolkits that aim to improve the business unit that you are working with. Use simple, clear language in these materials. Remember, value-based business may be a new business model for some of the people you deal with.

3   Build a set of case studies that demonstrates how your business

model works. Make the case studies examples from your business. This makes a compelling story that is hard to say no to.

4   Get customer insights. It is always useful to gain insights from the market you are trying to engage with. For example, if you are engaging with the business unit leaders of Germany, get to know that market. Even better, get some sound bites from customers in that market. Are they satisfied?

5   Complement and align with other functions. Value-based strategy can clash with learning and development, brand, product or strategy teams. Try not to fight with these teams, but align resources and have a joined up story. Politics stop lots of initiatives in businesses – be aware and play the game.

6   Get help from virtual teams. Seek to get members on board in the business unit you are targeting. Work *with* teams whenever you can.

7   Communicate and liaise often.

8   Listen to concerns (and make sure they know you have listened!).

9   Establish a working group with the business unit. Let them be seen to take the lead and own the transformation initiative (you are there as a guiding hand and process owner – never forget it is their business and they may feel threatened).

10 Seek great results and write them up. Praising results (and celebrating success) will give the business unit kudos but will also provide yet more ammunition that you can add into your chest of 'successful best practice case studies'.

Working as an internal consultant, designing and initiating change that can lead to a significant competitive advantage for the organization, can be a highly rewarding role. It is a different style of leadership to traditional line management roles. When establishing value management teams, care should be taken in selecting the right members and ensuring that they are developed to have internal sales, consulting and transformation competencies.

Value matters

1 Transformation is the hardest and most challenging aspect of implementing a value-based business model.

2 Infinite Value recommends Kotter's eight-step transformation model. This model is explored and described for the purpose of value-based business. It is a proven and robust transformation model, and is proven when applied to value-based business projects.

3 The first step is the most critical – organizations must recognize that they need a value-based business model. When this recognition is missing or weak it is difficult to get commitment from management and leadership.

4 Some organizations have customer management teams that focus on building strategy, capability standards and assisting the organization to change. In many organizations, this is a missing function.

5 For value-based business, it is suggested that the customer management team be broadened to become a value management team, looking at several critical relationships and activities, not just the customer agenda.

6 Value management teams need to act as internal consultants, constantly advising, selling concepts and supporting change with business unit leaders that run the business operations.

7 Several options are provided to consider how to structure and resource the value management team. The team can evolve as the programme develops, with a mix of full-time and supporting tags.

8 The value management team should comprise respected, commercial, general management and account management leaders. Experienced and respected leaders know how to get things done in the organization, and they are seen as peers when they look to implement new ways of working.

Chapter 13

Developing value management standards

There are only two ways to establish competitive advantage.

Do things better than other people or do things differently.

Karl Albrecht

Questions

How do I assess my business and evaluate where I have value management capability gaps?

How can I present and structure a set of guiding value-based business capability standards for my organization?

The capability standards model

This chapter is primarily concerned with providing an expanded set of standards for each of the seven elements of value-based business. These standards seek to provide a framework to enable organizations to conduct an assessment of where there may be gaps in their business capability. The model is intended to provide a structured approach to pull together all of the models that are provided in Part Two of this book.

Capability is an organizational construct. It looks at considering leadership (and culture), people, planning and process aspects. Figure 13.1 shows how the seven value-based business standards should be described as a capability. This chapter provides a structure and a set of questions that will enable an initial high-level assessment of an organization and help to identify where capability gaps are.

The model should be used as part of a strategic review process, and is usually adopted by the value management team as part of the process that identifies where effort is required to improve organization performance. When conducting assessments using this process, it is recommended that a team of eight to ten people forms the strategic steering group, with additional experts consulted for specific activities.

While quite detailed, it is recommended that the process should be used as a guide. Stay focused on what you are trying to achieve – you simply want to have a framework that provides a series of structured discussions and gets the team thinking about what you need to do in order to improve being a value-based business. Parts of the framework may not be relevant to your business (you may not use channel partners, for instance, so this section will obviously be omitted).

This is a starting point. Many organizations that I have worked with take this framework as a starting point, and adapt it to their business needs and particular industry terminology.

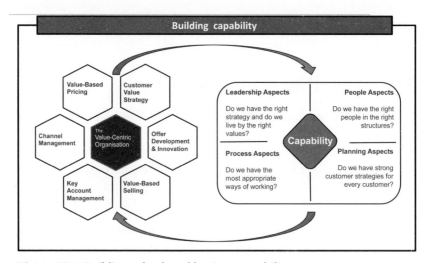

Figure 13.1 Building value-based business capability

Mind the gap!

Figure 13.2 indicates the output of a strategic review using the capability framework. (This is a summary radar chart from a review conducted with a global engineering organization.)

The seven analysis lines represent the elements of a value-based business, and each axis on the chart captures three performance points:

1 The inner radar is the performance of the organization TODAY;
2 The middle radar is the performance level/score that the team wanted to achieve in one year's time;
3 The outer radar is the target performance for the business in five years' time.

Scores are introduced on a 1–5 basis for each question, and each standard. The scoring can be as indicated on the attached key (Table 13.1).

The longer (five-year) period was selected since the team was realistic in assessing the effort it takes to change their organization. Change

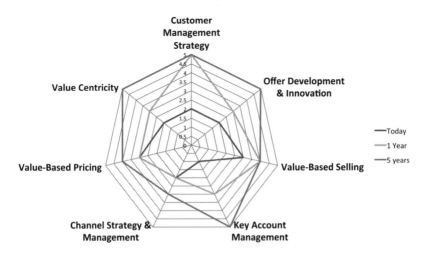

Figure 13.2 Mind the gap!

initiatives for this company can be slow – they are a large group and change takes time to filter down through all departments in all countries. (This is actually a very typical scenario for many organizations – this realistic view of the time this work would take is very refreshing and honest!)

Each standard poses a question against which is a 'good practice' answer (these are typical responses gained from organizations I have worked with, using this model). You judge your score for each question against how you think you compare against the answer. Honesty is a prerequisite when conducting capability self-analysis.

While I would like to claim that the framework is magical and by simply answering the questions in order you will miraculously have an assessment of your business, sadly, I cannot state that. The model does, however, act as a thought-provoking guide that prompts some probing questions and should make you and your team think.

The framework spits each of the seven elements into a series of standards. Elements 1.0 to 4.0 can be seen on Table 13.2 (value-based standards). Elements 5.0 to 7.0 are on Table 13.3.

Table 13.1 Key for assessing and scoring performance

Performance	Score
Not required	**0**
Basic – some ability but very rudimentary	**1**
Foundation – we have the intent, but lack process	**2**
Average (models/systems have been developed but not implemented)	**3**
Models/systems have been developed and implemented (not all areas)	**4**
Best practice – performance is industry leading	**5**

Table 13.2 The value-based business standards (1.0–4.0)

1.0 Customer Value Strategy	2.0 Offer Development & Innovation (ODI)	3.0 Value-Based Selling	4.0 Key Account Management
1.1 Purpose & Objectives	2.1 Value Understanding	3.1 Trust and the Decision-Making Unit	4.1 KAM Definitions
1.2 External Analysis	2.2 Creativity & Innovation	3.2 Gaining Customer Insights	4.2 GAM SAM RAM
1.3 Customer Segmentation	2.3 Customer Needs Analysis	3.3 Value Alignment	4.3 The KAM Plan
1.4 Competitive Advantage	2.4 Lifetime Value Analysis	3.4 Value-Based Negotiation	4.4 KAM Teams
1.5 Internal (Value Management) Analysis	2.5 Product Service Systems	3.5 Value Capture	4.4 Dashboards & Reviewing
1.6 Offer Analysis	2.6 Offer Construction	3.6 Value Co-Creation	4.5 KAM & PSS
1.7 Strategies & Actions	2.7 Testing Value Strength	3.7 Infinite Value (Sustainability)	4.6 KAM Evolution

Table 13.3 The value-based business standards (5.0 – 7.0)

5.0 Channel Strategy & Management	6.0 Value-Based Pricing	7.0 Value-Centric Organization
5.1 Route to Market Analysis	6.1 Pricing Capability Team	7.1 Culture & Leadership
5.2 Channel Segmentation	6.2 Strategic Pricing	7.2 People Aspects
5.3 Channel Value Proposition	6.3 Tactical (Value) Pricing	7.3 Structure Aspects
5.4 Channel Partner Development	6.4 Value. Cost. Price	7.4 Process Aspects
5.5 Channel Alumni	6.5 Pricing Framework	7.5 Value Resource Alignment
5.6 Channel Partner Collaboration	6.6 Value-Based Bidding	7.6 Value-Celling
5.7 Channel Strategy Review	6.7 Value-Based Pricing Reviews	7.7 Value-Centric Transformation

Customer value strategy standards

Standard 1.0: Customer value strategy

Do you have an effective customer value strategy? (Figure 13.3)

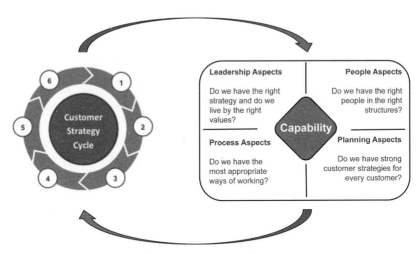

Figure 13.3 Customer value strategy standards

Standard 1.1: Purpose and objectives

Have you defined your customer value vision and business objective(s) for the next one to five years?

There is a clear purpose statement for the customer value programme. Leadership and the wider organization are aligned behind the vision. There is a mix of clearly defined qualitative and quantitative objectives with target dates for completion.

Standard 1.2: External analysis

Do you assess the external macro and industry forces acting on your business?

The business scans the macro-environmental and industry trends to establish the short- and long-term impact these could have on trading positions with our customers. We analyse the customers, the wider-value chain and our own external environment. There is a strong focus on future trends, recognizing that we have to adapt our business (and collaborate with our value partners) to respond to changing market forces.

Standard 1.3: Customer segmentation

Have you classified different customer types within your portfolio?

We have a customer segmentation process in place. There are classifications for customer types based on their strategic importance to us and how important we are to them. The customer segmentation process helps us to develop where we will allocate resources (we apply more resources for higher potential customers and less for lower potential customers).

Standard 1.4: Competitive advantage

What do you have that enables you to consistently win business with your customers?

Brands and products provide a good starting point, but it is our ability to provide tailored value-based offerings to customers that is our major competitive advantage. We have shifted from having a few people who form a sales force, to having the entire business functioning as a value force. By looking to the future, predicting trends and collaborating with our partners, we are able to adapt and compete consistently.

Standard 1.5: Internal (value management) analysis

Do you know the strengths and weaknesses of your own customer value business model?

We gain insights and feedback regarding our internal strengths and weaknesses by constantly reviewing ourselves against our competitors. Additionally, we seek feedback from customers, channel partners, associates and suppliers. We recognize that strengths and weaknesses are hard to assess and require honesty and careful consideration.

Standard 1.6: Offer analysis

How strong is your customer offer?

We assess our offers with each customer. We assess that the value we are providing is sufficient to meet customer needs and is better than our competitor offerings. When our offering is too similar to competitor offerings, we assess how to improve our understanding and introduce appropriate methods to increase the value we provide.

Standard 1.7: Strategies and actions

What strategies and actions are you following over the next one to five years?

The customer value strategy that we have developed has a detailed plan that identifies several key strategic areas that we have to work on. Each strategy is split into a list of actions.

Offer development and innovation standards

Standard 2.0: Offer development and innovation

Do you have an understanding in offer development and innovation? (Figure 13.4)

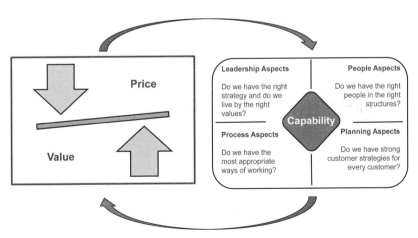

Figure 13.4 Offer development and innovation standards

Standard 2.1: Value (and offer development and innovation)

Is there an understanding of what your customer values?

We connect offer development and innovation directly to our selling and account management techniques. These models start by looking to understand the customer business and to assess what they need to meet their strategic goals and challenges. We seek to understand customers and what they value (our resulting offers are built on this foundation understanding).

Standard 2.2: Creativity and innovation

Do your customers see you as a source of innovation?

Because we work hard to understand our customers and to 'walk a mile in their shoes', we are seen as vital sources of innovation because our value propositions deliver solutions that meet their needs. We co-create value with our customers: this leads to constantly delivering greater value-enhancing solutions.

Standard 2.3: Customer needs analysis

How do you establish a deep understanding of what your customer needs?

Customer needs are assessed in five areas:

- Assisting the customer to improve top-line sales performance;
- Taking out costs from the customer's business;
- Improving the customer's reputation and compliance;
- Providing strategic and management advice/support;
- Understanding the customer's customer and market.

Our value propositions are based on having a deep understanding of the customer business and quantifying these resulting needs.

Standard 2.4: Lifetime value analysis

Do you establish long-term understanding about the products and services being used in your customer's business?

Our offerings have an impact over a sustained period in our customer's business. By analysing 'the total cost of ownership' for the customer we can build stronger offerings and demonstrate a more complete value benefit assessment. We quantify lifetime value analysis for every customer.

(Note: total cost of partnership is used for service-based offerings.)

Standard 2.5: Product service systems

Do you enhance your core product offering with service?

We are able to offer customers a range of offers, based on the level of support they require. We can offer:

- Product,
- Product + basic service,
- Product + advanced service,
- Total integrated solution.

We assess customer needs and, if appropriate for them and ourselves, we can provide value-based service packages.

Standard 2.6: Offer construction

Are your customer value propositions clear, believable and compelling?

There are definitions and systems that we adopt for customer value propositions and customer offers. We have very clear processes in place and our people are trained to use these techniques. Our customer value propositions are written in language that is compelling, believable, quantifiable and clear.

Standard 2.7: Testing value strength

How do you ensure that your value propositions are consistently effective?

We always seek feedback from customers after a value proposition is presented (whether we win or lose the bid). This feedback is assessed and reviewed to enhance the ways that we work in the future.

Value-based selling standards

Standard 3.0: Value-based selling

Do you sell to customers based on the value you add to their business? (Figure 13.5)

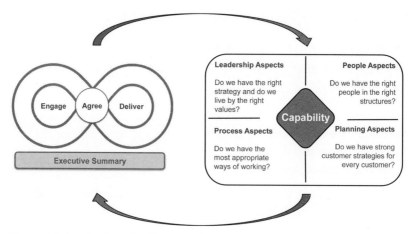

Figure 13.5 Value-based selling standards

Standard 3.1: Trust and the customer decision-making unit

Do you have trusted relationships with the right customer decision makers?

We seek to understand multiple decision makers in our customer business. We look beyond the buyer. It is important that we align the right people in our organization with the right people in the customer organization. Conversations about value are much more effective if more people talk about the breadth of our offer.

Standard 3.2: Gaining customer insights

Do your sales people know what the customer needs and values?

There is considerable effort researching the customer's business and developing strong relationships to gain an understanding about strategic, operational and personal needs. We look beyond just understanding how to sell product to the customer.

Standard 3.3: Value alignment

Are you able to align your offer with the customer needs?

Having an understanding of the customer's business always helps us to describe our offer in an aligned and complementary manner. If we don't understand the customer's needs, we cannot even begin to articulate our value proposition.

Standard 3.4: Value-based negotiation

Do you negotiate based on the value you add to the customer?

Value-based selling complements the principle-based negotiating techniques that we use. We always negotiate using a projection on the value that we can add to the customer business.

Standard 3.5: Value capture

Do you demonstrate the value that you have created for the customer?

We always capture the value that we promise in our customer value proposition. We do this by agreeing with the customer areas that we will measure with agreed critical performance indicators and key performance indicators. We present the value that we create and look to the customer to agree our contribution to adding value to their business.

Standard 3.6: Value co-creation

Is there mutual trust between you and the customer to create value?

The foundation of our sales and account management ethos is to do business with our customers based on the value we can provide to them. We seek to work jointly with customers by value co-creation. Even when our products are a commodity item, we seek to demonstrate the long-term value of choosing us as a supplier over our competitors. We work hard to build trust with customers so that we can work in a value co-creation style.

Standard 3.7: Infinite value

Do you have long-term relationships with customers?

Complex customer value propositions that deliver results over a prolonged period in the customer's business (such as advanced service packages) are built on long-term relationships and trust between ourselves and the customer. Our business model relies on long-term trust-based relationships with customers.

Key account management standards

Standard 4.0: Key account management

Do you manage your strategically important clients effectively? (Figure 13.6)

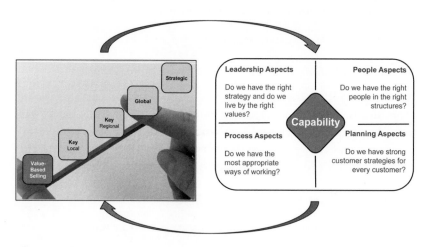

Figure 13.6 Key account management standards

Standard 4.1: KAM definitions

Are you clear how to identify and select a key customer?

There is clarity in our customer segmentation model that describes what a key customer is. We have selected our key customers based on existing and future business opportunities.

Standard 4.2: GAM SAM RAM

Are global, regional and local key accounts managed appropriately?

We recognize that managing key customers becomes more complex as they span countries, regions and our business units. We have carefully designed our planning processes and cross-business working to accommodate this complexity to good effect.

Standard 4.3: The KAM plan

Do you have strategic plans in place for every key customer?

Every key customer has a key account plan. We have developed our own key account plan template, which is designed with differing levels of detail to align with the customer.

Standard 4.4: KAM teams

Do cross-functional teams support each key account manager?

Each key account has an allocated key account manager and a nominated support team. This team may be allocated full-time to the customer, part-time or a mix of full- and part-time. We recognize that key account management is more than just the key account manager.

Standard 4.5: Dashboards and performance monitoring

Are there systems in place to track key account performance?

We consistently deliver 80 per cent of our business from the top 20 per cent of our customers. We achieve this by adopting key account management principles. A bespoke, developed, dashboard monitors the performance of our top thirty customers. This dashboard tracks the value that we are creating for the customer and for ourselves. Leadership reviews the dashboard on a regular (monthly) basis – since it represents 80 per cent of our business.

Standard 4.6: KAM-enabled PSS

Are your KAM teams aligned with your service-based offerings?

KAM is an integral part of our service package offering. Without KAM we would not have strong enough relationships with the customers that adopt our service and solution packages. We regard PSS as the ultimate value co-creation relationship. KAM is the foundation capability that enables these offers.

Standard 4.7: KAM evolution

Is there a focus on developing KAM capability as your business evolves?

We constantly review our KAM programme, recognizing that it is one of the most critical and advanced elements of our overall value-based business. We anticipate that in the future there will be an even larger need to focus on KAM than today.

Channel management standards

Standard 5.0: Channel strategy and management

Do you create value by working with your channel partners? (Figure 13.7)

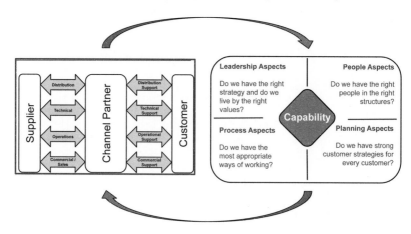

Figure 13.7 Channel management standards

Standard 5.1: Route to market

Are channel decisions being made effectively?

As part of the customer segmentation process, the first decision-making stage is whether to serve customers directly, indirectly (via channels) or by a mixture of direct and indirect. We also make decisions about customers that can be served via on-line channels. There is a very carefully constructed process to decide the best channel/route to market for every customer interaction.

Standard 5.2: Channel segmentation

Do you have systems in place to classify channel partners?

We have a separate channel segmentation process. There are core, key and strategic channel partners. We also classify by the role that the channel partner fulfils (commercial, technical, operational, logistical). We are very clear about all of our channel partners and the role they play with us (and us with them).

Standard 5.3: Channel value proposition

Do you have strong value propositions for every channel member?

Value propositions are created for every channel partner. We also work with them to develop joint value propositions when we work together serving our key customers.

Standard 5.4: Channel partner development

Do you develop channel partners to be effective at value-based business?

We have a fully developed value-based business programme that we provide to selected channel partners. They see this as a significant benefit when partnering with us. The programme is a suite of processes, training, coaching support and advisory sessions.

Standard 5.5: Alumni

Do you have a network to keep connections alive with channel partners?

Once selected, channel partners become part of our alumni. We hold regular conferences, webex sessions and an on-line community. We work hard with channel partners to keep the concepts of value co-creation alive and active.

Standard 5.6: Channel partner collaboration

Do you work with channel partners to understand and access the entire value chain?

There are regular review sessions where we work with channel partners and we 'stand back' to look at the key players in our market as we take our products and services to market. Assessing these relationships helps to maintain a strategic view of the 'bigger picture'.

Standard 5.7: The channel strategy review

Is there an on-going process to review your channel partner capability?

Channel partners are recognized as a vital part of our business model. We access 80 per cent of our customers in partnership with channel partners – they deserve our utmost focus and attention to collaborate. We constantly meet and discuss our channel partner strategy to accommodate changing market forces.

Value-based pricing standards

Standard 6.0: Pricing and commercial framework

Is pricing recognized as a critical part of your business? (Figure 13.8)

Standard 6.1: Pricing capability team

Do you have specialists who focus on pricing?

A pricing director is responsible for setting out all aspects of pricing capability.

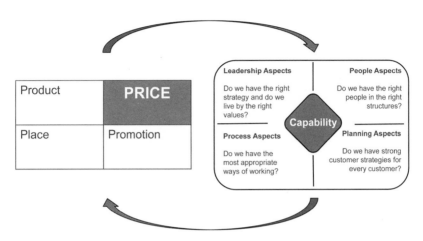

Figure 13.8 Value-based pricing standards

Standard 6.2: Strategic pricing

Do you have systems in place to set price strategies for products and services?

There are clear guidelines that set out the prices of our products and service ranges.

Standard 6.3: Tactical (value) pricing

Do you have value-based pricing integrated into your sales processes?

Value-based pricing techniques are closely aligned with the value-based selling, negotiation and KAM processes. Price and value proposition development are closely aligned. All commercial aspects when constructing contracts are part of the value-based pricing processes.

Standard 6.4: Value. Cost. Price

Is there clarity about the difference between value, cost and price?

The business trains all commercial people with the ability to understand and then articulate the difference between value, cost and price.

Standard 6.5: The pricing framework

Do you have ways to structure pricing options?

There are commercial frameworks that describe various options to structure price and commercial contracts.

Standard 6.6: Value-based bidding

Are your bidding processes aligned with value-based pricing?

We always provide bids that discuss the value we will provide to the customer. There are occasions when we have to 'fight on price', but we always quantify the value that our products and services offer. Competing on price is an option we take as a final resort. We would rather lose the business than have to supply on a lowest price basis.

Standard 6.7: Value-based pricing reviews

Are there strategic reviews to maintain your value-based pricing capability?

Management recognizes that value-based pricing is a critical component to our business model and our ability to compete on value. We constantly review our performance in this area, and seek continuous improvement.

Value-based business capability

Standard 7.0: Value-centric relationships

Does your organization build strong relationships with external parties to co-create value? (Figure 13.9)

Standard 7.1: Culture and leadership

Do the senior leadership teams establish a value-based culture?

The board has decided that we will be a value-based business. They recognize that we need to focus on building strong customer value propositions. This is achieved by co-creating value with customers and other critical external parties.

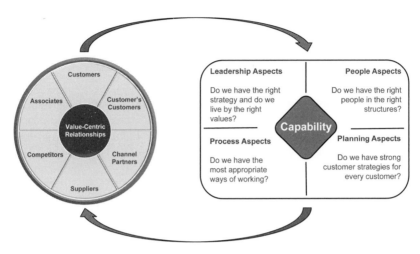

Figure 13.9 The value-based business

Standard 7.2: People aspects

Are people recruited, developed and motivated to enable a value-based business?

There are clear competency standards in place for all people directly and indirectly involved in managing value relationships. We recruit, train, coach and motivate our staff based on these competency standards. The organization focuses on discussing value and its benefits.

Standard 7.3: Structure aspects

Does the business align teams to optimize the creation of value?

The sales and account management structure is designed to support the customer management strategy and is aligned with the customer segmentation model. Larger strategic/key customers tend to have more dedicated resources, with larger teams. Smaller customers are served via our channel partners. Support functions allocate resources to teams as required.

Standard 7.4: Process aspects

Are there appropriate processes and procedures in place to focus on value co-creation?

We have developed a suite of processes that provide our teams with enough guidance to create and deliver strong customer value propositions. These processes are frameworks and techniques – they aim to provide a loose structure without being overly cumbersome and restrictive. Our systems are not overly complex.

Standard 7.5: Value resource alignment

Are value-tensions recognized and managed?

The business recognizes that a number of tensions exist when operating a value-based business. We understand these, and encourage management to discuss practical ways to address them.

Standard 7.6: Value-celling

Does your organization collaborate effectively with other value-partners?

We collaborate with customers, suppliers, associates and channel partners. When appropriate, we also collaborate with competitors. The focus of our organization is to create strong value – this requires working with other parties to expand our expertise.

Standard 7.7: Value-centric transformation

Do you regularly review and re-focus your organization's pathway to become a value-based business?

Addressing performance issues (you can't boil the ocean)

Conducting a workshop using the framework as a guide to spotting gaps can be very insightful and revealing. It will flush out many ideas and potential activities to improve the business. Care should be taken over tackling some of these strategic projects, however. Organizations take time to respond to change, and trying to implement too many things out of sequence can lead to a failed start. In short, you can't boil the ocean, and transformation takes planning and time.

As the radar chart in Figure 13.2 indicated, organizations can schedule initiatives for the next year, two years and more, possibly aiming for a five-year final target. The aim should always be to consider where you should place effort to gain the best results in the quickest time. This is quite possible; for instance, organizations can gain very fast results by introducing a value-based selling approach.

There are, however, certain things that should be in place as foundation activities for almost any organization. These are organizational capability 'key-stone' building blocks:

1 Gaining market and customer insights: you want to have a good feel for future trends so that you can build your business with an ability to trade in these coming conditions.
2 Customer segmentation: value-based business is a strategy that is built around the customer. If you over-serve lower value-potential customers, and under-serve higher-value potential customers, there will be a lack of performance. Any organization has limited resources: use them wisely and build your strategy around the customer portfolio.
3 Planning tools: there are plenty of generic account and key account planning tools on the market. They are useful, but force you into following somebody else's view about developing customer strategies and plans. You should develop your own account planning tools. Who else knows your business as well as you do?
4 Understanding value: there are generic definitions in this book regarding value. This is a starting point: it is strongly advised that your offer development and innovation modules are developed for your business and your customers (this can be linked to the account planning activity, but warrants recognition as a separate activity).

It is also advisable to take on a manageable list of projects. Five to seven main strategic initiatives are a sensible amount. If you complete them in good time, of course, you can start additional activities, but from experience in medium- to larger-scale organizations there is a limit to how many new concepts can be introduced at once.

Finally, remember the management advice offered by Alfred Chandler: 'Unless structure follows strategy, inefficiency results.'

I would add to this: Unless recruitment follows strategy and careful value-based business design, then inefficiency will result!

You need to develop what you want to be and how you want to perform before you place people in key jobs. In the value-based business, highly capable people with great attitudes are always required. Let your strategic capability review help you to define these individual characteristics.

Value matters

1   To assist in assessing your organization and determining where gaps may lie in your overall capability, the value-based business framework is offered as a self-assessment tool.
2   Use the framework to facilitate a workshop with a capable cross-functional team of experts. Discuss and agree your strengths and weaknesses and look for capability gaps.
3   The framework structures discussions and provides insights. It is not intended to be 100 per cent right for each organization, but rather a means to ask some probing questions and guide your conversations in a structured manner.
4   The framework asks a question and provides a 'good practice' answer. The answers have been observed and captured from organizations that I have worked with. Score yourself 1–5 based on your performance versus the answers provided.
5   It is recommended that over time you develop your own framework.
6   Radar charts are a very useful means of capturing a lot of analysis and spotting where your performance gaps are.
7   Plan to implement corrective actions over a number of years. Foundation projects tend to be customer segmentation, account

plan development, solid customer insights and developing your own value proposition models.

8   When running workshops, be challenging and question each other. It is sometimes hard to admit that you are weak at something – but look for evidence, discuss it and be honest.

9   The best honesty comes from 'the voice of the customer'.

10   Remember that structure follows strategy. How can you develop new structures if you don't have a clear strategy describing what you want to be?

Chapter 14

Value-based business transformation

Everybody has a strategy until they take a punch in the face.

Mike Tyson

Question

Value-based business is a different way of doing things: How can I get my organization to adopt these new business principles and ways of working?

Why transformation is difficult

Peter Drucker mused that 'The greatest danger in times of turbulence is not the turbulence itself – it is to act with yesterday's logic.' The start of *Infinite Value* was a reflection on the accelerating pace of change occurring across most economic factors. For many organizations, the need to change and adapt is apparent, but the act of transformation, and implementing some of the ideas and concepts of value-based business, can be challenging.

As Kotter proposed in his eight-step process for leading change, the main reason that organizations fail to change is at Step 1: Is there a real sense of urgency and a belief that this is something the organization needs to do? Chapter 13 advised how to deal with this challenge (and how to apply Kotter's model to value-based business). This chapter addresses some of the more practical aspects of transformation; it provides a few simple techniques that can help to make change stick in a large organization. Value-based business is a different way of working which requires careful planning and alignment of resources. In larger organizations, transformation also needs to be conducted at

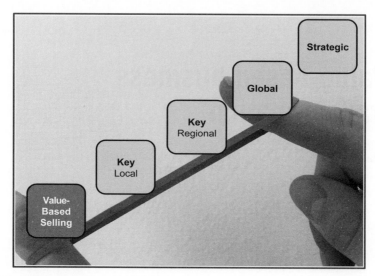

Figure 14.1 Stretch and width

a manageable 'pace'. Figure 14.1 shows an elastic band that is being stretched out. As the band is stretched it lengthens, but also reduces in width. While there is an extension in one direction, the strength and performance of the elastic band change. Stretch too far and it snaps. This can be an analogy for an organization as it attempts to develop and manage larger, more complex customers. Strategic, global and key customers present an attractive prize – they can each deliver increased profit. But this profit comes with an additional requirement to invest in people, systems, support and time, which often requires strengthening organizational capability.

Organizations can often manage two or three strategic customers. They allocate resources and put the best people on these teams. Replicating this model to cope with ten to twenty strategic customers strains resources. There are not enough good people; the wider organization is not so aligned regarding the new ways of working; and there may even be resistance to change. Large organizations have to work really hard to get a consistent alignment of hearts and minds regarding any new way of working.

The steering group for the programme (better still, a value management team, if established) needs to plan transformation very carefully. Three techniques are demonstrated in the next few sections that are simple to use but really help to plan and drive transformation.

Analysing transformation forces

Assessing the organization to understand what is helping to drive the transformation towards a value-based business (and factors that might cause resistance) is invaluable. An honest assessment conducted early on can get key challenges on the table so that they can be addressed. Organizational issues can fester if they are not addressed. Ignore blockers to your programme and it could be derailed several months down the track. Typical festering wounds might be:

- General managers who have their own agenda;
- CRM/IT systems that are not capable;
- External influencers that have personal agendas;
- Other projects that are hogging budget, energy and time.

Of course, there are also positive enabling forces. These might include:

- Board-level support;
- Competitors moving into this space (we need to catch up);
- Customer feedback.

A simple model to help identify and 'balance' these positive and negative forces is Lewin's force field analysis. It is a simple model, and works effectively when looking to implement a value-based business programme. Figure 14.2 shows the concept of Lewin's model (it is constructed using insights from an organization looking to implement a value-based stategy).

To construct the model, work in a team (use the steering group). Follow these steps:

1 Put a large piece of paper on a wall (A0 Poster size works best).
2 Draw the two axes as shown on Figure 14.2.
3 At the right hand side – write the 'desired change' objective. Describe what it is that you are trying to move to (this could

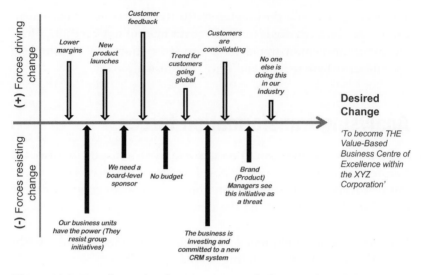

Figure 14.2 Transformation forces – an example (Lewin's force field analysis)

be the purpose statement and objectives for the overall programme).

4   Arrows at the top of the line (pointing down) are positive forces driving change. The length of the arrow represents the strength of the force.

5   Arrows at the bottom of the line (pointing up) are forces resisting change. Again, the arrow length correlates to strength of the force.

6   Brainstorm in small sub-groups: what do people think are positive and negative forces? How strong do they think they are? Why?

7   Finally, draw the arrows on the chart. This is a picture that captures a lot of emotion, practical thinking and analysis of your organization. It is the view of the team (once they have had a few healthy arguments!).

8   The final step is to consider how to build on the positive forces, and how to counter the negative forces. This will provide an invaluable transformation pathway to navigate the obstacles to change in the organization.

Figure 14.2 is a Lewin's transformation force diagram for a client that I worked with. They were a European division of a global food/meal processing and packaging organization. They wanted to be the best division in the group and be seen as the guiding blueprint for value-based business. The main negative force that they had to deal with was aligning local general managers to support the central programme. They overcame the resistance by developing a value-based business model with just one business unit as a pilot. It was a great success, and became the business model that the board wanted to adopt (it also achieved greater financial results – it became very difficult to say no to this new way of working).

Lewin's transformation model helped the team to make this assessment and build in activities for a successful transformation.

A transformation 'top tip'

Regardless of how well you think about your organization and try to predict every possible positive and negative transformation force, there will always be a level of uncertainty about how the organization will look and how effective the new ways of working will be. Even when leadership is very enthusiastic and keen to get started, it is always advisable to plan carefully and make sure that you have a construct that will be effective and will work for your business and culture.

Value in practice
Building a glider in the loft …

A supply chain organization spent several months assessing and developing a new key account management strategy. They had developed a good strategy, and identified several customers that could benefit from having strategic KAM plans to both protect existing business and secure organic growth in the future. The Managing Director of the business, however, was eager to proceed:

'It feels like we have been building a glider in the loft for ages! ... when can I see it fly ...?'

The project team was keen to please, and there was a feeling that it would be good to get KAM training established and start to make an impact. After some consideration, however, they decided that it would be better to build a KAM template and focus on ONE customer. While they were confident about the broad concept of KAM, they were not 100 per cent certain.

The solution. They followed the number 1 tip to establish a successful customer management transformation. They focused on ONE customer. This involved developing a KAM strategy and plan for a single customer. They managed this quickly and had a commercial success (20 per cent growth was identified).

The outcome was a happy managing director (as he saw a picture of what was possible). The project team also had a much-improved model and KAM template that worked for their business. Focusing on ONE customer led to an improved overall KAM programme.

The 'glider in the loft' story captures the challenge of transformation perfectly. You need to balance analysing, development and planning with 'getting into action'. Focusing on one customer as a pilot stage satisfies several issues:

1   You can test the model that you have developed;
2   The pilot will provide valuable data that can be written up and become your case study, and these case studies can be used in training;
3   When engaging with wider parts of the organization, it is hard for them to reject a value-based business model that delivers 'proven growth';
4   Members of the pilot will become 'value ambassadors' and can spread the word across the wider organization about how the new model produces commercial results;
5   In certain circumstances, you can seek feedback from the customer. These can be written or recorded sound bites. Having

the voice of the customer added to your call for action is incredibly effective to establish change!

In principle, the idea of focusing on one customer is really just adding to Kotter's eight steps of change. His sixth step is to 'plan and create quick wins'. This is exactly what your pilot will provide. In fact, if you want to build the idea, swiftly move from one to two to three plus customer's pilots. As long as you are creating good results there will be a vortex of evidence and experience that will provide a solid platform to drive change.

It is easy for the wider reaches of your organization to say no to a concept or idea.

Conversely, it is very difficult for them to say no to a suite of case studies that have been developed within your organization, provided your new business model accelerates growth.

Planning transformation: Adopting a balanced scorecard approach

Once a strategy is developed, and the positive and negative transformation forces identified that affect its success, a period of careful implementation planning is required. Part of this planning can be project planning, whereby activities are identified and described in terms of who will deliver these activities and by when. This is relatively straightforward and can be conducted by the project team.

A much harder (and critical) aspect however is looking across the organization and establishing a means to engage with key department heads to ensure that they understand what is required from them in terms of the tasks they have to perform to support the transformation to become a value-based organization. This is no easy task, and is often greatly underestimated by project teams as they seek to gain traction and implement new ways of working. The challenge has been covered several times throughout this book: a value-based business model is a different way of working since it requires co-operation between departments and a re-alignment of focus. To get different teams, departments, functions and key individuals aligned and doing 'things a different way' requires a convincing set of reasons delivered in an engaging way. The secret here is that effective transformation comes from persuasion and engagement, not direction and management. It is great to have a remit from a senior leader stating, 'This is the way that things will be done from now on,' but unless they are convinced and genuinely buy into the concepts, there will always be a resistance.

Following the transformation ideas that have so far been suggested helps. Having a small portfolio of successful case studies is invaluable. There needs to be a 'body of evidence' that keeps building and gaining momentum – eventually with this knowledge being bigger than those parts of the organization not following the new ways of working, the job of seeking engagement and co-operation will get easier.

In order to establish commitment and establish accountability, the balanced scorecard is suggested. Developed by Kaplan and Norton (1992), it is a means of aligning management activity with strategy. This is exactly the challenge of implementing value-based business, except that it is potentially a very different way of doing business. Kaplan and Norton advised that the balanced scorecard should have four main components to describe the activities that management departments, teams and individuals should follow. These are:

- Financial perspective,
- Business perspective,
- Customer perspective,
- Learning and growth perspective.

Balancing these themes in terms of effort and reward is the key consideration of a balanced scorecard. There is recognition that organizations have to spend time establishing a customer focus, building organizational capability and developing competence in order to be competitive and to achieve vision and strategy. This concept fits with value-based business perfectly. There is often a new strategy, with identified new standards that have to be built, and organizational/individual development. The entire programme is focused on the customer, making the balanced scorecard an ideal fit to plan, monitor and reward transformation and implementation.

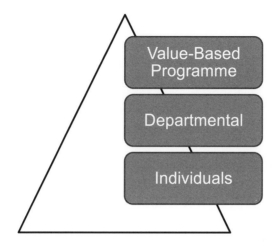

Figure 14.3 Connecting balanced scorecards

Connecting strategic objectives and actions with the wider organization is something that a balanced scorecard approach can allow. Figure 14.3 shows three levels to enable this. At the highest level, there should be a single value-based programme scorecard. This sets out at the highest level what is required to ensure that the main strategic initiatives are described and split into activities to enable a successful transformation. This then splits into a series of departmental scorecards. There will be one for each department, function or business unit that needs to support the programme (for example there could be scorecards for marketing, product development and several countries). This level of planning and establishing who is required to support the programme needs to be carefully considered by the project team. The final level is for individuals that operate in each business unit. Things only happen when individuals are motivated and rewarded to achieve these activities, and it is at this level that these goals are established and agreed with the people who make things happen. This pyramid connects a high-level balanced scorecard (representing the strategic intent of the programme) to key departments and finally to key individuals.

Figure 14.4 shows a four-stage model that can be used to bring strategy to life with an adapted version of the balanced scorecard concept. An initial overview of this model will help to understand the overall idea,

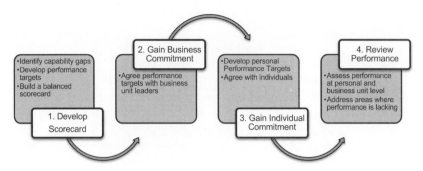

Figure 14.4 Cascading targets (bring strategy to life with targets)

with a deeper focus on how to construct the balanced scorecard afterwards. Taking each of the stages:

1 **Stage 1: *Develop the scorecard***
   The scorecard is built around the strategy (a model to develop a strategy is explained in Chapter 5) and is the first of the seven elements of a value-based business. The scorecard is split into two sections, a capability section that is organized around the seven elements of value-based business, and a commercial section that lists the financial and customer objectives.

   Each of these objectives is then divided into a set of targets that need to be achieved over a set period (usually twelve months since the overall process aligns with the review cycle for the organization and individual appraisals). The targets can be described in three levels of performance: threshold, target and stretch. The description for 'target' is what is most expected and will enable a satisfactory delivery of the programme. It represents 100 per cent performance. Stretch describes going beyond what is required and achieves a score of 100–120 per cent, and threshold is below performance, at 80–100 per cent.

   The advantage of splitting out targets like this on the scorecard is that it forces the project team to think hard and plan key activities that will deliver the overall vision and strategy. The other advantage is that it enables further discussions as the strategy is connected with the wider organization. It enables the discussion point: 'We are trying to achieve these things, and that means you need to do these tasks.' Without a balanced scorecard, it is very difficult to connect a strategy to a detailed action plan.

2 **Stage 2:** *Gain business commitment*
Once the single programme scorecard is developed, it can be taken to the relevant department heads that need to be aligned. This is an engagement exercise. Remember persuasion and engagement beats the directive approach!

Good engagement will make a clear business case to each business unit, providing context about what the programme is trying to achieve; what the benefits will be for the business; and (by using the balanced scorecard approach) exactly what is required from the department or team that you are talking to. They should be very clear about the benefits of the programme and what is required from their teams. Offering support, advice and multiple communication sessions will help this stage to happen more effectively. Make the teams feel that change is being conducted with them, not to them.

3 **Stage 3:** *Gain individual commitment*
Individual commitment comes by each department cascading down the wider objectives to individuals. Unless individuals are motivated and rewarded to support an initiative, they may not provide time, energy and effort. Why would they? Everybody is motivated to hit personal targets so that bonus payments and career development/promotion can occur. Unless your objectives become their objectives, there will be limited support.

For example, if you need five days a month from a scientist in an R&D department to support a key customer team, why would they contribute these days if they were not going to be rewarded? By getting the five days on the scientist's personal performance contract (in agreement with his/her line manager) the exact input can be agreed and support will be achieved. Again, stipulate threshold, target and stretch performance for each individual that will support the programme.

4 **Stage 4:** *Review performance*
When the three levels of balanced scorecards are developed, agreed and implemented, the programme can start rolling out.

Reviews should fall in line with routine performance meetings – most probably on a quarterly basis. If there is any significant under-performance, especially in the early phases of the programme, it is always wise to establish reasons for it and put corrective actions in place.

These four steps are high level but do provide a simple framework to enable the development and implementation of a transformation model. An important point to stress is the need to have good engagement and communication alongside the mechanism of the balanced scorecard. While it is an excellent model that describes what is required, by whom and by when,

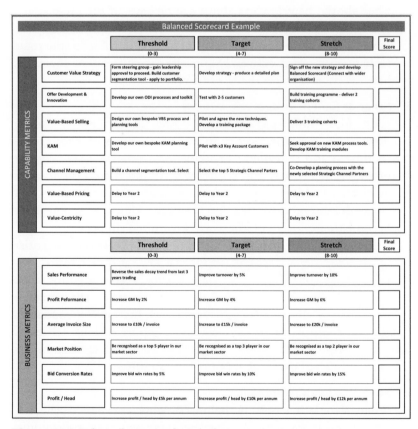

Figure 14.5 Balanced scorecard example

it is just a model and a framework. Good transformation programmes recognize that successful change occurs only when senior members of the organizations become convinced of the need to change and start to co-operate and support. This comes only following a period of careful discussion and communication. Engagement is always the key secret to any change management programme, and value-based business is no different.

An example of a balanced scorecard for a value-based business transformation programme

Figure 14.5 shows a completed balance scorecard (this is a top-level scorecard for the overall programme). This was completed for a supply chain organization. The capability metrics section highlights the seven elements, and describes threshold, target and stretch activities. The business metrics section describes the areas of business performance that are the targets to correct. In this case, these commercial targets were achieved after nine months of implementing the capability standards – there is always a lag.

The model worked well for this organization. It provided a clarity that had not existed previously and enabled alignment of key departments and section heads. They appreciated the balanced scorecard as it provided clarity. As one product manager stated:

> I was really unsure about this new customer transformation.... I had heard rumors about it, but I really was skeptical about what they wanted from my team. The balanced scorecard really made it simple though, it was a good model for me to talk with my team and agree the ways that we would commit our support.

Value matters

1   Gary Veynerchuk (CEO of Veynermedia) says: 'Ideas are shit, execution is the game.' He makes the observation as an entrepreneur for other entrepreneurs, but the sentiment applies to any scale of organization that is trying to introduce change.

Design and development is critical, but careful implementation is how change really happens.

2   Organizations need time to adjust. Like an elastic band, they can over-stretch and snap. Time is required to adapt to the new ways of working.

3   Two models are suggested to help with the implementation of a change programme – the first is Lewin's force field analysis. This is a simple technique to assess positive and negative forces within the organization that act upon executing the desired results.

4   The second model that is adopted is the balanced scorecard. This is an established model to identify and engage key departments and individuals and make them accountable with set targets. Threshold, target and stretch targets can be described and linked to individuals such that their performance and achievements are recognized and rewarded.

5   The transformation 'top tip' is suggested. This is to focus early stages of the transformation on one customer. Learn from this pilot, expand to the next few customers and gain momentum carefully. This can also be known as 'guerrilla' transformation or 'establishing change by a series of small wins'.

6   With a set suite of case studies that have been developed within your own organization, it is difficult for business leaders across your organization to say no to these new ways of working. It is easy for them to say no to high-level concepts and ideas, however.

7   Organizations are typically able to manage a handful of large transformation initiatives. Work hard to get value-based business recognized as a critical 'Top 5' strategic project.

8   As the programme gains momentum, establish a group of 'value ambassadors'. These are people who have been members of the pilots and have a good grasp about the new ways of working and the benefits that they deliver.

9   Keep communication alive with a series of formal progress reviews with senior leaders and plentiful smaller discussions across the business. Communicate the benefits of the new ways of working, but more importantly listen to the concerns that are coming back and establish responses that will ease these tensions.

10 The only thing in life that is constant is change. Organizations that are great at value-based business continuously review their performance and keep adapting to maintain their competitive advantage.

Chapter 15

Final thoughts and future predictions

The future depends on what you do today.

Mahatma Gandhi

Questions

What might be the future trends for enterprise organization selling?

Is Infinite Value a robust concept to cope with these challenges?

Final thoughts about Infinite Value

Finishing a book on Infinite Value entitled 'final thoughts' may seem like an odd idea, so actually this should maybe be called 'thoughts on the next five to ten years' but that doesn't sound quite so conclusive. In the true spirit of value and value creation, however, the whole concept is based on organizations embracing innovation in order to survive, grow and prosper. Value is infinite, the idea that suppliers and customers can keep working together to develop business, embracing methodologies, techniques and thinking that forms a value-based business model. If there is one trend we can be certain of, it is that change will keep happening and successful organizations will have to keep evolving.

Evolution, disruption, failure and advancement will all keep working hand in hand, placing new pressure and significance on the word *value* when organizations are trading together. The secret is not how resilient organizations are to these changes, but how they rebuild themselves to thrive in new markets. In whatever guise, value-based business models will remain the focus of organizational life. The detail of the design, however, will have to adapt.

To deal with the foreseeable future, from today over the next five to ten years, the following ten predictions have been made. As a short-term review, they build on many of the ideas that have already been set out in *Infinite Value*. This should be no surprise, since many enterprise organizations today are not following a value-based business model sufficiently. The predictions are not too fanciful, and in some cases are well on-track. This means that they are worthy of discussion and building into strategic planning sessions. Even if you throw out half of the predictions, at least you will have considered the thinking and context.

Ten predictions for the future

1   **Consumers will continue to gain more purchasing power**
    Technology advancement is already creating a platform that provides consumers with extensive purchasing information. They can compare prices, performance, experience and specifications at the click of a button (actually, the swipe of a mobile screen).

    As Simonson and Rosen maintain, consumers are living in an age of (nearly) perfect information, and given that the Internet is still in its infancy, there is still far more to technology benefits for consumers to come.

    This will play into the hands of consumers, with brand and marketing becoming less impactful (in isolation) for suppliers. Suppliers will also benefit from technology, they will be able to target consumers by their buying habits and history, but the over-riding power will shift to the consumer.

2   **Procurement in business marketing will continue to become more sophisticated and professional**
    Enterprise procurement is becoming savvier today: they have systems that compare supplier performance and they can easily commoditize transactional procurement and force suppliers to compete on price. The bigger challenge is that procurement is becoming a more respected and valued profession (certainly in the UK and Europe). Following the recession, greater emphasis

was placed on procurement – saving money could save the company, and as such, procurement gained a seat at the board.

Another financial shock and panicking markets would be bad for business, but it will also accelerate the power base of procurement. Sales, account management and corporate culture has to catch up: respecting the 'growth of the top line' has to be on parity with respecting 'shrinking costs to preserve the bottom line'.

Of course, both procurement and sales are important, but a bit of 'shared love' would be nice.

3 **Competition will increase**
Today, for many organizations (suppliers and customers) there is a constant threat of new competitors entering the industry in which they compete. With technology and globalization making it easier for organizations to develop offerings, the emergence of new organizations challenging and fighting for your share of the pie will increase. Technologies will fuel the emergence of new competitors with stealth-like ability. Uber has disrupted the global taxi industry with a clever use of technology. The London Black Cab industry, long established with set fees and a standard operating model (you flag them down by hand), has been changed forever, by utilizing a phone app. Payment, safety, price and convenience have all disrupted an established business (don't talk about Uber to your next Black Cab driver ... maybe talk about the weather instead).

4 **Product life cycles will decrease**
Several factors give rise to the length of service that can be enjoyed by organizations, as they take products and services to market:

- Consumers and customers are more demanding – they expect new products more frequently,
- Competitors change the game and match (or better) your product offering,
- Technology allows new entrants to disrupt your supply position,
- Global markets provide increased competition from new providers.

This all leads to a scenario whereby suppliers have to be re-inventing the products they bring to market – tweaking, advancing or breaking through performance barriers.

5   **The need for services and solutions will increase**
When suppliers seek to enhance their value propositions to suppliers, they generally wrap service packages around their product offerings. This is a way to innovate and co-create value. The advancement of services and solutions is also beneficial for customers, with suppliers delivering increased value for the customer and taking non-core activity out of their operations.

The advancement of cheaper technology to provide data, monitoring and analysis of equipment in use will make these solution-based packages more powerful, cost-effective and robust. The 'Internet of Things', or the connecting of devices and monitoring everything from vehicles to entire cities, will again boost the options available to suppliers and the attractiveness to customers.

Value co-creation, and value-based business when adopted correctly, will usually lead to enhanced value propositions – and this will fuel the development (and demand) for services and solutions.

6   **Outcome-based contracts will become more common**
Trends are already in place in which some customers prefer suppliers to enter contracts through which they are rewarded for delivering the promises described in their value propositions. Buyers are becoming more powerful, value propositions are becoming more complex (with enhancing service packages) and suppliers are seeking to be rewarded more for their efforts. The advancement of outcome-based contracting (for more complex supply agreements) will increase, since it makes commercial sense for all parties concerned.

7   **Key account management will take centre stage of organizational importance**
The commercial teams in organizations have already started to shift in the way they are structured to serve their customers. With digital channels offering a highly cost-effective and

totally appropriate way to access smaller or more transactional customers, many organizations can shift to a digital model and eliminate direct selling.

The customers are strategically important: a smaller footprint of key customers is critical in the way that they are managed. As industries consolidate, globalize and become more complex, the response to these customers has to increase. This is key account management, and rather than its position today of having to fight to be recognized as an essential function, it will evolve to become a critically important activity.

Key account management will take centre stage in many organizations, with key account management being a highly valued and recognized profession. In many industries, sales will become an endangered species, whereas highly skilled key account managers will evolve into business leaders. Look after your good key account managers. They will become the architects of value-based business in the future.

8 **The need for highly developed channel partners will accelerate**
The historical reasons for using channel partners remain intact. They are flexible, adaptive, offer access to markets and create a cost-effective means to extend an organization's logistics, sales, technical and operational reach. But as organizations seek to displace sales, retaining focus on key and strategic customers on one side, and transacting through digital channels on the other side, the need for collaborative channels to maintain connections with all customers will intensify.

In a value-based business model, channel partners will become far more strategic and called upon to extend value creation (not just as a cost-effective provider, managed on a transactional basis). Of all relationships, collaboration can become especially effective by working more closely with the teams that are based in channels. It will be an essential way to operate in an environment of increasing disruption and accelerating change.

9 **Collaboration will become essential, not fanciful**
Collaboration across a wide group of strategic partners may be the only way of responding to disruptive forces quickly. Today automotive producers that have competed aggressively for

decades are now having to work together to develop and operate new technology centres. In some cases, it is the only way that they can stay in the game.

Collaboration needs a different mindset and management style. A good place for many organizations would be to start collaborating with partners that you should be working with anyway (like suppliers and channel partners). Again, due to disruption and the pace of change, collaboration will become essential to survive, not a fanciful activity for the latest R&D experiment.

Value-selling will evolve into value-'celling': suppliers, customers, associates and other key stakeholder organizations will draw upon their combined resources to compete and develop value.

10 **Customer centricity will evolve into value centricity**
In my consulting work, I come across many key account managers trying to align the collective resources of their organization to create and deliver new value propositions for customers. And with this requirement comes a recurring major challenge from them: 'How do I get the rest of my organization to support me in serving the customer?' This is a problem. If organizations need to shift from being solely customer-centric, they need to become value-centric. There needs to be alignment and co-operation to support customer challenges, but also with other external strategic partners.

Is Infinite Value robust enough to cope with the future?

The rationale laid out in Part One of this book for a value-based business approach today will remain a robust business model for the future. If anything, the pace of change from macro-economic and technological forces will increase, as will competition from within industries. This strengthens the case to build a business model that can handle such changes.

Organizations can take one of two responses. They can either fight on price to continue winning business, or they can stand up to the changing forces and fight with new value propositions (thus becoming disruptive forces themselves).

Of course, the need to develop new products will remain a means to develop competitive advantage. Innovative products and services built and delivered to robust quality standards will always be critical to build the foundation of an organization's brand. The challenge for suppliers is to determine what those products and services should look like.

Figure 15.1 shows how a value-based business approach develops a competitive advantage in a virtuous cycle. Stronger relationships that focus on effectively building knowledge around understanding what the customer values when connected to the new product development will enable the development of stronger core offerings. Organizations that truly want to embrace value-based business in the future need to make this connection between sales and new product R&D robust and seamless.

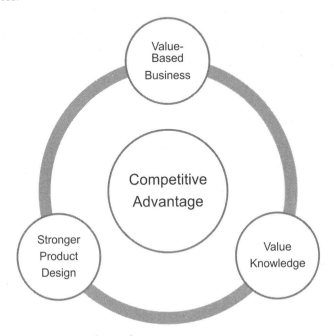

Figure 15.1 Virtuous value cycle

The seven elements of value-based business make a solid foundation. As sales transform such that key account management becomes the 'direct' selling model, and channels become even more important, the seven elements will strengthen. The one extension to the model that has not been discussed is the use of serving customers digitally and on-line. Already a growing trend, on-line will continue to grow, offering significant advantages for customers looking to engage with suppliers on a transactional basis (or even to research features and prices) and suppliers that want to access markets with a cost-effective cost to serve model.

Some organizations will look to shift as much business as possible through digital channels (of course there will also need to be third-party supply chain distributors if physical goods are being sold). With larger, more complex customers requiring a more advanced and bespoke solution, a value-based business approach is critical. Businesses have to collaborate and work together. Opportunities and threats will appear that require a 'value-cell' approach, so that new competitive offerings and ways of working can be found.

Disruption and change will continue to occur. However, the practical ideas and concepts that form the foundation principles of Infinite Value can provide a defensive response mechanism. It is time for sales and account management teams to take centre stage of organizations and be the driving force behind strategy development and delivery. Organizations that are brave enough will prosper with a value-based business model.

Please send me your thoughts: mark@segmentpulse.com

Mark Davies
Autumn 2016

Bibliography

BOOKS

Chapter 1

Dobbs, R., J. Manyika and J. Woetzel (2015). *No Ordinary Disruption. The Four Global Forces Breaking All the Trends.* New York: PublicAffairs Books.

Handy, C. (1989). *The Age of Unreason – New Thinking for a New World.* Arrow Books.

Simonson, I. and E. Rosen (2014). *Absolute Value. What Really Influences Customers in the Age of (Nearly) Perfect Information.* HarperBusiness.

Chapter 3

Lemmens, R., W. Donaldson and J. Marcos (2014). *From Selling to Co-Creating. New Trends, Practices and Tools to Upgrade Your Sales Force.* BIS Publishers.

Raynor, M. E. and M. Ahmed (2013). *The Three Rules – How Exceptional Companies Think.* New York: Portfolio Penguin.

Chapter 5

Drucker, P. F. (2008). *The Five Most Important Questions You Will Ever Ask About Your Organization.* Wiley.

Chapter 6

Maslow, A.H. (1954). *Motivation & Personality. A general theory of human motivation based upon a synthesis primarily of holistic and dynamic principles.* Harper & Brothers.

Chapter 7

Chan, Kim W. and R. Mauborgne (2005). *Blue Ocean Strategy. How to Create Uncontested Market Space and Make the Competition Irrelevant.* Harvard Business School Press.

Fisher, R. and W. Ury (1982). *Getting to Yes. Negotiating an Agreement Without Giving In*. Random House Business Books.

Kotler, Armstrong and Piercy Harris (2013). *Principles of Marketing, 6th European Edition*. Pearson.

Lane Keller, K. (2013). *Strategic Brand Management, 4th Global Edition*. Pearson.

Chapter 9

Wilson, H., R. Street and L. Bruce (2008). *The Multichannel Challenge – Integrating Customer Experiences for Profit*. Butterworth/Heinemann.

JOURNALS AND BLOGS

Chapter 1

Eversheds. 'Law Firm of the 21st Century. The Clients' Revolution'. Eversheds own publication, 2010.

Goodwin, T. F. 'The Battle is for the Customer Interface'. *Blog: Techcrunch*. Posted 3 March 2015.

Moore, G. E. 'Cramming More Components onto Integrated Circuits', *Electronics* 38/8 (1965).

Chapter 3

Marn, M. V., E. V. Roegner and C. C. Zawada. 'The Power of Pricing'. *The McKinsey Quarterly* 1 (2003).

Chapter 4

'Where Thinking is King'. *Economist* (13 July 2013) Print Edition.

Chapter 5

Collis, D. J. and M. G. Rukstad. 'Can You Say What Your Strategy Is?' *Harvard Business Review* (April 2008).

Porter, M. E. 'The Five Competitive Forces that Shape Strategy'. *Harvard Business Review* (January 2008, first published 1979).

Chapter 8

Gulati, R. Silo Busting. 'How to Execute on the Promise of Customer Focus'. *Harvard Business Review* (May 2007).

Chapter 10

Marn, M. V., E. V. Roegner and C. C. Zawada. 'The Power of Pricing'. *The McKinsey Quarterly* 1 (2003).

Chapter 11

Schumpeter. 'Managing Partners. The Pressure on Companies to Form Alliances with Rivals is Growing Inexorably'. *Economist* (23 May 2015). Print Edition.

Chapter 12

Kotter, J. P. 'Leading Change – Why Transformation Efforts Fail'. *Harvard Business Review* (January 2007, first published 1995).

Chapter 14

Kaplan, R. S. and D. P. Norton. 'The Balanced Scorecard – Measures that Drive Performance'. *Harvard Business Review* (January–February 1992).

Index